The Liberal Invasion of Red State America

The
LIBERAL INVASION
of RED STATE
AMERICA

KRISTIN B. TATE

REGNERY
PUBLISHING
A Division of Salem Media Group

Regnery® is a registered trademark of Salem Communications Holding Corporation

Cataloging-in-Publication data on file with the Library of Congress

ISBN 978-1-62157-957-1
ebook ISBN 978-1-62157-965-6

Published in the United States by
Regnery Publishing
A Division of Salem Media Group
300 New Jersey Ave NW
Washington, DC 20001
www.Regnery.com

Manufactured in the United States of America

10 9 8 7 6 5 4 3 2 1

Books are available in quantity for promotional or premium use. For information on discounts and terms, please visit our website: www.Regnery.com.

To Leonard, with love

CONTENTS

CHAPTER ONE
The Decline and Fall of the Blue States
Why States the Democrats Control Are Losing Residents   1

CHAPTER TWO
The New Economic Reality
The Ramifications of the Liberal Invasion, in Dollars and Cents   25

CHAPTER THREE
Political Impacts on Receiving States
How Liberal Migration Is Changing Politics at Every Level   51

CHAPTER FOUR
The Rise of the Purple State
What Happened to New Hampshire, Colorado, and Virginia?   69

CHAPTER FIVE
The New City-States
How Red State Cities Explain Blue Victories   91

CHAPTER SIX
Washington, D.C.
The Exception That Proves the Rule   109

CHAPTER SEVEN
The New Exurbs
How Moving Vans and Rural Pushback Explain the Election of Donald Trump   121

CHAPTER EIGHT
More Divided Than Ever
How Echo Chambers Are Polarizing Our Politics—and Our Nation   137

CHAPTER NINE

Reading the Tea Leaves

A Look into the Not-Too-Distant Future   151

CHAPTER TEN

The Case for Optimism

Even Hipsters Can Help Make America Great Again   167

Acknowledgments   191

Notes   193

Index   227

CHAPTER ONE

The Decline and Fall of the Blue States
Why States the Democrats Control Are Losing Residents

Was I the only one at my spinning class in Manhattan fed up with paying $120 every month to belong to a gym with clean showers, $3,000 rent every month for an apartment without cockroaches, and $7 every morning for a cup of coffee? Was I the only one fed up with the inexorable march of urban decay in the greater part of New York City's boroughs, matched with the discomfort of crowding and the inexplicably ever-rising costs?

I was not.

My move to New York City fresh out of college was exciting—as it is for many other young people. But for many, New York gets real old, real fast. A few years of living in the Big Apple leaves many recent college grads penniless and stressed out.

New York is the most expensive city in America.[1] Its lower-cost neighborhoods are ridden with crime[2] and homelessness.[3] Its public schools, among the worst in the nation,[4] look more like prisons than places of learning. Its streets are lined with panhandlers and trash. And with up to 50 percent of their paychecks going to a combination of federal, local, and city taxes—not including other consumer taxes baked into every aspect of their everyday lives—residents don't even have the comfort of knowing that their taxes are going to the improvement of their lives. New York infamously misuses the hard-earned money of its citizens in ways that scarcely benefit them. The beleaguered working population finds encouragement these days in sadly outdated refrains like, "It's the greatest city in the world" and, "If I can make it there, I'll make it anywhere." These days, most simply aren't making it, and the city and state governments are little help.

Take the New York City subway system, the Metropolitan Transportation Authority (MTA), which loses more than $6 billion per year thanks to corrupt management and wildly above-market worker salaries.[5] In order to increase cash flow to the subway system, city officials routinely burden New Yorkers with increases in ticket prices—today, a one-way ride costs $3, up from $2.75 last year. But it's more than just fare hikes; the MTA also imposes heavy corporate taxes on electric, utility, and phone companies. These charges, used to support a tangle of financial waste, simply get passed on to New York City's residents and commuters.

And that's just the MTA. The city's bloated and infamously mismanaged school system, taxi cartel, and housing programs are just a few of the other programs driving New Yorkers to financial ruin and desperation. How can they hope to thrive when big-spending programs are emptying the city's coffers and wrecking its economy?

They can't.

Eventually city and state taxes, fees, and regulations become so burdensome that people and corporations jump ship. More people are currently fleeing New York than any other metropolitan area in the nation. Over a million people have moved out of New York City since 2010 in search of greener pastures, which amounts to a negative net migration rate of 4.4 percent.[6] In 2018 alone, 180,306 more people moved out of New York than moved in from other states.[7]

Corporate growth in the city has also declined dramatically. Last year New York had one of the slowest-growing economies in the nation. Business owners complain that the unfavorable regulatory environment—including the newly instated $15-an-hour minimum wage—has simply made it too costly to operate in the city.[8]

What's happening in the Big Apple is a microcosm of what's happening in the nation's blue state cities and towns. New York, Los Angeles, Chicago—the places where power and capital have historically congregated—have become so overregulated, so overpriced and mismanaged, and so morally bankrupt and soft on crime that people are leaving in droves.

The cost of popular moving truck services, such as U-Haul, is largely determined by the ironclad laws of supply and demand. Turns out, the demand for trucks leaving blue states like New York and heading to red states exceeds the demand for trucks going in the opposite direction. A route from California to Texas, for example, costs more than twice as much as a route from Texas to California. Want to go from Los Angeles to Dallas? $2,558. The trip in the opposite direction? Just $1,232. Texas is the number one state people drive moving trucks to, with states like Florida, South Carolina, Tennessee, North Carolina, and Colorado rounding out the top ten. The states people are fleeing? California, New York, New Jersey, Massachusetts, Michigan, Pennsylvania, and Illinois.

Census data reflect these trends. Between 2017 and 2018, Texas and Florida were the big winners in overall population gains; during that time span, the Lone Star State gained more than 379,000 residents while the Sunshine State gained more than 322,000. The biggest losers? New York, California, and Illinois.[9]

California alone saw a net loss of over one million residents between 2007 and 2016. The overwhelming top destination for those ex-Californians was Texas, followed by Arizona, Nevada, and Oregon. The largest socioeconomic segment moving from California is the middle class.[10] The state is home to some of the most burdensome taxes and regulations in the nation, and its social engineering—from green energy to wealth redistribution—has made many working families poorer. As California continues its long decline, the exodus of middle-class, working families accelerates.

The last decade has seen a significant exodus from some of the nation's biggest blue states, while many red states continue to gain population. Figures from the U.S. Census Bureau show that between July 2017 and July 2018 the nation's biggest population losers were the high-tax states of New York and Illinois. During that one year alone, the total populations of New York and Illinois declined by 48,510 and 45,116, respectively.[11] 2018 marked the fifth straight year in which Illinois saw a population decline. Democrat-controlled Hawaii and Connecticut were also among the top population losers.

We have seen how Texas, which topped the list of states in population growth, saw an addition of nearly 380,000 people during that same time span, and Florida, a close second, added 322,000. Both are traditional Republican strongholds. When you break the census data down in percentage terms, Republican-controlled Nevada, Idaho, Utah, Arizona, and Florida saw the nation's biggest population gains.

These are no coincidences.

While the bulk of out-migration from these states is the result of people fleeing cities, the trend extends to rural areas situated in blue states as well. Small communities in states like Connecticut are unable to counteract the drag of bad governance at the state level. Generally, only immigration from foreign nations is propping up population figures in blue states. And the new arrivals from other countries tend to be lower skilled and rely more heavily on government services than the residents they are replacing. Americans just don't want to live in the blue states governed by Democrats anymore.

It's easy to understand why. In New York, a combination of increasing costs and worsening conditions under Sandinista-supporting New York City mayor Bill de Blasio, together with restrictive policies strangling corporate growth in the rest of the state, make the state a demographic disaster. All told, the number of citizens leaving the state is at its highest rate since the bad old days of the 1970s.

Heavy taxes burden rural areas in blue states. There's no more ease in having a little home on the prairie; in Illinois, "the Prairie State," the average household turns over an incredible $8,162 in taxes per year (more than what California households shell out). But the state still wants *more* of its residents' hard-earned money. To plug an ever-widening budget hole, Illinois is now considering hiking the income tax and cutting several exemptions.

Not surprisingly, the populations of each of Illinois's neighboring states have grown over the last several years. Illinois now is undergoing population loss at a rate approaching Michigan's in the run-up to Detroit's collapse a decade ago.

You may be thinking these figures simply bear out conservative economic principles: higher taxes, more regulation, and a lax approach to law enforcement drive population out of the badly governed blue states into the better-governed red ones. That's true enough. But sadly, the ultimate result is not a triumph for sound conservative public policy. Instead, the blue state cancer has metastasized and is traveling to other parts of the body politic.

While Adam Smith's economic invisible hand seems to be doing its work—the residents of blue states recognize the bleak future of their homes, so they vote with their feet—the problem is that many of these domestic migrants, once they arrive in red states, proudly vote for the same policies they just fled.

There's ample evidence that residents who leave blue states for red states cause their new homes to trend leftward. Look at Texas, which is growing faster than any state,[12] with the majority of its growth from domestic migration coming from California and New York.[13] Texas doesn't register voters by political party, so the only way to measure the voting habits of the new residents is to track voter turnout over time. Check out the increase in Democratic votes cast in Texas's successive gubernatorial primaries, as the state's population exploded with blue state refugees:

Election Year	Texas's Total Population	Democratic Votes Cast	Republican Votes Cast
2010	25 million	680,548	1.4 million
2014	27 million	560,000	1.3 million
2018	29 million	1 million	1.5 million

2014 was a midterm election year, so both parties saw decreased turnout across the board in that year. But over time, as Texas's population grew by leaps and bounds, Democratic votes have made up a significantly larger portion of total ballots cast. Between 2010 and 2018, Democratic votes increased by 50 percent while Republican votes increased by just 10 percent.

A deeper dive into Texas domestic migration figures reveals the top states where new residents are moving from. According to census statistics, the top states losing residents to the Lone Star State each year have consistently been California, Illinois, and New York.

Year	Total Domestic Migration to Texas	New Residents from California	New Residents from Illinois	New Residents from New York
2011	508,000	63,000	20,000	20,000
2012	538,000	66,000	29,000	20,000
2013	539,000	64,000	23,000	21,000
2014	553,000	65,500	22,000	26,000
2015	532,000	70,000	22,000	18,000
2016	525,000	63,000	26,000	20,700

During the same time span, the margin of Democratic votes cast increased significantly—especially in Texas cities like Houston, Dallas, and Austin, which absorb the majority of domestic migrants.

In chapter 3, we'll take a deeper dive into the political ramifications of the blue state exodus for receiving red states. Shifting demographics are transforming politics at every level of government and will have a profound impact on red state cities and rural communities alike. But first, let's take a closer look at what's driving blue state residents into red states in the first place.

The Blue State Blues

Joanne and Vince Intrieri were true New Yorkers who had lived in the city for decades. But increasingly burdensome state and city taxes were chipping away at their bank account, and the new federal tax law passed in 2017, the first year of the Trump administration, just made the situation worse. So in 2018 the couple traded their Manhattan flat for a three-bedroom condominium in sunny Miami.

The Tax Cuts and Jobs Act of 2017 reduced state and local tax (SALT) deductions to $10,000, a cap which many New Yorkers easily exceed. New York City already had the highest tax burden in the nation; its residents on average pay 12.7 percent of their income in state and local taxes. But for the city's middle- and high-income earners, the new federal tax law drove up their tax bills even further, since they can no longer deduct steep state and local taxes. New Yorkers earning a million dollars now owe the IRS $21,000 more than they did before the law went into effect.[14] To hundreds of thousands in the city, "fair" became instantly "unfair": an estimated one in twenty-five New Yorkers is a millionaire—over 380,000 people total.[15] And New York's millionaires drive the city's economy by investing in and spending money at businesses that employ millions of people.

"My husband and I have been in New York City for more than 20 years, but we aren't tied to an office anymore and our kids are older," Ms. Intrieri told the *New York Times*. "Between the state and city taxes, plus about $50,000 in property taxes, it is a lot of money going out the door. Why do it?"[16]

The Intrieris aren't the only ones; in the wake of the new tax bill, scores of New York's middle-income families and high earners have already fled south to Texas and Florida, which have no personal income tax.

In February 2019, New York governor Andrew Cuomo announced that New York faced an unexpected $2.3 billion budget shortfall. The governor attempted to blame President Trump and Florida for his own state's economic woes. Cuomo complained about the removal of the SALT deductions under Trump's tax bill and said New Yorkers are fleeing to the Sunshine State to save on taxes.[17] But the fact is, New York is killing the goose that laid the golden egg through decades of poor policy decisions and an unfair tax system. Rather than blame Trump and Florida, Cuomo would be better off grabbing the paddles of fiscal reform to keep his flatlining patient alive.

The new law, which also lowered the federal corporate tax rate to a flat 21 percent, will only speed up the rate of capital investment and job creation in red state cities such as Dallas, Phoenix, and Miami. It will also drive more high-skilled labor out of blue state cities. Bruce McGuire, founder of the Connecticut Hedge Fund Association, told Bloomberg News that in light of the new tax laws "it would be almost irresponsible if you weren't thinking about moving" out of meccas like Los Angeles, New York, and Chicago.[18]

Blue state politicians' dismay at the SALT credit change highlighted their hypocrisy: finally, they were concerned about a tax hike. Blue state politicians love SALT deductions, which allow them to continually raise state and local taxes with little political blowback. At the time of this writing, veteran House Democrat Nita Lowey from New York's suburbs is touting a bill to reinstate SALT deductions.[19] "The new tax law is kind of like icing on the cake for some who were thinking about moving out of the state," said a candidate for California state treasurer. Pretty upsetting, considering the state's history of taxation—and the fact that over half of the financial impact of the SALT changes will be the burden of the dastardly "1 percent" that Sacramento has been blaming for everything wrong with America.[20]

California politicians especially fear the new tax law's effect on middle-class residents.[21] California's existing exorbitant tax rates already leave families squeezed. Cali's top marginal income tax rate of 13.3 percent is the highest state income tax rate in the nation. The marginal rate on the state's median annual income, $61,320, is a burdensome 8 percent. Shedding crocodile tears for the minimal impact of the SALT write-off on middle-class families does nothing about the much more burdensome taxes and fees that Sacramento imposes on those same residents directly.

Blue state politicians knew they could continuously increase local taxes with few political consequences, because their constituents could write those taxes off on their federal income tax returns. The removal of SALT deductions removed that assurance, pushing left-leaning voters out of blue state mega-cities into more affordable red state cities. For years, SALT deductions allowed blue states and their more left-leaning citizens to decrease their federal tax burden. But why should residents in conservative states be forced to shoulder more of the overall federal tax burden just because liberal states like to increase local taxes to spend within their own geographic areas? Why should fiscally conservative New Hampshire, with no income tax on its residents, subsidize tax-and-spend schemes that benefit the richest inhabitants of Massachusetts and New York?

On top of exorbitant income and property taxes, high rent and mortgage payments are often a significant burden in blue states. And bloated taxpayer-funded handouts are yet another contributing factor in the great blue state exodus. The highest welfare spending rates correlate strongly with the largest out-migration rates. New York, which leads the pack with $3,100 in annual per capita welfare spending, is losing 9.6 percent of its population each year! Connecticut spends $2,100 and says goodbye to 6.2 percent of its residents. In California and Massachusetts, respectively, it's $2,600 and 3.5 percent and $2,700 and 3.4 percent. Illinois, which spends less on welfare but taxes more, has an appalling 8.9 percent annual domestic out-migration rate.[22] The leaders of these states are running out of taxpayers to soak.

This toxic mix of progressive politics, increasing state taxes, and increased social spending acts as a vicious vise squeezing out working-class families. Middle-class families typically earn too much to receive government welfare and get hit with higher property and income taxes. People eventually pack up and head to greener pastures (places with lower costs of living). *No need to chase me out—I'll just go. Thanks for the memories.*

Take a look at how "taxing the rich" actually affects blue states. In the 1980s, Connecticut was a corporate safe haven for businesses fleeing the high taxation and crime of New York and Boston. Now it's just the opposite. The state is suffering what CNBC calls a "business migration crisis."[23] Major hedge funds are leaving. Corporate headquarters for GE and Aetna are bidding farewell to the state (Aetna, after 164 years). A massive 45 percent of Connecticut's top hundred taxpayers left the state between 2015 and 2016, and the state saw a tax revenue decline of $2.2 billion between 2017 and 2018.[24] The thing about states is they can't print money to pay off their debt like the federal government can. They need to attract jobs and taxpayers to pay it off. Connecticut lawmakers don't seem to understand this. Perhaps they are hoping for another $700 billion federal bailout, like the one in 2008.

In New Jersey, we see the folly of taxing the small sliver of the population that has the means of moving away—and fast. In 2016, the state's legislature passed a comprehensive new "millionaire's tax," on top of tax rates that were already among the highest in the nation. The result? You could have flunked high school economics and still gotten this one right: as a money manager from northern New Jersey told the *Wall Street Journal*, his clients were leaving like the state was "on fire."[25]

A hedge fund manager named David Tepper, one of the wealthiest taxpayers in the state, left for Florida in 2016 (which has no state income tax) to escape New Jersey's outrageous taxes and took his business with him.[26] The result? New Jersey coffers collapsed a full percent.[27] As of that year, New Jersey's top tax rate had increased almost 50 percent since 1996, to 8.97 percent. Trenton didn't reveal the total lost revenue from Tepper's business and personal income taxes, but hundreds of millions per year is a reasonable estimate.

And what did Tepper do with the money he saved by leaving New Jersey? For starters, he bought a major stake in the Carolina Panthers.[28] Imagine what you could do if you got a 9 percent raise. Thinking of a new deck? Need a new car? Saving for your kids' college tuition? These are your dreams, and they are real, but New Jersey wants to be your dream catcher and destroyer. No, the state of New Jersey does not endorse that message.

So did Trenton learn its lesson from the Tepper affair and the mass loss of residents and capital? Of course not. In 2018 it adopted a new top tax rate of 10.75 percent.[29] Every 10 percent hike in states' income taxes results in a one percent loss of their millionaire population.[30]

Since high-tax states increasingly rely on a declining number of high-earner taxpayers, even a handful of households leaving can be deleterious. Consider this: California relies on just *1 percent* of its population for a full half (!) of its tax haul.[31] These residents represent just 24 percent of all state income but bear 48 percent of the tax burden.[32] The Golden State relies on fifteen thousand tax filers for 25 percent of its overall tax intake.[33] What happens if (or, dare I say, *when*) those taxpayers decide to pack up and leave? If the past is any indication, their solution will be yet another tax hike on the poor suckers who remain.

This reliance on the ultra-rich, coupled with exorbitant spending, led to California's dead-last ranking from Moody's among large states' abilities to grapple with a future recession. Conservative Texas was ranked number one.[34] California's solution to perennial budgetary problems almost always involves implementing "temporary" taxes...which never go away. Case in point: in 2012, a sales tax hike was passed, along with higher marginal income tax rates for high earners. Now millionaires get stuck with an income tax of 13.3 percent, while households earning $250,000 hand over 9.3 percent of their income. These tax increases were supposed to be temporary, but they were renewed in 2016. They didn't go away at the end of 2018, either, having now been extended all the way until the end of 2030. And nobody believes they will be phased out then, either. Government only grows.

Stephanie, a good friend of mine from college, is from an immigrant family that moved to San Diego from China in the early '90s. Stephanie's parents epitomize the American dream. They came to the U.S. with few resources and no education, and today they proudly own a chain of hip restaurants in Southern California. But rather than reward Stephanie's family for contributing to California's economy and culture, state politicians go to great lengths to soak them with burdensome tax hikes that strain the family's finances and ability to expand their business. Today Stephanie's parents pay 10.3 percent in state taxes plus 35 percent in federal taxes on their $300,000 annual household income. In other words, nearly half of the family's hard-earned money is going straight to government coffers—and that's in addition to the exorbitant cost of living in California created by absurd regulation and business-killing policies that drive up the cost of nearly everything. It should come as no shock that Stephanie's parents are currently considering selling their restaurants and moving to low-cost Florida.

They aren't the only ones thinking about leaving. A 2019 poll by Edelman Intelligence found that 53 percent of California residents are considering leaving the state on account of the exorbitant cost of living. The poll also found that nearly two-thirds of Californians believe the best days of the Golden State are in the past.[35]

So how did California bureaucrats use all the extra money the state received as the result of its recent tax hikes? Lawmakers initially assured voters that the funds would be put toward public education. But instead (surprise, surprise!) most of the money goes straight to California's insolvent pension system (translation: cushy pensions and benefits for California's army of bureaucrats). The state of California employs nearly nine hundred thousand government workers.[36] The rest of the money, which totals a whopping $2 billion per year, goes toward the state's equivalent of Medicaid, the costs of which are about to skyrocket to even higher levels, as California politicians have pledged to pass legislation allowing illegal immigrants to receive medical care subsidized by the government.[37]

During the past decade, overall state pension debt has increased by almost $200 billion[38]—almost the size of the entire economy of South Carolina or Oregon.[39] This is also about the size of California's entire annual budget.[40] San Francisco's solution for their portion of the pension shortfall? Raising taxes, of course! In 2018, city bureaucrats implemented a $298-per-property annual real estate tax on the excuse of "increasing teacher pay."[41]

These increased taxes leave California with little slack if a recession hits. As of 2016, the state had just *one-tenth* of the rainy day funds it would need to weather such a storm.[42] And if a handful of wealthy earners leave before then, the situation will be even worse...and likely lead to *another* tax increase on remaining Californians.

Adding insult to injury, those who leave California for a state with a lower cost of living are forced to pay yet another fee. Yes, California punishes people who try to leave. The state's Franchise Tax Board will charge your small business *ex post facto* taxes of up to an additional 100 percent of taxes already paid if its members believe you fled to avoid taxes, or if you make more than $200,000 in income per year as an individual.[43] ID Analytics, a company eventually bought out by LifeLock, was forced to pay several hundred thousand dollars in retroactive taxes.[44] How absolutely infuriating.

Don't think it can get worse? If you live in California, it can. While the IRS may make your life hell by auditing six years of income, the state of California can audit you for your entire life.[45] One web entrepreneur was charged $200,000 in back taxes and $47,000 in penalties for a legitimate stock sale six years before.[46] It's a literal "Hotel California." You can check out, but your money can never leave.

What's happening to the accumulated wealth in high-tax states? It's increasingly fleeing those states, along with the people who earned it. Between 2015 and 2016, those who moved out of Connecticut took over $6 billion in income with them, while those who moved in during that same time period brought just $3.36 billion in income.[47] That's a $2.7 billion total net loss to Connecticut in just one year. About $2 billion of that revenue followed residents to Florida alone.

Next door, high-tax New Jersey's anti-business, high-tax policies chased out $18 billion in net income from 2005 to 2016.[48] The state lost ten thousand wealthy families in just one year, after a "millionaire tax" was imposed.[49] Illinois lost a net $3.4 billion in adjusted gross income in 2014 alone, with half going to Florida and Texas.[50] One state's loss often becomes another state's gain.

As blue states chase out jobs and local investment, they become increasingly reliant on taxing the wealthy earners and middle-class families who remain. The pressure to raise taxes continually increases as a state's economic situation becomes grim. Liberals also see more government spending as the solution to a weakening economy, so spending goes up further, requiring—you guessed it—*more* tax increases.

So What Do You Get for All Those Tax Payments?

"Moral hazard" is when someone takes more risks because someone else bears the cost of those risks. Left-wing policy is one of the greatest generators of moral hazard in history. Democrat-controlled cities and states have to live with the accumulative effects of the tax-and-spend policies of cynical politicians and un-fireable bureaucrats.

Sure, you may be saying to yourself (especially if this book was gifted to you by your conservative nephew), *but don't Republican states do the same thing?* Yes! Not every folly in American politics is confined to the Democratic Party. But the states losing residents at the highest rates tend to excel in individualizing rewards and socializing risk—a hallmark of the American Left. There is no mass exit from the nation's largest red states.

What we see in blue states is that other priorities and promises go by the wayside to keep up with ever-mounting entitlements. One of the closest correlates of reduced public funding for education is increased public healthcare spending. Since 1990, the proportion of all state spending on higher education has been halved to 9 percent. Students are getting stuck with tuition increases and nickeled-and-dimed with student fees while Medicaid spending has nearly doubled.[51] There is no such thing as a free lunch, so much of the increased Medicaid spending is simply passed on to taxpaying stiffs like you.

In blue state after blue state, discretionary spending has been crowded out by entitlements. Money once spent on education and tangible infrastructure such as roads and bridges has been diverted to increases in social welfare programs. Before Obamacare, California spent 13 percent of its budget on higher education and 19 percent on Medicaid.[52] By financial year 2016 these numbers had changed dramatically, to just 7 percent on education and 34 percent on Medicaid! During the same period the number of Californians on Medi-Cal, the state's Medicaid equivalent, nearly doubled from 6.9 million to 13.5 million. This is a massive increase, of course, but the amount spent tells a more revealing story. Spending skyrocketed from $35.7 to $82.8 billion. This caused a severe shortage of available doctors for patients. In 2013, there were on average fifty-nine primary care physicians and ninety-one specialists serving every 100,000 Medi-Cal enrollees. Just two years later, with increased spending and new patients, the number of available doctors per patient fell by a third.[53]

What does this mean for the average Californian? Hospitals are overcrowded and more people are dying. Meanwhile, as California expands taxpayer-funded medicine to illegal aliens, emergency room wait times have gone up significantly—patients who get admitted to hospitals in the state are forced to wait an hour longer in the ER than patients nationally.[54] Imagine rushing your elderly father to the hospital after he has had a heart attack and being forced to wait hours because illegal immigrants are flooding the ER. When you're dealing with a medical emergency, every minute counts. The difference between a twenty-minute wait time and a one-hour wait time could easily determine whether a patient lives or dies.

The overall trend in blue states is spending cuts against those who need basic, non-individualized services from their state governments. Below is data from the nine states with the highest percentages of citizens covered by Medicaid. In general, the more a state spends on Medicaid, the less it spends on education and transportation. This makes sense. All budgets have limits.

State	Percentage of population receiving Medicaid	Medicaid as total percentage of spending for FY 2017	Higher-education spending as total percentage of spending for FY 2017	Transportation as total percentage of spending for FY 2017
New Mexico	33.8%	30.2%	16.6%	4.7%
Vermont	33.3%	28.8%	1.7%	9.7%
New York	30.9%	32.6%	6.7%	6.7%
California	28.1%	33.3%	7.0%	5.4%
West Virginia	28.1%	22.2%	12.1%	7.3%
Arkansas	26.4%	29.2%	15.0%	4.8%
Delaware	25.0%	19.3%	3.9%	8.6%
Oregon	24.8%	23.6%	3.7%	5.5%
Rhode Island	24.4%	29.3%	12.6%	6.6%
National Average	22.5%	29.0%	10.4%	8.1%

Sources: 2017 Medicaid data,[55] Medicaid and CHIP Payment and Access Commission,[56] National Association of State Budget Officers[57]

The reallocation of funds to social welfare programs and cratering pension funds harms students at every level. California governor Jerry Brown boasted about an increase in tax revenue, but California isn't using it boost education. The governor recommended that the University of California system increase tuition *and* cap scholarships.[58] There are already 5,400 pensioners retired from the UC system, each bringing home well over $100,000 per year, which comes to a total cost of over $5.5 billion annually—an increase of 60 percent between 2012 and 2016![59] Did *you* get a 60 percent raise over the last five years?

The average pension for a UC employee retiring after thirty years is $88,000. Some are much, much higher. The former head of the UC system collects $357,000 annually for just seven years' work. Former Clinton adviser Robert Reich pulls down $300,000 to teach one class[60] on income inequality (and will get a sweet pension when he retires).

And some UC employees are allowed pensions and six-figure salaries...at the same time! Sweet deal! The UC system pays one former professor, Dr. Fawzy I. Fawzy, a $369,000 annual pension. But Fawzy simultaneously draws a UC salary, as he is one of several hundred retirees in the University of California system brought back to teach after retirement. These "recalled" retirees draw both a pension and a salary. Fawzy currently makes over $650,000 a year off the UC system.

Twelve of the top twenty-five UC pension holders aren't even professors—many of them are administrators. The system is, in common parlance, FUBAR (search it). Unsurprisingly, university administrators don't want these shocking taxpayer-funded compensation figures released to the public. The numbers were kept private until a California-based think tank sent the university system's president a Public Records Act request for pension data. After a six-month battle with university administrators, a limited amount of data was finally released.[61]

The University of California continues to grapple with a $15 billion shortfall due to horrific policy choices, including not asking its employees to contribute to the pension fund for twenty years. This type of fiscal irresponsibility would have bankrupted a private company long ago. But this is part of the massive California state government, so all they need to do is raise taxes. UC at one point allowed a minimum retirement age of fifty, since raised to fifty-five. Can you name a single private-sector job that offers full retirement benefits at age fifty? Me neither. California has made some changes, including a large bailout in 2015 in exchange for a new pension cap and a choice for employees to join a 401(k) program.

Meanwhile, the Golden State keeps throwing more tax dollars at public workers even as its pension plan is going broke. Lee Baca, the former LA county sheriff who narrowly escaped jail time for covering up inmate abuse by lying to the FBI, is collecting a $342,000-per-year pension.[62] California's public-sector unions are—surprise, surprise!—fighting any efforts at reform, and they persuaded the state's supreme court to gut the 401(k) reform mentioned above.[63]

The pension bloat affects K–12 education as well. Increases in "education spending" for the poorest districts seldom make it to the classroom. These increases instead have to cover skyrocketing pension costs, which have now climbed to over $100 billion in state obligations.[64] There is no trickle-down to the students who need it at the elementary and high school levels. Just over half of students in these disadvantaged districts are proficient in English and math.[65]

At some point this house of cards will collapse, and California lawmakers will be asking for a federal bailout. They will never blame their own mismanagement, but rather someone or something else: Trump's policies, China, Wall Street—anything but themselves. They will demand the bailout to support "working families." But it will be the fiscal mismanagement of California lawmakers making the bailout necessary—at the expense of *you*, the American taxpayer.

Think that's bad? California's massive pension shortfall is only part of a national gap of $1.4 trillion in state pension funds[66]—almost the size of Texas's economy.[67] Four states don't even have half of their future obligations covered. The states with the worst shortfalls include the same blue states that keep coming up in this book—New York, California, New Jersey, Illinois, and Massachusetts.

So ultimately, what's left for a middle-class family? You're paying high taxes and getting poor services. Liberals love to say that's just the cost of a civilized society. But blue state budgets rarely provide the benefits you expect. Among the ten states with the worst-quality roads?[68] The same old names you've memorized by now are on that list too.

Dealing with state bureaucracies is particularly distasteful in states dominated by Democrats. Twenty-one DMVs in California require making an appointment at least a month in advance in order to get your paperwork done. The DMV in Fremont, California, requires a full seventy-three-day wait, on average. And once you're there, you have to do even more waiting—in 2018 the average was sixty-nine minutes, up dramatically from forty-eight minutes the year before. In Sacramento, the wait is an average of over an hour and a half.[69] So what's going on? State auditors found employees regularly shirking their job responsibilities, including one who slept three hours a day on the clock.[70] It has gotten so out of control that an enterprising little private company has sprung up to send someone to wait in line for you at San Francisco DMVs for the low price of twenty-five dollars per hour.[71] Connecticut has a similar problem, with some of the longest waits in the nation.[72] With public-sector unions calling the shots, your family is paying more in taxes to get far less in services. And despite all that egregious napping on the job, most of these DMV employees are cranky, miserable people.

Poorly managed and fiscally incompetent states are finding new ways to raise more revenue. One of them is through liberal (heh) use of speeding tickets. Among the top ten states to hand out tickets: Pennsylvania, New York, California, Massachusetts, and Connecticut.[73] As a proud Texan, I'm ashamed to admit that Texas made this list as well.

States and cities also utilize red-light and speed cameras to plug funding gaps, with the highest concentrations of them in New York, California, Maryland, Illinois, and D.C.[74] And while some states and cities are lightening up on the practice in response to commuter outrage, there is a financial price to pay. From a *Governing* magazine piece on red light cameras: "When New Jersey ended its pilot program, Moody's, the credit rating agency, warned of the impact the development could have on the two dozen municipalities that had the devices."[75] The cameras are used to pick your pocket. But studies suggest they actually make us less safe. An analysis found an *increase* of 22 percent in rear-end collisions and of 15 percent in crashes resulting in injuries on account of the cameras.[76] Drivers realize the cameras are there and often slam on their brakes, causing crashes. The cameras are money-making machines for lawyers, lawsuits, and states. California takes in, on average, an astounding $490 for every violation.[77] Chicago's traffic violation revenue increased 50 percent between 2014 and 2016, to $67 million.[78] Like most government programs, this one has been terribly mismanaged. Three hundred and ninety thousand Chicago drivers are receiving refunds as a result of the city breaking its own rules by not sending second violation notices before passing judgement and issuing $100 late fees four days before the deadline to pay the tickets.[79] The city is, predictably, offering only 50 percent refunds.

If you're not paying for the privilege of driving in blue states through taxes or tickets, you're paying for it every time you fill up your gas tank. The top ten gas-taxed states in America include some familiar faces. Pennsylvania, California, Washington, Hawaii, New York, Michigan, and Connecticut make up the top seven. Gas is almost *forty cents* more expensive in Pennsylvania (#1) than in Texas (#44)! The states with the most tolls, by far, include New York, Illinois, Pennsylvania, Connecticut, and Massachusetts.[80] Commuters in these states get screwed every single day. And of course, higher transportation expenses drive up the cost of consumer goods as well.

Left-wing policies make your general standard of living more expensive in plenty of other ways, too. California's infamous rent control rules, which bureaucrats want to expand significantly, severely crimp the supply of housing. Take San Francisco, where the average monthly rent for a one-bedroom apartment is nearly $4,000.[81] Restrictive building codes curtail new construction in the area, driving up housing costs even further. Residents are making do as they can—some people live in their cars or even storage units (yes, really). Luke Iseman, a thirty-one-year-old Wharton grad, is renting shipping containers to people seeking affordable housing for $1,000 a month. Others live in their vehicles; one twenty-three-year-old engineer at Google lives in the back of a moving truck in the company's parking lot. A few people who work in the Bay Area live in lower-cost Las Vegas and commute to San Francisco by flight—they claim to save about $700 a month by flying to the Bay Area every day instead of living there.[82]

Building and zoning restrictions have made California an astonishingly 2.5 times more expensive than the national average. A modest single-family home will set you back over a half-million bucks. Since building is so expensive, only 80,000 houses are built annually, even though there's an estimated need of 180,000 per year.[83]

Burdensome regulations yield negative outcomes for residents…with no end in sight. California leads the nation in homelessness[84] and poverty. The nominal 2014 poverty rate in California was 16.4 percent (#35) but after adjusting for rent, food, and geography, it was 23.8 percent (#1). New York is officially ranked thirty-second in poverty, but after cost-of-living adjustments it skyrockets to number seven. Poverty in blue states is obscured by the fact that higher incomes go significantly less far there. You can make $80,000 per year and be rich in South Dakota but feel relatively poor in Manhattan. A hundred dollars will buy you just $86.43 worth of goods in New York, $93.37 in Massachusetts, $87.34 in New Jersey, and $88.97 in California. But take that same $100 to nearly every state that voted for Trump in 2016, and it will buy you well over $100 worth of goods. Is it really worth living in New York if you lose 14 percent of your income just by paying higher food, gas, and home prices?

Put yourself in the shoes of a young family raising kids or a retiree living on a fixed income. Is this the best possible use of your hard-earned money? What matters more to you: your quality of life, or your state's "needs"? Why not jump the fence from California to Nevada or New York to North Carolina or Illinois to Florida? Good weather, lower taxation, and fewer restrictions on your personal freedom. But please, leave your politics in the state you're leaving.

There are many reasons to uproot your family and leave everything you know. But many people move without a proper assessment of why they left New York for North Carolina in the first place. This lack of reflection has voters moving to Florida or Texas or Colorado or New Hampshire and then registering once again as Democrats. After all, maybe making Texas blue will finally bring some culture to the Lone Star State, they think. More likely, it will just bring the same dimwitted policies they were trying to escape in the first place.

Maybe we can compromise. You can keep Austin weird, and we'll keep Texas red. Deal?

Federalism (Gasp!) Works!

There is a reason why Edward Gibbon's multi-volume treatise *The History of the Decline and Fall of the Roman Empire* is a must-read among historians. It is a lengthy primer for anyone hoping to understand civilizational decline.

Mark Steyn's recent bestseller *America Alone* echoes many lessons from Oswald Spengler's classic work *The Decline of the West*, giving us a glimmer of understanding of how socialist and social-democratic experiments usually bring about the exact opposite of what they promise. Thank God Illinois and Rhode Island cannot print their own currency. Within a year people would be wallpapering their homes with the worthless money, like the Germans after World War I.

In our sovereign republic, the burdens of these failing states are borne by the other members of the Union. Springfield cannot print its own dollars, but it can saturate the bond market with billions in riskier and riskier bonds, to the detriment of investors and more responsible states. Bridgeport and Detroit can beg their states and the federal government for bailouts. California and Connecticut can beseech Congress to plug holes in their annual budgets and support their flailing social experiments. Meanwhile, taxpayers from all fifty states have to pick up the tab with each federal bailout.

States (and to a lesser extent, local municipalities) are constitutionally designed laboratories of democracy. They provide arenas in which policies can be tested, rejected if they fail, and adopted elsewhere if they succeed. This model has worked well over the last two and a half centuries. But where there is single-party control the model doesn't work as intended. Liberal policies fail—and then liberals simply double down on their failed policies.

Historians today believe that instead of a sudden collapse in AD 476, the Roman Empire fell slowly and gradually as a result of migration, government interventions in markets, costly foreign adventures, poor border enforcement, dilution of the currency, and intergenerational poverty abetted by the government dole. Does this sound familiar? The empire was undermined by incremental changes that were difficult for the average person to see.

Future students of today's America will be able to trace a timeline of what happens when states tax their citizens' earnings and wealth away. States that have run their finances into the ground for generations will be the most severely impacted from the next recession and will be unable to meet their obligations they made during good economic periods (like now). But the coming bailouts will mean that even if you and your family leave Illinois or California, you will still pay for those states' unfunded pension liabilities and some of the worst roads in the country.

There has only been one period of state bankruptcies in the U.S., in the economic calamity of the 1840s.[85] Inflation and a spike in unemployment led to a major recession called the Panic of 1837; as a result, nineteen of the twenty-six U.S. states, as well as two of the three territories, incurred state debt and declared bankruptcy. But today there's another calamity in the making in the blue states: runaway pension costs, a hollowing middle class, and experiments with socialist programs such as single-payer healthcare boondoggles and high-speed rail.

Some California cities have already declared bankruptcy. And with average municipal pension costs doubling in the next seven years, many others are spiraling towards financial ruin. California cities like Vallejo, Stockton, and San Bernardino all followed Detroit into debtor's prison and do not have levers to get out. They are locked into high-spending habits and have tapped out sales and property tax rates. There are calls to make city bailouts a state responsibility.[86] Then in the next major recession, there will be calls to federalize state debts—so farmers in Missouri can subsidize overpaid San Francisco pensioners.

As liberals abandon their blue states for economic survival, many will infect their new home states with the same bad voting habits. They will elect leaders they see as hip and enlightened. Politicians like Beto O'Rourke and Alexandria Ocasio-Cortez will start popping up in the heartland. New Hampshire, which in the mid-1990s was arguably the most Republican state in the nation, now boasts far-left moonbat congressional representatives like Chris Pappas, Annie Kuster, and Carol Shea-Porter. These New Hampshire progressives all support the Green New Deal, proposed by Ocasio-Cortez,[87] which would drastically increase the government's role in nearly every area of American life and nudge the nation closer to socialism. This new breed of politician did not come to New Hampshire because citizens in the state became enlightened. They came to power because Massachusetts residents, fed up with high taxes and expensive regulations in their own state, moved north into the Granite State. Locals from New Hampshire have been watching their home go slowly from red, to purple, to blue. There is no longer a single Republican in Congress from any state in New England—a frightening harbinger for the rest of America.

CHAPTER TWO

The New Economic Reality
The Ramifications of the Liberal Invasion, in Dollars and Cents

O bscure hipster music, lively chatter, and the ambient scent of coffee grounds filled the air during my weekend trip to visit my dear friend Ruth—a spunky mid-twenties gender-nonconforming master's student in postcolonial studies. Pushing through a crowd of gender-studies majors and young professionals in thick-rimmed glasses and skinny jeans, I made my way to the barista and ordered my usual: a black coffee.

Sipping on caffeine bliss, I strolled the urban promenade and peered into ornate storefront windows with artful displays: Fashion boutiques showcased the elegant handiwork of leading designers, global and regional; two new microbreweries boasted award-winning beers crafted from unique sources of water and wheat; a used-vinyl store overflowed with white men sporting dreadlocks. Further down, a large museum advertised a coming Dalí exhibition, with works on loan from museums in Spain and France.

I finally met Ruth at a "fusion bistro"—because who wouldn't want a brunch menu that combines haute Vietnamese cuisine with Peruvian "street" motifs. After stuffing ourselves with octopus baguettes (I swear, they taste like chicken—just more expensive), we headed off to the farmer's market to buy organic yams—worlds away from the GMO orgy at Sam's Club outside of the city center. We planned our evening as we strolled, most likely a late-night stop at Peter Kern's. What better place to take in an old-fashioned than an old-world speakeasy hidden away downtown, dimly lit, with ample leather seating and bartenders with caps like Sherlock Holmes's and red beards like Yosemite Sam's.

Welcome to Seattle.

Nah. Just kidding.

Welcome to good ole Knoxville, Tennessee!

Knoxville is fast becoming a hipster utopia—or, as I like to call it, a "hipstertopia." The Tennessee city, not historically synonymous with cool, is quietly becoming a hot spot of innovation, enterprise, fashion, and trendy locales that attract youth, talent, and young families. Startups and high-tech companies are flocking to the city to take advantage of its business-friendly environment and increasingly young, educated population. Grow Bioplastics, a quickly growing startup that takes organic waste from the paper industry and turns it into biodegradable mulch for farming,[1] is a prime example of the creative entrepreneurship taking Knoxville by storm.

Millennials and parents of young children are coming to the city for its good jobs, low cost of living, and tax structure that leaves more money in their pockets. The average age of a Knoxville resident is thirty-three.[2] This influx of new, aspiring residents has spurred the opening of trendy bars, cozy cafes, and top-ranked eateries, with edginess and coolness. Without walking more than a few blocks from the city center, Knoxvillians can eat an upscale dinner and enjoy a panoramic view at the city's iconic Sunsphere, get a five-cent coffee at the Mast General Store, grill their own steaks at the hip joint Udders, and catch a movie at a historic 1920s-era movie palace. The urban area is chock-full of quirky art installations and even some world-class museums. The World's Fair Park, located at the heart of the city, is a sprawling green space for picnics and frisbee sessions, complete with mammoth fountains and lush gardens.

Meanwhile, the city's job market is booming. The unemployment rate is 2.6 percent, well below the national rate of 4.1 percent. Knoxville consistently ranks as one of the nation's top cities for job creation. Residents enjoy no state or city income tax on wages and salaries.

The best part? You don't have to be rich or work three jobs to pay your rent. The average monthly rent for a one-bedroom apartment in Knoxville is $765.[3] Compare that to the going monthly rate for a one-bedroom rental in New York City, San Francisco, or Los Angeles—$2,662,[4] $3,372,[5] and $2,168, respectively.[6] In 2012 I lived in a downtrodden, dangerous Brooklyn neighborhood and paid $2,000 per month for the privilege.

Knoxville is clearly on the upswing, but if the city follows the path of the nation's other more developed hipstertopias, it will eventually peak and then begin to decay into a less than ideal community. As liberal-minded young residents flock to the city for job opportunities, they bring with them a buzzing nightlife and culture (good)—but also vote in favor of ignorant and destructive policies that squash economic growth (bad).

A few years ago, Houston went through a similar transformation. As the local job market boomed in 2012, mostly because of a strong gas and oil market, the city grew faster than any other major metropolitan area in the nation; there were more good-paying jobs available than people to fill them. Recent college grads and young professionals flocked to the city as trendy bars, high-end restaurants, and cute boutiques popped up in parts of the city that were once desolate and dangerous. Breathtaking high-rise apartment buildings with rooftop pools were erected downtown to accommodate all the new arrivals. I lived in Houston during this mini-Renaissance, and saw the transformation unfold before my eyes. Every weekend there were chic neighborhood pool parties and impressive new exhibits at every local art museum. During the height of its growth, in 2013, Houston was even ranked the best city for dating.

But things have changed in Houston. The city, which used to be extremely conservative and reliably red, has become a stronghold for liberals in large part because of the new residents moving in from other states. Harris County, in which Houston is located, boasted a forty-four-year Republican presidential voting streak up until 2008, when Barack

Obama took the county.[7] That same year, the offices of sheriff, county attorney, and district clerk fell into Democratic hands. The county went Democrat again—by larger margins—in 2012 and 2016. Then in the 2018 midterm elections, remaining Republican judges were swept out by voters in Houston.[8] Today, only Democratic judges preside on the bench in civil, criminal, family, juvenile, and probate courts.

During the same time span, between 2008 and 2018, Houston's population surged more than 15 percent, from 2 million to 2.3 million. And the top out-of-state metro areas sending new residents to Houston were Los Angeles, New York City, and Chicago.[9]

The successive Democratic wins in Harris County are already ushering in policy changes. In 2018, the liberal Houston City Council approved a property tax increase.[10] Meanwhile, the city's increasingly left-wing population is demanding new, restrictive regulations on the gas and oil industry[11]—you know, the industry that caused the city's economy to thrive in the first place.

Far beyond traditional Democrat-controlled cities like New York, San Francisco, and Los Angeles, left-wing policies are slowly taking hold and transforming cities situated in formerly solid red states. At first these changes manifest themselves in positive ways: new museums, state-of-the-art bike paths, and an influx of world-class restaurants. But over time, burdensome taxation and regulation demanded by newly elected activist politicians begins to chase businesses, and ultimately jobs, out of town. We've pointed to the logical end points of Democratic governance in their traditional strongholds. Unfortunately, formerly conservative places such as Colorado, New Hampshire, North Carolina, and even Texas could be headed for the same dead end. These states provide a template for what will likely happen to many western and southern states like Tennessee over the next generation. The profound economic, political, and cultural changes will first be most apparent in large cities and then, slowly but steadily, infect rural communities as well. The demographic transformation of the nation could end up undermining America's economic exceptionalism.

U-Haul renter beware.

The growth of cities like Knoxville, Seattle, Portland, and Denver showcases so much economic potential...that inevitably gets extinguished. And the electoral clout of such cities—their veto of the preferences of residents who live outside of city centers but also call Tennessee, Washington, Oregon, and Colorado home—will bring on a bust in these states, shaping places that are vastly different, culturally and politically, from these formerly red states as we have known them in the past.

Thousands of college-educated, young, upper-middle-class whites continue to move into the cities of conservative states, like Knoxville and Houston, and change them into boutique economies. Knoxville will likely suffer a fate similar to that of Denver, which in the early 2000s experienced an economic boom as a result of a combination of accumulated wealth and fresh residents who changed the status quo. Formerly run-down parts of town were remade with microbreweries, cupcake bakeries, coffee shops, music, and graphic design firms. But then things started to change for the worse, and Denver's growth came to a screeching halt. The city's low rents, which had originally ignited the population boom, skyrocketed, and as a result many young people (and original residents, too) began moving away.

The liberal population that remained elected moonbats like Rafael Espinoza and Kendra Black to the city council, and they changed Denver's priorities from affordable housing to banning plastic straws[12] and designating Denver as a "sanctuary city,"[13] inviting any illegal immigrant needing municipal services into the community. These initiatives don't help the working middle class, but gosh darnit, they make everyone feel so much better about themselves!

How long can you constrict anything that is living—even thriving—before the oxygen is sucked right out of it? Sure, some economic boomlets can last longer, especially if they're accentuated by gobs of state and federal dollars (see Northern Virginia as Example A). But usually such areas end up in worse shape than they were before the boom began. The bust is especially damaging when the affected state has implemented high taxes and restrictive regulations. Once the cost of living gets too high, many of these disenchanted liberals simply pack their bags and take their high culture to the next up-and-coming city or town, where they impose their destructive ideas and politics onto their new neighbors.

Some states have been able to pull themselves out of the doldrums of economic decline; take what happened in New York City when Rudy Giuliani became mayor in 1994. During the two previous decades, the city was in a steep decline caused by job-killing left-wing policies and lax law enforcement. Violent crimes had skyrocketed in the five boroughs; in 1990 alone, there were 2,245 murders in the city (a record high).[14] Residents were fleeing in record numbers—between 1970 and 1990, New York City's population declined by more than half a million.[15]

Giuliani reversed the decline by implementing a more business-friendly regulatory climate and strict, common-sense law enforcement policies. Sadly, after Giuliani brought New York City back to its glory days, a series of left-wing mayors, including Bill de Blasio, brought misery back to the Big Apple. Subway muggings are on the rise[16] and the city's homeless population has soared to over sixty thousand, with the city spending $117 in tax revenue per day to house each homeless person.[17]

But New York's story of revival is rare. It would seem to be more difficult for small-population cities and states to go back to their former days of economic prosperity once their populations have been significantly transformed by an influx of new, more liberal residents. A tiny fraction of the huge population of Californians or New Yorkers can have enormous impacts on the electoral politics of states they're moving to, such as North Carolina or Colorado or Tennessee. Sometimes, if the offending state is right next door (as in the case of the constant waves of Massachusetts residents flooding into New Hampshire), it's especially difficult to stem the blue tide.

And sadly, failed policies often lead to politicians doubling down on the original failures, believing that they just didn't go far enough the first time.

The rise of hipstertopias like Knoxville, Portland, and Austin might seem like perfect examples of how changes in demography help the receiving cities and states. After all, these residents, especially those who are wealthy and well educated, do inject new life, new culture, and new money into an area. Fixing up formerly disadvantaged neighborhoods can play a role in the transformation of urban neighborhoods from no-go zones to rustic farm-to-table locales. But if the population boom comes with misguided political activism, the money eventually dries up as economic growth is stifled by restrictive taxes and burdensome regulation.

This is not to say that there aren't significant benefits early on from thousands of young people flooding the next trendy city. Up-and-coming cities often rely on boutique businesses, based around food and art, to make the new economy turn. Consider the following:

- Portland, Oregon, ranked as the number one city in the country for "foodies" in 2018[18] on account of its eclectic mix of traditional and bandwagon food crazes. It also tied for the number one city for coffeehouses and craft beer.
- Oregon, Colorado, and Washington each brought in millions of dollars in tax revenue through the legalization of marijuana, which has caused an economic boom for potheads and retailers alike.
- Colorado has gained a reputation for its craft beer. Consider donning a handlebar moustache and taking a daylong steam locomotive ride to tour a number of major craft brewers.[19] Or catch a documentary on the craft during a film festival.[20] The state has the second most breweries of any state, at 204, with workers who enjoy an average salary of over $50,000.[21] Washington ranks number three. Colorado also hosts the annual Great American Beer Festival, which draws thousands.[22]
- Growing cities are typically quick to install beautiful public spaces equipped to host events and young families.

Portland and Seattle have among the highest-rated parks in the nation.[23] (Today, though, these beautiful gathering places are on the brink of never being enjoyed again due to harassment from "city official welcome" protestors—kind of unfriendly protestors, at that.)

• A number of anchor businesses in Seattle such as Microsoft, Boeing, and Amazon attract thousands of young people, especially highly educated programmers and engineers.

And as long as these rapidly growing cities often benefit from the residual effects of former, more conservative local governments that understood the principles of what makes an economy tick, they can continue to thrive. Washington State still does not have an income tax, and Oregon is considering banning sales taxes on groceries. Colorado still retains some tax competitiveness. New Mexico was smart enough not to regulate gas and oil fracking out of existence. There are some vestiges of two-party government in these states, but each grows a deeper shade of blue every day.

So the past policies that made today's growth cannot last forever. The new liberal residents of these states are living on the declining dividends of a saner political past. The hard work of earlier generations is being squandered to feed fresh youth who never consider how that wealth was built in the first place.

Red to Purple to Blue

When my friend Rebekah told me in 2015 that she was moving to Virginia, I scoffed. "You won't last long down there," I told her, "with all those Southern hicks. You're a prep from Boston—you'll never fit in." She was making the move to an area about forty-five minutes west of D.C. to take a job in a town called Oakton. I imagined tractor trailers and scruffy rednecks doing keg stands before jumping into their "pools," which were, no doubt, pickup trucks with hose water–filled beds (as seen on Instagram). My friend, a Wellesley-educated feminist, would run back to Boston with her tail between her legs in no time. Poor, poor, naive Rebekah had no idea what she was getting herself into.

Rebekah simply rolled her eyes and told me to come visit her soon. Months later, when I finally did, I was shocked by what I saw: rows and rows and rows of McMansions sitting on well-manicured yards, preppy little bakeries selling ten-dollar gourmet cupcakes that looked like works of art, and moms in collared shirts pushing strollers down quiet, tree-lined streets. It was January 2016, and I saw more Hillary Clinton yard signs than I could count.

What?! Where were the canned beers, "Git 'r Done" bumper stickers, and jokey church signs?

Turns out, Virginia has undergone a complete transformation over the last two decades—and the changes haven't been exclusive to areas right outside of D.C. Demographic shifts have turned Virginia from a conservative Southern state into an increasingly left-leaning territory of Democrats. After conservatives gained control of the state legislature in 2000, it looked like the first colony's feet were firmly planted on Republican soil. But when a population boom hit the state as a result of the exploding size of the federal government under George W. Bush and Barack Obama, the politics of Virginia started to change.

Today, Northern Virginia's population is dominated by throngs of federal employees commuting to D.C. and people who work for industries dependent on government spending. Virginia's population in 1990 was 6.2 million; that same year, the combined population of Alexandria City, Arlington County, Fairfax City, and Fairfax County (D.C.'s suburbs) was 1.12 million—or about 18 percent of the state. Today, those D.C. environs make up about 1.88 million people, or 22 percent of Virginia's current 8.4 million residents. The high proportion of residents in Virginia's D.C suburban areas is key to the demographic shift of the state. The greater D.C. area is full of federal workers, a group that reliably votes to increase government spending because it is in their own best interests. In fact, the votes from Virginia's four counties considered D.C. suburbs made the difference in the 2017 governor's race. Democrat (and winner) Ralph Northam beat Ed Gillespie by 232,000 votes—almost precisely the margin of votes that came from the wider D.C. area. The rest of Virginia was effectively 50–50 on the candidates.

Take a look at the three largest population centers' votes for Democrats and how they have pulled Virginia leftward:[24]

Year	Fairfax County	Alexandria City	Arlington County	Virginia
2005	D: 60.1% R: 38.0%	D: 71.9% R: 26.3%	D: 74.3% R: 23.9%	D: 51.7% R: 46.0%
2009	R: 50.7% D: 49.1%	D: 62.8% R: 37.0%	D: 65.5% R: 34.3%	R: 58.6% D: 41.26
2013	D: 58.4% R: 36.4%	D: 71.9% R: 22.3%	D: 72.0% R: 22.9%	D: 48.0% R: 45.5%
2017	D: 67.9%, R: 31.3%	D: 78.4% R: 20.8%	D: 80.1% R: 19.0%	D: 53.9% R: 45.0%

Fairfax County leans so far left—no GOPer has won there since 1980 (not even Reagan in the 1984 Republican wave)—that Democratic party officials don't count the county's votes until the end of election night, when they will inevitably drown out any chance of a Republican victory. Both in Virginia's 2014 Senate race and in the 2016 presidential election, it initially looked as though the GOP had pulled off astonishing victories...before the votes of Northern Virginia were counted. The rest of Virginia is solid red, while a tiny corner packed with bureaucrats on the government dole consistently gives Democrats a final push over the top. The GOP holds a narrow 51–49 lead in the House of Delegates and a similar 21–19 lead in the state senate. Four of the last five governors have been Democrats, as are both of the state's current senators (each former governors themselves).

No matter what the rest of the state does, the newcomers have a solid veto. As much of the nation moved rightward, Virginia has moved in the opposite direction. The state's new residents want nothing more than to keep the federal government growing—it's in their own best interests, after all.

The leftward turn of Virginia is only going to become more drastic as the federal government employs an increasing number of bureaucrats who move to the state. Just look at some of the most prominent recent trends under Governor Terry McAuliffe, a progressive Democrat. McAuliffe barely failed (by just a single vote) in his attempt to expand Medicaid. He also tried to increase voter rolls by two hundred thousand ex-felons by executive fiat, before being overruled by the state's supreme court. McAuliffe did succeed in utilizing his authority to allow almost thirteen thousand former felons the right to vote. He called for (but was ultimately unable to pass) an assault weapons ban in the state and attempted to restrict the number of handguns purchased and the carry rights of interstate travelers.

There's a pretty ironclad rule, a bit of a reverse of Milton Friedman's old axiom: places that begin to restrict economic freedoms will usually go on to restrict personal freedoms. In a glaring example of the legislation of upper-middle-class, public-sector, liberal sensibilities, a kid over the age of twelve who trick-or-treats in Chesapeake, Virginia, can now be fined up to one hundred dollars or jailed up to six months (really).[25] And the economic outlook for the state? A combination of good and bad news. Virginia's economy grew significantly over the last ten years, but now that growth has largely come to a halt. The state's unemployment rate, for example, was still under but steadily creeping toward the national average in August 2018.

And this advantage has shrunk considerably over time. During the depths of the Great Recession, Virginia's unemployment rate under Republican governor Bob McDonnell was a consistent third lower than the rest of the country's. But before the recent Trump boom, the state's unemployment rate started trending upward during 2016 and has lost much of its lead over the rest of the nation. Virginia's overall economy avoided shrinking during the Great Recession, as federal spending exploded in the Obama years, and has grown by about a quarter since 2008. Sounds pretty neat until you realize that the economy of Texas grew by a third during that same time—without all that federal money.

Most purple states like Virginia fared relatively well during the Great Recession, and in some instances they have strong economies today. But as progressive policies take effect in these states, their growth often lags behind that of Republican-controlled parts of the nation. To better understand where Colorado, New Hampshire, and Virginia are heading, we have to look at states that have shaded from purple to solid blue.

Washington and Oregon have been radically transformed from moderate states into unwilling rural counties dragged leftward by Seattle and Portland. Today, both states have unemployment rates significantly higher than the national average. They're not saddled with the same long-term Democratic dominance that is threatening complete collapse in blue states like California or Illinois, but they have seen firm left-wing control for the last generation now. And they're starting the slow but distinct lurch toward economic trouble as liberal policies are finally bearing their poison fruit.

There's every reason for these two states to be among the national leaders in GDP growth and unemployment rate. And for a long time they were. Both Washington and Oregon have good weather, exceptional natural beauty and tourist attractions, and they are home to some of the most significant corporations in the world. Washington alone has Amazon, Microsoft, Starbucks, and Boeing.

What happened? Politics happened.

I talked earlier about Seattle and Portland's shift to the left. Washington hasn't had a Republican governor since 1985; Oregon, since 1987. Democrats have increased their share of control of each state's legislatures and implemented predictable policies…and results. The effects are obvious. Both states had higher unemployment rates than the rest of the country during the Great Recession and early 2000s economic stall, and higher unemployment rates during both the 1990s and 2000s expansions, and after 2010. How is that possible? Oregon's GDP was largely stagnant during the Great Recession and only started growing again in 2015, while Washington's GDP has increased at a quicker pace and even led the nation in 2016 and 2017.

But well-intentioned left-wing policies drag down the economies of each state. Oregon has instituted tax structures similar to California's, with a maximum personal income tax of 9.9 percent and a maximum corporate tax of 7.6 percent. Oregon's tax haul has increased; residents shell out 10.3 percent of their overall income in state and local taxes, compared to 9.7 percent in 2002.[26] Washington's taxes have also increased since the early 2000s.

The two states have been tax-happy, with few moments of sanity. Washington voters rejected a carbon tax in 2016 by a large margin, and then legislators shot it down the following year. In November 2018, voters will have to face yet another such proposal.[27] The liberal politicians just don't know when to quit. Washington's cigarette taxes are over three dollars a pack, triple that of Oregon and *over five times* that of neighboring Idaho—especially punishing to the poor. Not surprisingly, as a result of the oppressive taxes, over 35 percent of all cigarette sales in the state are contraband.[28] Washington imposes the third-highest gas taxes in the nation, at 49.4 cents per gallon, and Oregon is number twelve, at 36.77 cents.[29] Washington's gas taxes have rocketed up in recent years—more than doubling from the 1990s rate of 22 cents per gallon. Oregon even considered a *$1,000* tax on owning a vehicle over twenty years old[30] (which thankfully failed). It also increased payroll taxes by .1 percent for a state transportation fund in 2018.[31] Anything that can be taxed seems to be subject to taxation. After all, who will notice another .1 percent here or there?

Eventually, people do notice.

Businesses see which way the wind is blowing, and they are making many of their long-term plans outside the state. In 2013, Boeing built a major new manufacturing complex in Missouri rather than in Washington State, where the company has been headquartered since 1916.[32] There are now fifteen thousand Boeing jobs near St. Louis,[33] and the company is hiring so fast in the area that it's having trouble finding enough skilled workers.[34] Maybe threats made by a socialist on the Seattle city council that the government should seize control of Amazon, Boeing, and Microsoft had something to do with it.[35] Or maybe it was the same city council's push to install a head tax, which literally punishes (taxes) companies like Amazon for each Seattle resident they employ.

Vestiges of pro-business policies in both states keep them relatively competitive on a national scale. But the bureaucrats who run both states' largest cities seem hell-bent on destroying any employment or business within their confines.

The tax environments in these states are getting worse—almost always disproportionately punishing poor people, despite all of the class warfare rhetoric. The left-leaning Economic Opportunity Institute published a ranking of taxes in Washington cities, and Seattle ranked...drumroll, please...the most regressive in the state *and among the worst in the nation.*[36] Meanwhile, the three cities in Washington with the least regressive taxes are all in Republican-dominated areas. A family earning just $25,000 in Seattle pays a full 17 percent of their income (about $4,200) in state and local taxes, while a rich family earning $250,000 pays just 4.4 percent of their income. Heavy sales and excise taxes make a toxic regressive mix.

But the cost burdens of liberal policies extend far beyond just taxes. The same Seattle politicians who claim to loathe those rich "1 percenters" drive living expenses higher and higher for people who can't afford to own property, thanks to restrictive regulatory policies that jack up rents. Cities such as Seattle are actively "pro-tenant"—with rules that make it difficult for landlords and property managers to evict tenants in a timely manner. *Pro-tenant!* Sounds good, right? *I'm a tenant, so pro-tenant laws are surely good for me!* While these "pro-tenant" laws make it less likely that you'll be tossed out on the street if you're late mailing the rent check, they ultimately *raise* your rent and *damage* your living experience.

How do they do that? "Pro-tenant" rules make it harder for landlords to discern who might actually pay rent, as opposed to, say, trashing the place and skipping town. Many states' data regarding nonpayments and evictions are placed into a "tenant blacklist," which gives landlords a way to weed out risky tenants. But Washington State doesn't collect this data, and calls it a "tenants' rights" issue. Wait, whose rights—those who didn't pay their rent?

The result of this policy is that landlords face a higher risk that more tenants will fail to pay rent. Landlords protect against this risk by increasing your rent—the rent of the responsible tenant—to ensure they won't face a shortfall in rent income at the end of the year. And so you, as a result, pay more in the end. At first glance this may not look to you like a tax. But when your rent goes up, you are paying for a government policy that you were never consulted on.

And then there are Seattle's restrictive building policies, which also jack up costs for property owners. Think landlords swallow these costs themselves? Hah! They get passed down to you in the form of higher rent. Poor Seattle residents pay an average of $2,500 extra each year in rent (about 15 percent) as a result of property taxes and building regulations.

Seattle and Washington's "progressive" taxation is anything but. And we haven't even touched on subsidized housing. Where do the subsidies come from? Taxpayer dollars, of course. Everyone pays a price for progressive policies, one way or the other.

And the costs don't end there for Seattle residents. The city's sales tax is a whopping 10.1 percent, a staggering amount for poor families. The city also slapped a soda and sugary-drink tax of over a dollar per two-liter bottle on its residents.[37] It should shock absolutely nobody to learn that Seattle is ranked as the seventh most expensive city in the nation. Seattleites need to earn a minimum of $89,000 annually per person to live comfortably.[38]

So how exactly does Seattle spend its residents' hard-earned tax dollars? Taxes may be high, but surely the city is putting that money to good use...right? Wrong.

Some of the city's biggest expenditures in recent years have been its ever growing social justice programs, including the Race and Social

Justice Initiative, which uses city funds to subsidize a variety of "necessary" initiatives, including "Achieving Racial Equity with Art Investment" and "Transgender Economic Empowerment," which has an annual budget of $100,000.[39] In their wisdom, the overpaid bureaucrats running Seattle also imposed fines of up to $50 for not composting food scraps,[40] spent $52 million for streetcars too large for their tracks,[41] and created the "Democracy Vouchers" program intended to reduce money in government—by shoveling public funds straight to Democrats.

Here's how Seattle's Democracy Vouchers work: Each voter is given four $25 vouchers by the city, which they can then donate to political causes or candidates. The idea was to enable candidates with fewer resources to win elections because they wouldn't have to fundraise…but the program doesn't help those it was supposed to (you're shocked, SHOCKED, aren't you?!). Instead, the money goes straight to establishment figures. During the last election cycle, 92 percent of the money went to the three most popular candidates. One city council candidate, Hisam Goueli, backed the program believing he would have a shot. Not only did he have difficulty dealing with the city's regulation of the program, he only received $20,000, right before the election. Another candidate, Sheley Secrest, allegedly used the vouchers as a money laundering scheme to funnel her own money into the campaign. The total cost of Democracy Vouchers? Three million dollars per year.[42]

Take out your wallet, sucker.

It may shock you (or it may not) to learn that efforts to help the city's working class haven't helped much at all. Seattle's attempted employment "head tax" would have charged large companies $275 per employee. It was eventually unceremoniously repealed under pressure from Amazon[43] (which is rather ironic, given Amazon's stated liberal ethos).

It's easy to understand why companies were so offended by Seattle's head tax proposal. Employers there are already squeezed enough. In 2014, the city council enacted one of the first $15 minimum wages in the country. Hailed as the next progressive solution, the higher minimum wage ended up increasing unemployment.[44] A University of Washington study found that companies pared back employee hours as a direct result of the minimum wage hike. The average employee lost 9 percent of his or her (or zir's) hours, which equated to $125 in earnings each month. The study also found that employment of low-wage earners declined by 1 percent.[45] Meanwhile, businesses have been relocating to new cities or simply closing—especially restaurants.[46]

These liberal policies have created a permanent underclass where there should instead be dramatic growth. High rents, lax law enforcement, and backwards tax policy have also created arguably the worst homelessness problem in the United States.[47] The *Seattle Times* describes the situation as "definitely worse than New York or LA." One out of every two hundred people in Seattle's county are homeless. It's now so bad that City Hall has been transformed into a massive homeless shelter. The building's basement is filled on the average night, and most nights the homeless spill into the lobby as well. Nearly all of the city's two-thousand-plus shelters are fully occupied on the average night, at all times of the year.[48] Crime is increasing along with homelessness, despite attempted actions of local government to clamp down on the problem with "community policing." The city council is now considering sheltering the large vagrant population in giant tents (imagine the aesthetics alone)[49] but is concerned that it can't even afford the tents.

Rather than implement pro-growth policies to bolster the local job market, which might actually improve the homelessness situation, Seattle bureaucrats just keep throwing money at the homeless. In 2017 alone, Seattle spent more than $50 million attempting to solve its homeless crisis—that's about $16,000 per homeless person. And what did the city have to show for it? Even more homeless people in 2018 than in 2017.

Recent Democratic Party control and heavy reliance on a few big businesses that toe the left-wing political line have created an environment characterized by stark inequality. Liberal politicians in cities like Seattle campaign against inequality; Seattle even elected an avowed socialist to their city council. But the system that these left-wing politicians and the voters who put them in office have created has resulted in the poor being taxed in incredibly regressive fashion, increased youth poverty and homelessness, and reduced wages and employment for the working class. Poor neighborhoods in the city have doubled since 2000.[50] It takes a bunch of Democrats to live up to stereotypes of moustache-twirling Republican villains that hate the poor.

Similarly, to the south, things in Portland, Oregon, are proceeding exactly as you would imagine. Portland's population has jumped over 20 percent since 2000. White hipsters have driven out traditionally black residents and are now destroying the fragile boutique economy they created.

The city's residents and politicians plan to tax everything. It's their solution to every problem! A 1 percent tax on big retailers to fund green energy initiatives is on the ballot. The *Willamette Week*'s description of the proposal, Measure 26-201, sounds like a Mad Libs game: Tax revenue will be "used to fund energy efficiency and carbon reduction projects for low-income Portlanders and communities of color and to provide job training in the energy field for those groups."[51] Add to that a 3.8 percent tax increase in 2018[52] that still couldn't prevent school closures[53] and a 2.2 percent business tax on companies that gross more than $50,000 a year (and a proposal that may increase the business tax by almost half).[54] Unsurprisingly, the city faces high rates of tax avoidance.[55]

And still there are more:

- A thirty-five-dollar-per-person arts tax, which you have to file each year *even if you don't owe anything*. If you don't pay it, the amount owed doubles. Thirty-two percent of Portland residents evade the tax.[56]
- A neighborhood leaf-cleanup fee that ranged from fifteen dollars to sixty-five dollars,[57] repealed in 2018. Why? The city's interim transportation manager said it best: "The fee we started collecting in 2010 never met its goal of covering the city's costs. In addition, the costs of administering the fee have been quite significant, adding up to almost 20

percent of program costs. We decided it made financial and policy sense to return to providing this service free of charge."[58]

- A statewide $15 tax on each bicycle, which falls most heavily on Portlanders. Maybe you're against cheap, clean transportation and healthy exercise? Well, the state spent $47,000 in the first quarter of 2018 to collect just $77,000 in taxes. The original projections estimated an annual administrative cost of $50,000 and revenue of $1.05 million.[59]

- In 2017, Portland's city council agreed to end investment in *all* corporate bonds and securities. Not a tax? Well, if the city's new investments generate less revenue, the shortfall will be paid for—wait for it—by residents. And estimates of lost revenue total $4.5 million per year.[60]

- Need to install a sign on your business? Charges for that start at $157 and run all the way up to $468. Need your plans reviewed by the city? It's only $142 an hour (heh). Can't make it during business hours? Be prepared for the city to charge you $194 per hour—minimum one hour, even if it takes just a few minutes.[61]

For all of the money pouring into Portland and the state of Oregon's coffers, you'd think they'd be running massive surpluses. Nope! Portland carries $4.4 billion in public debt (over $21,000 per resident) and came in seventieth in a ranking of the debt loads of seventy-five cities studied by a Chicago think tank.[62] Meanwhile Oregon is facing a huge $1.6 billion biennial budget shortfall. One billion of that total was from the Beaver State's expansion of Medicaid, which enrolled almost double the number of anticipated participants. Do they not see this stuff coming, or don't they care?

At least *some* of that money has to be spent on something worthwhile, right? How about a $200,000-a-year Oregon state hotline to report wasteful government spending (sounds like my kind of idea!)? Except this hotline has received exactly *zero* significant tips.[63] What hotline gets a $200,000 budget, anyways? (Maybe somebody should call the *hotline* in to the hotline.) And Portland recently increased recycling fees sharply because the city wasn't recycling close to home—it was just dumping recyclables in China, which rejected them for being contaminated.[64] Oregon spent $300 million to sign up Oregonians for health insurance that enrolled no one.[65] The solar panels on a new Portland courthouse will take only 109 years to pay off.

A similar leftward transformation is unfolding in increasingly deep-blue New Mexico. The state elected a number of Republicans in the recent past, but its state and federal legislators are solidly Democratic. The result? New Mexico currently has the second-highest poverty rate in the nation, at 19.7 percent,[66] and it ranks worst in the nation in rural poverty.[67] The state suffers from low rates of educational attainment, a high proportion of low-paying jobs, and a higher-than-average unemployment rate.

New Mexico is a unique mixture of policy and population, with programs like Medicaid and other poverty measures not doing much to assist the poor. A large percentage of the Native American and Latino populations in the state are simply left behind. Nearly a third of Native Americans in the state live in poverty,[68] as do over a fifth of Latinos.[69] Poor residents also pay higher effective tax rates than their rich compatriots.[70]

Not that rich New Mexicans aren't being forced to pay through the nose. New Mexicans shoulder the fifth-heaviest total tax burden in the country,[71] almost a fifth higher than California's. The average resident pays about 18.8 percent of his income in state and local taxes. Overall, New Mexico taxes have increased approximately 20 percent in just the last sixteen years. The taxes are particularly hard on poor residents, especially since the state has the second-highest sales tax burden in the nation; sales taxes eat up over 7.5 percent of the average resident's income. The sales tax applies to nearly all goods and services, which increases cost at every step along a supply chain. Add New Mexico's 12.5 percent tax on mineral extraction, and it's poison for businesses looking to succeed in the state.

Fortunately, even with the high tax rate the state took full advantage of the fracking boom—and now is the third-largest oil producer in the nation.[72] New Mexico's oil production has nearly doubled since Trump took office, leading to a surge in GDP growth. Perhaps Trump and Susana Martinez can reverse the long-standing trends and right the state before it's too late.

If New Mexico got oil extraction right—as its ace in the hole that counteracts its destructive Democratic policies—its northern neighbor Colorado has not learned from its example. In fact, Denver—floating along on the sugar high of hipsterism—is squandering Colorado's real economic potential. Oil and natural gas are solid resources, but trust funds eventually run out.

Colorado has benefited from the fracking boom—some. Its natural gas production is up a quarter from 2010, while oil extraction has increased by an incredible 500 percent. Sounds impressive, doesn't it? It is. But a ballot initiative in November 2018 would restrict hydrofracking within a half mile of buildings, which will effectively ban it from most of the state—and this initiative is leading in the polls.[73] The likely next governor, Democrat (and Bernie Sanders's choice) Jared Polis, is notoriously hostile to the industry, which incumbent Democrat John Hickenlooper knew better than to touch. Oil and gas companies make up $32 billion of the state's economy, and almost half of Colorado's economic growth.[74] As the state veers left, the Democrats are threatening to kill the goose laying the golden eggs.

Why does Denver feel it can kill off one of the most productive sectors in Colorado's economy? Well, the recent population surge might explain it. The population of Colorado has increased over 20 percent since 2000, with massive in-migration from California. Colorado's formerly low property values and taxes, as well as scenic vistas, drew many upper-middle-class residents fleeing Sacramento's reach.

The result is that Colorado has a higher-than-average educational attainment. But it has also veered substantially to the left. New residents bring their liberal political beliefs with them. Republicans had a

160,000-voter-registration lead in Colorado in 2000; by 2018, Democrats led by 1,800 registered voters.[75]

The state has a high rate of new business creation—and of business failure.[76] Colorado is catching up to California and Illinois with high-tax proposals—one headed to the ballot calls for a $1.6 billion tax hike on earners making over $150,000 and an increase in corporate taxes. Another initiative calls for a 21 percent increase in the statewide sales tax.[77] The state also considered (but nixed) a 2018 plan to quadruple taxes on Airbnb rentals.[78] Recent tax hikes have failed on account of voter input through referenda, but that dam appears to be weakening. Even the strong marijuana industry is growing more slowly, with a number of growers and retailers threatening to leave the state over proposed regulation.[79]

The biggest sign of Colorado's slow decline is the formerly libertarian state's flirtation with single-payer government healthcare. A 2016 ballot initiative to create "ColoradoCare," the state's own version of Obamacare, was rejected by a full 79 percent of residents. The plan was a bit of a convoluted mess, but one thing was clear—residents would have to pay out the nose for it. This would include a 6.67 percent employer tax, a 3.33 percent employee payroll tax, and 10 percent taxes on self-employment, capital gains, and Social Security benefits—an almost $25 billion tax increase in the first year alone. You can imagine how popular that idea was. And even those massive tax increases would not have been enough to fund ColoradoCare. Proponents of the plan said it would save money compared to current healthcare spending. (Numbers and facts, who needs those pesky details?) But even a friendly accounting found the plan would run a massive deficit.[80] The state would have created an extra-legislative twenty-one-person body to run the system. Elected by Colorado residents (including illegal immigrants), they would have had the power to raise copays and reduce services. It was a recipe for disaster—like similar single-payer fantasies in Vermont and California. The conservative site The Daily Wire summed it up nicely: "The more voters learned about the plan, the less they liked it."[81]

But that doesn't mean Democrats seeking office aren't still peddling the idea and others like it. Gubernatorial hopeful Jared Polis was against the 2016 proposition but is now backing "Medicare for All."[82] As Democrats swamped the state's legislative elections in 2018, such propositions are back in the limelight.

If you don't live in a purple state like Colorado now, don't assume your state won't soon be headed in the same direction—toward tax increases, severe restrictions on businesses, and government-run healthcare. Such changes are likely coming to a community near you, sooner than you may think.

Après Nous, le Déluge

What happens as residents in historically red regions start realizing their state is slipping from their grasp? What happens when their "social betters" in positions of power realize that their authority is now nearly unchecked? The political changes, economic hardships, and deepening cultural divide that inevitably accompany the transformation of a state from blue to red threatens to tear the societal fabric apart.

After the Sandy Hook shooting in late 2012, Governor Hickenlooper led Colorado to enact some of the toughest gun control laws in the country and certainly the most restrictive in the Mountain West. Colorado instituted universal background checks and banned magazines holding more than fifteen rounds. The proposed laws were unpopular. Only 31 percent of Coloradans supported them in 2014.[83] But Democrats controlled both chambers of the state legislature—as a result not only of the 2012 Obama wave, but also of the demographic transformation of the state. The gun control measures passed in a partisan vote.

Efforts to remove the new restrictive gun laws failed. Today the state legislature is deadlocked between the two parties, with Republicans largely representing the rural parts of the state—the areas pushing for the gun restrictions to be overturned—and Democrats representing the blue cities.

Many born-and-bred Coloradans feel that their state is slipping away from them—that the reality of their lives in rural areas, which often include hunting or enjoying the utility of guns on a ranch, is not respected by the politicians who now control their lives or by the voters who put them in office. With Republicans in the Colorado Senate wanting no-permit constitutional carry[84] and Democrats pushing for "red flag" laws to pull guns from non-criminals who may be deemed unfit to possess a firearm by a doctor,[85] the ongoing gun debate is not just a political fight anymore—it's about the state's identity.

There's also an economic cost to the state's new gun restrictions. Colorado's formerly healthy firearms industry saw the writing on the wall as Democrats increasingly took control of the state and didn't want to be boogeymen on the Denver social scene. So they started moving out. Magpul Industries pulled up the stakes on their 200-employee business producing bullet magazines. The company, which had previously considered a larger facility within Colorado, instead moved to a much friendlier environment, Wyoming. Magpul now operates a new 380-employee facility in Cheyenne, just two hours north of Denver. The company received a lucrative contract with the United States Marine Corps that swelled revenue and employment that could have been in Colorado. Two of Magpul's suppliers also moved some of their operations out of the state. A gun-sight fabricator also left. Four hunting-themed television shows canceled their shoots, and a hunting-trip company in the state faced boycott from out-of-state hunters. As NPR reported,

> Wes Atkinson runs Fort Collins, Colo.-based Atkinson Expeditions, which offers multiday hunts for elk and deer. People who use outfitters like his spent an estimated $231 million in the state in 2007, the last year such spending was measured. But now, businesses like Atkinson's are the target of a boycott by out-of-state hunters.
>
> Atkinson says the changes in Colorado are a slippery slope. "It's a foot in the door. It's the beginning of the end,"

he says. "That's how everyone relates to it. If you're going to do this, what's next? So this is their way of trying to put a stop to it. Colorado outfitters and business owners that deal with guns are the ones that pay the price."[86]

The identity and economic landscape of Colorado have been altered by laws that over half of Colorado's sheriffs oppose[87] and that are considered generally "unenforceable," according to Larimer County sheriff Justin Smith.[88]

What is worth the complete transformation of your state? The upper-middle-class scolds who import the failed policies of their former homes with them can bring a temporary economic boost. But in Portland and Seattle they have effectively snuffed out traditional American lifestyles—and they're coming for second-tier cities in traditionally conservative states with their condescending view of your lifestyle: expect the Cultural Revolution in Denver, Phoenix, and even Dallas next.

Low taxation, modest regulations, manufacturing, and the extraction of raw materials—the traditional levers of economic growth—are all under attack. Colorado, Washington, Virginia, and Oregon now bear more than a passing resemblance to Illinois, California, and New York. Large population centers like Denver, Seattle, Fairfax County, and Portland and their environs simply outvote and outweigh the Republican rural populations in the hinterlands. When residents from these cities start fleeing to the lower-tax and lower-cost parts of these states, even these Mayberrys will be overwhelmed and become purplish.

In Ronald Reagan's famous 1964 "A Time for Choosing" speech, he laid out a simple moral: "Not too long ago, two friends of mine were talking to a Cuban refugee, a businessman who had escaped from Castro, and in the midst of his story one of my friends turned to the other and said, 'We don't know how lucky we are.' And the Cuban stopped and said, 'How lucky you are? I had someplace to escape to.' And in that sentence he told us the entire story. If we lose freedom here, there's no place to escape to. This is the last stand on earth."[89]

Where do you go once your last stand is overrun?

CHAPTER THREE

Political Impacts on Receiving States
How Liberal Migration Is Changing Politics at Every Level

D emocrat Robert "Beto" O'Rourke almost pulled off the electoral upset of this young century. He pulled within a 3 percent margin of incumbent Texas senator and 2016 presidential contender Ted Cruz in the 2018 midterm election. The near win by the left-wing Democrat was impressive (especially in Texas... *Texas!*), and it's even more stunning when you look at the raw number of votes. A mere 220,000 votes, out of over the 8 million cast, separated the candidates.

O'Rourke pulled within the margin of error for a number of reasons, including impressive retail politicking. But one of the largest reasons was demographic changes in a state that has a reputation as one of the reddest in the nation. Beto pulled in over a hundred thousand more votes in Texas than Hillary Clinton did in the 2016 presidential election, and he was only slightly more than a half million behind Donald Trump's winning total in the Lone Star State. These numbers suggest that Texas could actually be a battleground state in 2020—especially if the native son is nominated by the Democrats for president or vice president.

Texas isn't blue... yet. There's no firm certainty that it will be, but a combination of immigration from Latin America and migration from the rest of the United States will likely place it in the toss-up column by the 2030s.

There's a clear correlation between Texas's booming population and the increasing share of Democratic votes in successive elections. Domestic net migration—the difference between the number of migrants leaving Texas for other states and the number of migrants coming to Texas—totaled 867,000 between 2010 and 2016.[1] The top state, by far, losing residents to the Lone Star State during that period was California. Since Texas doesn't allow voters to register by party affiliation, it's especially difficult to estimate the number of blue-state expats who have continued to vote for Democrats in their new home. But the share of Democratic votes in Texas elections increased significantly between 2010 and 2016 as the state's booming economy attracted new residents from California and other states. Look at the jump in Democratic votes between the 2012 and 2016 presidential election primaries:

Election Year	Democratic Turnout	Republican Turnout
2012	590,000	1.5 million
2016	1.4 million	2.8 million

While the turnout increased for both parties, the Democrats saw an incredible 137 percent increase in votes, a significantly larger uptick than the Republicans. Of course, other factors in addition to demographics were at play in these elections, including excitement around the candidates themselves. But there is every indication that new residents played a significant role in the political shift.

Between 2014 and 2018 alone, Texas voter rolls increased by 1.6 million. Counties bordering Austin saw the largest percentage gains.[2] Note that the Austin metropolitan area is a top destination for domestic migrants, as the Lone Star State's capital is America's fastest-growing city.[3] The counties bordering Austin used to be solidly red but currently see close congressional races on a regular basis.

If Texas moves out of the Republican column, the effects on the national level will be disastrous for the GOP. The time to wake up to this threat is now: by the time the party elite realize what's happening, it will likely be a decade or more too late. The transformation of Texas—with its enormous political clout and thirty-eight electoral votes—from solid red to deep-blue islands in a sea of red country will set off immense shock waves.

Austin can be the butt of jokes and the exception that proves the rule in 2019, but it represents Texas's future better than the rest of the state.

Don't say I didn't warn you.

The Blue Dog Threat

I'm not going to say that Beto is a moderate. He's not. But he certainly Tex-ified his approach to the 2016 Senate election. He wasn't an outsider who parachuted into the state, speaking down to Texans. By presenting himself as a born-and-bred Texan, Beto gained where another left-leaning candidate couldn't have. And it helped that he had represented El Paso in Congress, rather than a district in Austin. He also speaks Spanish fluently and made a point of using a Latino nickname on his signs, rather than the Anglo "Robert." Ted Cruz, whose father escaped the prison state of communist Cuba, cannot speak Spanish fluently. Voters noticed.

There is also a strong argument that Beto benefited from constant fawning media coverage. But that can't be counted against him or seen as some sort of a fluke; it's going to keep happening. In fact, the media will likely move further to the left in the coming generation. As will rich campaign donors. The $70 million Beto raised for his Senate campaign will prove a harbinger of bigger and better Democrat fundraising to come.

Beto leveraged his "authenticity" factor against Cruz, who had been a master debater at Harvard Law—and spoke like one, to his detriment. Cruz's challenger spoke in sound bites of his own making, while the incumbent talked in his own clunky manner, trying to nationalize the race to frighten Texans about a left-wing takeover of the state—a strategy that just barely succeeded.

Beto's rehearsed but smooth manner of speaking, outreach to young voters, and belief in the Democrats' thesis about the "coalition of the ascendant" paid dividends—pushing Beto far ahead of where Hillary was in Texas just two years before. If, two years later, in the 2020 presidential election, Texans face a choice between arch–New Yorker Trump and a homegrown young politician willing to campaign in nearly every county, there is a very real possibility that the state might go blue for the first time since 1976.

Rinse and repeat for the next several election cycles. Hillary Clinton's team believed that high turnout in blue states and an impenetrable "Blue Wall" in the Midwest would keep Trump far from 270 electoral votes. While we all know how that story ended, the analysis may have been merely premature.

Clinton's choice of Tim Kaine as her running mate was a smart one: a white, Southern former governor who didn't rock the boat. Apart from his disastrous effort in the vice-presidential debate against Mike Pence, Kaine didn't move the needle for a large number of voters. He wasn't a drag on the ticket like Joe Lieberman or Sarah Palin were; he avoided being a lightning rod or the butt of late-night jokes. He was a low-risk, low-reward gamble who recalled the Democrats' successes in the 2000s. Kaine had been elected governor of Virginia in 2005 as a blue dog Democrat, a moderate who oversaw the transition of Virginia from red to blue in under a generation. The Democratic Party has now won four of the last five races for the state house. Virginia, once reliably red, is now likely out of reach for Republicans in 2020.

None of this makes a figure with Kaine's moderate levels of charisma a good choice to lead a ticket. But his rise should be a lesson to Texas. If Tim Kaine and Mark Warner could be the catalysts turning a state as red as Virginia once was into a state that elected former DNC chairman Terry McAuliffe as its governor, something similar can and eventually probably will happen in the Lone Star State.

Cities are the vanguard of demographic change in these states. We see thousands of new residents entering into the major metro areas of

Texas, Virginia, and Colorado. Given the seemingly one-directional demographic ratchet, Republicans could become as rare in major metro areas as they already are in former Reagan territory in Orange County, California.

The Democrats need to catch a break to crack open Texas and other states that currently vote reliably red. But presenting candidates that sound moderate but will vote left of center, combined with changes to the composition of the electorate, is a method the Democrats have used convincingly time and again. There may very well be a blue Texas...and Georgia...and Florida in our future.

You Can Go to Hell, They're Going to Texas

Businesses move to Texas for many reasons, but the most commonly cited is its competitive tax environment. The state has no income tax, and its property and business taxes are unusually low. It's heaven for anyone looking to succeed in America's market economy.

Believe it or not, that was Connecticut—forty years ago. Before it became one of the nation's worst-run states, Connecticut was often red at the local level. It had a wonderful business climate that lured corporations from New York City during the city's implosion in the 1970s and 1980s. Then a combination of Republican squishes and Democrats passing "temporary" or "limited" tax increases turned the state into Illinois 2.0.

Today Connecticut comes in forty-seventh out of fifty in a ranking of the states' tax environments, and dead last in the nation in property taxes.[4] For a long time, Connecticut, like Nevada, Florida, New Hampshire, Texas, and Wyoming, had no personal income tax. It was an oasis in the Northeast for earners at all levels. But in 1991 Connecticut became the last state without an income tax to implement one.

The original tax on incomes was supposed to be "fair"—a flat 4.5 percent income tax rate for all income levels. But government only grows. It came as a shock to absolutely nobody when, after the implementation of the tax, Connecticut's state government ballooned in size. Between

1991 and 2014 state spending increased 71 percent faster than inflation, while the population grew by just 9 percent.[5] The state increased its spending on debt service, pensions, and employee healthcare by an astonishing 174 percent.[6] At the same time, Connecticut bureaucrats also jacked up spending on welfare programs by 70 percent.

The sharp increase in tax revenue allowed an even larger spike in government bureaucracy and spending. Today a full 94 percent of the state's public workforce is controlled by public-sector unions, and the average full-time union employee on the state payroll makes an astonishing $73,036 per year. That's over $21,000 more than the average employee in the state. Wouldn't it be nice if you got a $21,000 raise, insane job security and benefits, and every holiday in the book off? Twenty-three percent of all full-time public employees in the state make over $100,000, and 617 of them are paid over $200,000.[7] Must be nice.

Connecticut pays public union members a total of $3.4 billion per year, which explains much of the projected deficit for 2019–20 of $4.6 billion. Do the public-sector unions care about the debt? Hah! Just ask union boss John Olsen. Questioned about high public-sector compensation in 2010, Olsen said, "That's like saying that someone beats their wife, therefore I should. Just because someone in the private sector doesn't get a pension doesn't mean union workers should give up negotiated pensions."[8]

Efforts to have state employees chip in for their own retirement are met with fierce resistance. A modest 1 percent increase in Connecticut teachers' retirement contributions to a very reasonable 7 percent—representing just $20 million toward the state's $50 *billion* unfunded pension liability—was immediately followed by a rollback effort.[9] As Stephen McKeever, the VP of the state's branch of the American Federation of Teachers, said, "From the beginning, our members made clear that a targeted tax on teachers was an unjust approach to balancing Connecticut's finances." New taxes create new opportunities for government bloat. Paid for by working stiffs, like you.

Connecticut is now entering into death-spiral territory, raising taxes higher and higher to cover spending and pension promises it can never keep. The state was already in the danger zone before Governor Dannel Malloy took office in 2011, but he has pushed the envelope even further with two major waves of taxes that put the top earners' rates at nearly 7 percent. Connecticut also levies a staggering 8.25 percent corporate tax. Pension and union pressures are also causing cities and towns to tax middle-class residents—out of the state.

Translation: Rather than scaling back spending and public pensions, the geniuses running Connecticut instead continue to double down on the tax-and-spend policies that got them in trouble in the first place.

The state's economic and fiscal woes began as the result of Democrats' spending in the late 1980s under Governor William O'Neill. Earlier, in 1971, public resentment of a new tax hike was so deep among residents that although one was passed, it was repealed after just six weeks following a massive public outcry and the governor's refusal to sign it into law. Then, in 1990, Republican Lowell Weicker, who had represented Connecticut in the House and Senate, ran a firebrand third-party campaign for governor under the banner of "A Connecticut Party." Weicker ran on a platform of vehemently opposing a state income tax—and won.

But once elected governor, Weicker went back on his word. When he took office, the state had a projected $2.4 billion deficit and his "solution" was...wait for it...an income tax! The move was deeply unpopular. Weicker said, "My policy when I came in was no income tax, but that fell apart on the rocks of fiscal fact." In a purported "compromise," the 1991 budget set the state income tax rate at 6 percent. Did the income tax solve the state's budget problems? Nope. Since the installation of an income tax, Connecticut's budget has exploded, and the state faces a yawning deficit.

A similar "compromise" under Republican governor John Rowland allowed lower pension contributions in the 1990s—setting up ballooning payments decades later. Another "deal" increased healthcare spending for public employees. Do these "compromises" sound familiar? They should. Democrats use such agreements to trick Republicans into more spending all the time. Look no further than George H. W. Bush's 1990 tax increase, which Democrats turned around and used as a cudgel to kick him out of the White House in 1992. The move looked particularly bad for Bush, who had been elected on his pledge: "Read my lips, no new taxes."

Connecticut's tax increases chased out the corporations that had flocked to the state in earlier years. So long, General Electric. Au revoir, Aetna. The state has offered companies that are considering leaving generous corporate welfare to stay,[10] as we'll discuss more later. But none of this economic decay can happen in Texas…right? Not so fast. There are surprising similarities between the struggles in Connecticut in the 1990s and the situation unfolding in Texas today.

First, there is the increasing influence on state politics of the large cities that are gaining population faster than the rural areas. Texas's population has increased enormously over the last generation, but that growth has been heavily concentrated in Dallas, Houston, San Antonio, and Austin. The very same population trends drowned out the influence of Connecticut's towns and small cities, which fell under the shadow of Hartford, Manchester, and Danbury as those big cities became both increasingly bluer and larger than the surrounding areas. Their outsized populations and influence helped drive Connecticut into deep blue territory.

Second, business in the state (comprising both startups and companies that relocated to Texas because of its business-friendly red-state political climate) looks more and more like a piggy bank waiting to be smashed. Someone like Governor Greg Abbott is not going to be baited. But over time, especially during the next recession, there will be a serious temptation to kill the goose that lays the golden eggs.

Don't just take my word for it. There is plenty of census and economic data showing that population shifts are already leading Texas down this path.

Population of Major Cities and Their Share of State Population from 1990 to the Present

	1990	2000	2010	2017 (est.)
Texas	17.1 million	20.9 million	25.2 million	28.3 million
Austin metro	846,000 (4.9%)	1,250,000 (6.0%)	1,716,000 (6.8%)	2,056,000 (7.3%)
Houston metro	3,302,000 (19.3%)	4,178,000 (19.9%)	5,920,000 (23.5%)	6,892,000 (24.4%)
San Antonio metro	1,408,000 (8.2%)	1,712,000 (8.2%)	2,142,000 (8.5%)	2,474,000 (8.7%)
Dallas–Fort Worth metro	3,885,000 (22.7%)	5,221,000 (25.0%)	6,426,000 (25.5%)	7,399,000 (26.1%)

These four greater metro areas have seen a massive increase in their influence on Texas politics as their populations have exploded over the last few years. While these areas made up 55.1 percent of the state's population in 1990, today they include 66.5 percent. Austin and San Antonio are growing at such a rapid clip that each is likely to become a megalopolis like Dallas–Fort Worth over the next decade.[11] As the areas gain in residents, all four cities are trending distinctly bluer. Both the cities themselves and their surrounding suburbs vote increasingly Democratic, and this shift has massive implications for Texas as a whole.

Presidential Election Results by Metro Area, Winning Margins by Party

	2000	2004	2008	2012	2016
Texas	21% R	23% R	12% R	16% D	9% R
Austin metro	5% R	10% R	2% D	.08% D	12% D
Houston metro	11% R	10% R	1.6% D	.08% D	12% D
San Antonio metro	7% R	10% R	6% D	4% D	13% D
Dallas metro	24% R	24% R	10% R	6% R	7% R

Rural areas are losing political power to growing cities, which are leaning further and further left. Throw in the population growth of the increasingly Democratic Rio Grande–adjacent counties, and Texas is changing fast.

The major oil and natural drilling operations in the state have propelled Texas's economy and kept it growing during the last recession. Oil and gas production in the Permian and Eagle Ford basins has skyrocketed, with the Eagle Ford fields producing almost twice as much as all of Alaska. The Permian's production has tripled in the last ten years. Texas produced over four million barrels per day in 2018—about as much as Iraq. Yet despite the historically close relationship between the oil industry and major metropolitan areas like Houston, much of the actual oil production occurs far from the fastest-growing cities. To many new inhabitants, oil production and fracking are just an old and dirty source of fuel.

Fossil fuel production is a major boon for Texas's economy in tax revenue. The state levies a 4.6 percent tax on oil extraction and 7.5 percent for natural gas; the two together represented about $3 billion of 2017's annual tax haul.[12] This tax revenue is a massive chunk of the state's rainy-day fund—including disaster relief, the state highway fund, and the state education fund. It also helps the state make do without an income tax. Another $8 billion of taxes on energy extraction goes into local tax coffers.[13] That $11 billion in revenue helps keep pressure for other taxes and tax hikes in check.

But did any of that matter to the Austinites who—along with liberals in Boston, Brooklyn, and Washington, D.C.—put up signs for Beto O'Rourke in 2018? No! New Texans in the state's major metropolitan areas don't see oil and gas as the keystone of their local economies. Cruz's campaign launched a major ad campaign against O'Rourke for supporting a ten-dollar-per-barrel federal extraction tax and for voting against allowing oil exports[14]—both of which would have had severe adverse effects on Texas's economy. Cruz was right on the merits, but that wasn't enough for many voters.

These aren't the fantasies of a sacrificial lamb candidate. Exceptionally inclement weather in the rural areas where Republican candidates tend to excel last November might have put Beto over the top. And if Mother Nature doesn't do it, shifting demographics likely will. At some point in the near future a locally elected Democrat will start making major changes to Texas's economy.

And the changes won't be for the better. Remember what happened in Connecticut. If Texas boosts taxes on oil and gas production, adopts a state income tax, or hikes the statewide franchise tax, it will likely also adopt increased spending that will outpace the new tax revenue. We have seen how public-sector unions took full advantage of the opening of the tax faucet in Connecticut.

There is also the risk of tax money being used for specialized treatment for favored companies. To keep its business environment competitive, Texas uses multiple tools, one of which, in particular, comes with both promises and pitfalls. Texas Chapter 313 allows municipalities to offer major property tax reductions to large corporations willing to relocate to the state. Between 2001 and 2016, Chapter 313 cost state taxpayers $7.1 billion, $1.7 billion of which went to renewable energy—right in the midst of an increase in gas and oil production unparalleled in history. In other words, while efficient, inexpensive energy is abundant in Texas and the rest of the country, Texans were forced to shell out billions in subsidies for inefficient, expensive energy technologies. Similar schemes are becoming more common across the state: in San Patricio County, officials approved a 100 percent tax rebate for three years and 70 percent for the following seven for a large Exxon plant[15] to produce ethylene for agriculture. The city of Richardson offered 75 percent off local property taxes to convince Texas Instruments to build a $3.2 billion computer chip facility.

Chapter 313 has added business, yes, but at a high cost. Projects funded through these tax rebates have been exorbitantly expensive. Each job created by Chapter 313 projects costs the taxpayers a hefty $350,000.[16] The Texas Enterprise Fund, in contrast, has been able to create jobs at a cost of just over $3,700 each in public spending. Today there are over three hundred Chapter 313 projects total, and the program has cost state taxpayers over $7 billion since its creation in 2002—more than education budget cuts in the state during the Great Recession.

What's so bad about that, you might ask? Texas's economy has worked exceedingly well and these tax rebates are just one of many tools it uses to stay competitive. But Chapter 313 is an example of corporate cronyism getting a toehold in the Lone Star State. As Texas becomes bluer, programs like these will become larger and disproportionately help the wealthy. Don't believe me? Sadly, there are thousands of examples of liberal politicians in the highly taxed and regulated—and failing—blue states relying on such programs to help their political allies and punish companies that don't toe the line.

The Amazon Effect

In 2018, Amazon was seeking a city for "HQ2," its massive new headquarters and the twenty thousand new jobs it would bring. Jeff Bezos's pitch was impossible for politicians in places that desperately needed an economic boost to resist, but he was essentially looking for cities that would be willing to transfer local and property tax revenues to the pocket of the world's richest man: himself. Local elected officials scrabbled over each other for a brief glimpse of the new robber baron, eager to sell out their voters and their principles to curry favor with a company that is worth over $1 trillion. This shouldn't be the way a market economy works, but years and years of poor policy had opened the door for this sordid bidding war at the taxpayers' expense.

I'm glad that Amazon has grown by leaps and bounds over the last generation. Chances are pretty good that you bought this book from its site and are reading it on a Kindle (Jeff, if you're reading this paragraph, I want that royalty check stat). Amazon helped modernize the American economy and digitize commerce, while providing valuable products at your doorstep at low prices—and mediocre original content on Amazon Prime Video. The company is a valuable piece of millions of Americans' stock portfolios and retirement accounts. It didn't achieve a higher valuation than the GDP of *all of New England* by accident.[17]

On the other hand, the company has now become an eager participant in corporate welfare schemes at every level. In 2013 Bezos bought his way into the Beltway and gained national influence through his $250 million purchase of the *Washington Post*, whose website now drives more traffic than the *New York Times*. Once a center-left publication, the *Post* has taken a decisive turn to the harder left under Bezos's stewardship.

So Jeff Bezos now owns the largest e-commerce site in the nation *and* one of its largest media conglomerates. We all know how the competition for "HQ2" worked out. And we all saw how the bidding war exposed Amazon's immense influence on policymakers—and the extent to which targeted subsidies help the wealthiest individuals and corporations at the expense of the common person. Corporate welfare like this is only going to grow in states with terrible tax and regulatory environments.

BuzzFeed, of all sources, compiled a list of the most "outrageous" sweeteners local governments offered to try and snag Amazon's HQ:

- Atlanta and the state of Georgia rolled out $2 billion in incentives, including a program to create a twenty-four-week boot camp for training employees, free parking for Amazon bigwigs at the world's busiest airport, and the use of new train cars on the MARTA public transport system for the company's products. The offer was capped off with $1.7 billion in tax credits, including $1.3 billion from the state and $87 million from Atlanta.
- Boston offered 0 percent loans for Amazon employees to buy homes in the city.
- Chicago offered $2.25 billion in incentives and an additional $400 million for infrastructure projects for its notoriously

poor transport network. Windy City officials even commissioned a special video voiced by William Shatner to entice the Trekkie Bezos to come to the city (the Shatner video conveniently neglected to mention that Chicago is home to one of the highest tax and murder rates in the nation).

- Columbus, Ohio, put together a 1,300-page offer for Amazon with an incentive of $500 million. This included a fifteen-year full tax abatement, which would have saved the company nearly half of its investment costs. On top of that there was a 35 percent income tax refund. Columbus even offered to create a special police task force to deal with what the city called "an unacceptable murder rate."

- Dallas offered to build a new university called "Amazon U," on top of $600 million in incentives.

- Maryland made it to the final round of bidding with an astonishing offer of $6.5 billion in tax credits—equal to the amount the state spent on all higher education in 2018[18]— and an additional $2 billion in promised infrastructure spending to support the company's employees. The tax credits would have reimbursed Amazon almost 6 percent of the wages of each job created. The amount offered in tax rebates would have been *higher than the average amount paid by each employee in state income taxes!*

- Pennsylvania put up $4.6 billion.

- Newark, New Jersey, allocated $2 billion.

- Washington, D.C., offered up to $1.2 billion, including a 0 percent corporate tax rate for five years and *reducing the overall tax rate by a third as long as Amazon was there.*[19]

All of this flies in the face of classic American economic development. America became the world's most powerful economy not by corporate welfare and favoritism, but by the free market. Many of the locales in this bidding war—such as Newark, Columbus, and Philadelphia—have

staggering poverty rates and lethargic economic growth rates. Traditionally, companies have moved into poorer regions when city or state leaders
adjust their overall tax climate to encourage business. That kind of policy
creates prosperity that lifts all boats by fostering economic growth across
the board. Making singular exceptions for large companies without a
current presence in or connection to a jurisdiction is a different story—
likely with a much less happy ending.

The entire boondoggle revealed the depths of the political back-scratch-
ing that is a wider threat to business climates nationwide. The two
announced winners—New York City and Washington, D.C.'s Virginia
suburbs—ultimately triumphed partly because of the lavish incentives they
offered and partly because Bezos wants his company to be close to the
levers of power. The deal Amazon got will profit Amazon more than New
York or Virginia. The proposals from each region were blatant corporate
welfare. New York State offered the megacorporation $1.5 billion in direct
tax breaks.[20] This alone represents a whopping $48,000 in taxpayer fund-
ing per projected job created. Governor Cuomo said during the process,
"I'll change my name to Amazon Cuomo if that's what it takes." New York
utilized a PILOT (payment in lieu of taxes) program to sweeten the pot and
lower tax rates just for Amazon. Cuomo plans to bypass the state's Public
Authorities Control Board, which usually approves such tax giveaways.[21]

New York City offered the mega company another $1.5 billion—
under self-proclaimed Amazon critic Bill de Blasio. The mayor said the
HQ2 project would aid the city's development in the tradition of Karl
Marx (yeah, really).[22] He also said, "Using the power of government, we
dictate the terms in as many ways as we can. And in this case, we did
that." De Blasio discussed building a train station near the new Amazon
site, despite the entire MTA being one step above a rickshaw system.
Each New York City resident was set to be on the hook for $348 in
incentives to Amazon,[23] and that figure is much higher for the city's
actual taxpayers, since many who live in the city pay no income taxes.

Eventually Amazon decided to pull out of its plans for New York,
after left-wingers like freshman congresswoman and self-proclaimed

socialist Alexandria Ocasio-Cortez railed against the "greedy" company. Apparently the billions in incentives weren't worth subjecting the company to a political climate dominated by people who detest it.[24] There was a time when major companies had to have a presence in New York City. But those days have passed. As the prestige of being in New York has declined, state politicians increasingly rely on corporate subsidies to compensate for the negative political and business climate and lure businesses. In 2018 alone, New York gave away $10 billion in corporate incentives—more than any other state.[25] But in the case of Amazon, the subsidies simply didn't make up for the negatives.

The National Landing site in Virginia offered fewer sweeteners, but the state still had lower corporate and income taxes to lure Amazon. Virginia and Arlington offered the company "only" $573 million in incentives to move to the city. Still, there were some seriously concerning gems in the deal. Consider that of the $573 million, $23 million will come from the city of Arlington in the form of a "cash grant." And how will the city fund this cash grant? By raising its local hotel tax![26] Yes, you read that correctly: the city of Arlington is raising taxes to pay Amazon, one of the richest companies in the history of the world. This is crony capitalism at its finest, folks.

It seems clear that the way to bring big business into your newly blue-ified state is through special packages for special applicants. Politicians like Bill de Blasio campaigned on the idea of two cities, one rich and one poor, in the tradition of expensive-haircut enthusiast and third-place 2008 Democratic presidential finisher John Edwards, who spoke so eloquently of "two Americas." But when push comes to shove, instead of using taxpayer money to improve the subway, reform the public schools, or lower tax rates across the board, New York City's Democratic politicians are the very shills for corporate trickle-down economics that they accuse Republicans of being.

Such favoritism did not begin with the Amazon deal, and it will not end there either. We're seeing an incredible number of incentive giveaways that strongly correlate with the high taxes and burdensome regulatory schemes of the blue states and cities. Just wait until Texas has high corporate and income tax rates.

Payment in lieu of taxes (PILOT) programs provide targeted tax breaks for specific companies and projects. As of 2010, the most recent year for which data is available, the states with the most PILOT programs include New York, Massachusetts, Connecticut, New Jersey, Pennsylvania, Rhode Island, and Indiana.[27] What do all of those except the Hoosier State have in common? They're all solidly blue states. The New York Jets and Giants pay no property taxes for their shared MetLife Stadium in East Rutherford, New Jersey. In fact, all but three NFL teams pay nothing in property taxes.[28]

Not surprisingly, these plans often don't work out the way that they're promised to when they are sold to the public. The massive steel producer Alcoa received $5.7 million in discounted energy rates from New York State to prevent layoffs in what was the largest corporate welfare program in the nation's history to that point.[29] In exchange the company promised to save 185 jobs at its facility. Instead, in 2015 Alcoa announced layoffs totaling 487 jobs[30]—or two-thirds of their total capacity at a smelting plant. The state's response? A $69 million taxpayer-funded bailout, or about $65 million per preserved job to a company worth $11 billion.[31]

In 2016 alone there were multiple sweetheart deals handed out to large companies. California gave Disney $267 million for a new luxury hotel in Anaheim. Nearly bankrupt Connecticut paid $220 million to keep Lockheed Martin from up and leaving the state. Massachusetts spent $145 million to poach General Electric from Connecticut. Maryland put up $62 million to convince Marriott not to move its headquarters from the state.[32] The threat of cutting jobs is a political winner for major companies, keeping the spigot of taxpayer largesse flowing.

When Ronald Reagan campaigned against "welfare queens," I don't think he meant the world's richest corporations extracting more and more from states with uncompetitive tax structures. But this trend will only accelerate as more states move from frugal red governments towards the dreaded tax-and-spend label.

The truly low-tax states that make Cato Institute and Tax Foundation lists have been consistent in their application of tax rates. These healthy environments for business often feature not only lower tax rates but also a lack of the pressures that tend to bring about higher taxes: less spending on government bureaucracy and fewer individualized subsidies for large companies. While low-tax states are accused of favoring the wealthy, that's typically just not accurate. Usually, low-tax states don't pick winners and losers. They leave that up to the free market, which makes their economies flourish—to the benefit of rich corporations, poor citizens, and everyone in between.

Unfortunately, in the new blue state economic model, crony capitalism isn't just a fluke or an exception to the rule. It's the norm. Sweetheart deals for favored businesses like Amazon are not a bug in the system, *they're a feature*. Opposed to corporate welfare and giveaways? Keep Texas Texas, and don't make it into Connecticut.

CHAPTER FOUR

The Rise of the Purple State
What Happened to New Hampshire, Colorado, and Virginia?

New Hampshire's growth outpaces that of other states in the North-east, and for good reason. The state imposes no income or sales tax on residents. It boasts stunning mountain landscapes and vast wilder-ness. The Live Free or Die state offers its citizens the opportunity to be left alone to pursue their own lives on their own terms. But the state's domestic migrants typically hail from eastern Massachusetts and the area around Boston—a city of singular distinctions, but one with a superiority complex. Eastern Massachusetts has sent Democrats to city, state, and federal legislatures for decades. The citizens who make up its electoral majorities elect Democratic politicians to implement their pro-gressive social convictions, egalitarianism, and commitment to a robust welfare state. Partly as a consequence, Massachusetts also has a sluggish job market[1] and an exorbitant cost of living, each exacerbated by ever-increasing taxes and burdensome regulations that constrain business growth. And tens of thousands of Massachusetts residents have fled the policies they created for themselves—heading to New Hampshire to enjoy the tax benefits and the unobtrusiveness of the state, and in some cases to start a business.

You'd think the attitude of these migrants would be one of humility and deference to the traditions of New Hampshire. But you'd be wrong.

As New Hampshire shifted from solid red to purple over the last two decades, thanks to a growing population of voters from Massachusetts, longtime residents have seen their communities change in ways that were hard to pinpoint at first. For many lifelong New Hampshirites, things just began to feel…different.

New left-wing voters are having a significant impact on the state in ways that cut deeper than the economy or political map. They are fundamentally transforming the culture and way of life in the Live Free or Die state.

I noticed some of these changes firsthand last December when I went home to New Hampshire for Christmas. With a feeling of happy expectation, a smile formed on my face reaching from my lips to my eyes. There it was, glowing in the high beams of my rental car: our old mailbox. It was the same one we had when I was kid, still perched on its weathered post, the colorful red cardinal painted on its battered metal side. This mailbox, to which so many dreams had been delivered, had survived the snows and storms of the endless New England winters. I slowed down the rental car and let my mind drift back in time.

As a teenager, I had often kept my eyes on that mailbox, eagerly awaiting the postman's weekly delivery of *Teen Vogue* and *People* magazines—those missives from the far-off land of big cities and fast living, the glossy catalogues of fashion and gossip that were a vital link to the wider world for a girl in a small rural town. The scandals alone…no one had those in my hometown, at least not that I knew of.

But now that mailbox was full of flyers and notices of old businesses going under and new ones springing up. In a town where everybody used to know everybody else's name, new people had come in—and they were hardly concerned about the way things *used* to be. New Hampshire had the highest population growth rate in the northeastern United States between 2016 and 2017,[2] with most of its new residents coming from Massachusetts.[3] These new Granite Staters were eager to transform their new home in their own image.

While a lot was familiar, my small hometown didn't look the way it used to. I wondered if this was how people felt when they went to a big class reunion—like the thirty-year one—and tried to identify people they once knew. On the drive to my childhood house I noticed still-existing fragments of a previous era: a rustic barn, an antique covered bridge, a stone wall built back when people rode horses and shot deer with muskets. I had thought those things were lame when I was a kid. My high school friends and I had chafed at all the old things in our small town. We craved newness: new music, new clothes, new electronic gadgets. We were embarrassed by the folksy "old-timey" country stores and the white-steepled churches that smelled like grandma's house, musty and steeped in the smells of hair oil and peppermint soap. They weren't "cool." But now, after years of living in the big city, I longed for the familiar sights and smells of my old hometown.

After college I had done exactly what I used to dream I'd do and hightailed it out of my small rural town. I pulled a stint in New York City after college and then moved all the way south to Texas where the sun blazed hot, people spoke in sentences peppered with Spanish, and men in big cowboy hats pretended to own cattle. When I did return to my dad's New Hampshire farmhouse on occasion to give him a howdy or celebrate Christmas, I stayed just long enough to see that everybody was alive and well. And each time, I noticed my hometown had shifted a bit further away from what it once was. To my surprise, I found myself thinking fondly about the old homestead; in a world beset by what many people called "progress," it's good for some things to be consistent and reliable.

I drove up the long gravel driveway to my father's house and took in the snow-covered lawn, remembering how my brother and I had romped through all that snow when we were kids. The driveway was already plowed, cleared by Dad's trusty John Deere, with chunks of snow piled on each side. A jackrabbit darted through the bright beams of my headlights.

The house I grew up in hadn't changed, and I was grateful for it. It had the same front porch, bright red front door, and big oak tree at the corner that painted the sky with red leaves every autumn. Dad had put up the colored Christmas lights on the two bushes flanking the front steps.

Dad stepped onto the porch just as I turned the car off. I got out and waved.

"I hope you brought your snowshoes!" he said, pointing to my city-friendly sneakers. *I don't think he could quite grasp how a Texas transplant didn't need snowshoes.*

We went inside. The place smelled the same as it always had. It's funny how every house has its own smell. My friend Isabel's house always smelled like garlic and onions. Another friend's house smelled like disinfectant—her mom was a fanatic cleaner. Growing up, I didn't know what my house smelled like, because when it's your house, you can't identify anything particular about it. *Strange, I never would have thought it wasn't my home anymore.*

"Hungry?" asked Dad. "I've got some turkey in the refrigerator." He made me a sandwich, and we sat at the kitchen table. "What do you want to do while you're here? Anything special?"

I thought for a moment. "I know it seems silly, but I want to drive into Claremont and see the Nativity scene in front of the public library. Do they still have a live donkey and sheep there? I remember it was always one of my favorite things about Christmas here, with the animals and the life-size figures of Joseph and Mary and the Three Wise Men."

Claremont was one town over from my dad's house—just a ten-minute drive. Every Christmas, we'd go to Broad Street Park, in the center of Claremont, to see the life-size Nativity scene and menorah.

Dad looked concerned and said, "Good idea. This may be the last time you'll be able to see it. Most likely, it won't be there next year."

"Why not?" My stomach jumped like I'd just taken a ride down a disappointment rollercoaster.

"The atheist group Freedom From Religion is threatening to sue the town of Claremont! The controversy started a few months ago when a Claremont resident demanded the removal of the holiday displays.[4] A guy named Sam Killay," Dad said.

"But why?" I asked. "The Nativity scene and menorah in Broad Street Park are a decades-old tradition. Families in the area have gotten so much joy from seeing them, for generations."

Dad scoffed, "Not surprisingly, Killay is new to town. He only moved to Claremont a few years ago from Rhode Island.[5] Figures. He's an atheist who publicly complained about the holiday displays—and his complaints got the attention of Freedom From Religion. The group says the displays violate the separation of church and state. The town of Claremont likely won't want to spend thousands of dollars in legal fees, so they may just relent and take the displays down."

How could I not have known about this? The blue raids on red rural folks' homes, lifestyle, and traditions were getting ridiculous. The place I grew up was being invaded by people who wanted all the perks but none of the cultural identity that, frankly, in hindsight, seemed pretty damn special.

Yet I wasn't surprised. Rural traditions were being squashed all around the nation. In tiny Elmore, Ohio, the same the Freedom From Religion Foundation (FFRF), based in Madison, Wisconsin, threatened to sue the village, claiming placement of a Christmas Nativity scene in a public park violated the constitutional separation of church and state. A lawyer advised the village it could dodge the lawsuit by making the Nativity scene part of an overall holiday display: add a Santa Claus, Christmas trees, and a bunch of candy canes, and they might be off the hook.[6]

In Concord, Indiana, a group supported by the American Civil Liberties Union (ACLU) sued the Concord Community Schools in federal court because the annual Christmas pageant at Concord High School featured a twenty-minute live Nativity scene. The plaintiffs claimed that the Nativity scene and the story of the birth of Jesus were well-recognized symbols of the Christian faith. They said their presence at the Christmas Spectacular had no secular purpose, was coercive, represented an endorsement of religion by the high school, and had the primary effect of advancing religion.[7] These groups are cultural bullies, and they're helping blue state invaders transform red state America. If the in-migrants don't approve of the culture they find in their new neighborhoods, they threaten the longtime residents into submission. They pit deep-pocketed progressive advocacy groups against small towns, and the FFRF or the ACLU pushes the locals into a financial headlock and holds tight until the town taps out.

Suddenly my appetite was gone. I took my suitcase up to my old room. Aside from Dad using my room as a storage closet for a bunch of cardboard boxes and an old lamp or two, it hadn't changed much. No TV—my parents had forbidden it. The computer was an old Dell I had gotten in high school. We didn't get hooked up to the internet until I was in junior high. If you wanted to communicate with someone, you called them on the phone.

You might say we lived in a comfortable bubble, at least by today's standards.

The Big Shift

Later that week Dad and I attended holiday dinner in Grantham at the rural home of longtime family friends Craig and Mary Spaulding. Craig is the patriarch of a fairly large family, and he has the quintessential New England home. It looked especially quaint covered in white, thanks to the big snowstorm that had hit town the day before. When we arrived there were already more than a dozen people there, and a fire was roaring in a fireplace in the next room over. Ah, yes. This is how holidays in New England were supposed to be: smiling faces, roaring fireplace, and snow.

Moseying from the dinner buffet with a plate of food, I sat down next to a girl who looked about my age. Nicole was the best friend of the Spauldings' daughter, Megan. The two had attended college together at Boston University. After graduating last spring, they both took jobs at the same graphic design firm in Portsmouth, New Hampshire. I congratulated Nicole on being a new Granite Stater and asked how she liked her new home.

"Portsmouth is great," Meghan said, "but definitely not as progressive as Massachusetts."

"How so?" I asked.

"New Hampshire needs to get with the times. I grew up right outside Boston, in Somerville. We've been a sanctuary city for years.[8] It's the moral, right thing to do. Undocumented immigrants live in our communities and make all of our lives better. These people have families and shouldn't have to go about their daily lives worried about being rounded up and deported."

Nicole told me there was a growing effort in Portsmouth to declare the community an official sanctuary city.

"I joined a group of residents to put pressure on the local government in Portsmouth," she said. "We've been holding rallies and even started some phone banks to spread the word and put pressure on the city council. I actually think we're making an impact—our city councilor, Nancy Pearson, said she and the city manager are giving serious consideration to the proposition."[9]

I wasn't too surprised. Portsmouth is one of New Hampshire's fastest-growing cities and a top destination for Massachusetts exiles. Located on the seacoast, it's close enough to Boston to be a popular destination for commuters.

"Has there been any pushback?" I asked.

"Unfortunately, yes," Nicole said. "Some of the longtime locals, especially the older folks, are really opposed to the idea. A lot of the people involved in the pro-sanctuary effort are from Massachusetts originally, and to us it's just shocking that such a large number of people could be so unwelcoming."

A number of New Hampshire towns have declared themselves "sanctuary cities" in recent years. Manchester (New Hampshire's capital), Deerfield, Dublin, Harrisville, and Lyme have all instructed their police officers that they are no longer allowed to cooperate with ICE or inquire about a person's immigration status.

A few months after our dinner at the Spauldings, Nicole's group had a breakthrough: Portsmouth's city officials introduced a "welcoming and diversity" resolution, which essentially has the same effect as declaring sanctuary status but without the risk of losing federal funding.[10]

For decades New Hampshire was a solid red law-and-order state. Native residents are seeing their home fundamentally transformed by blue state newcomers who do not share their values. As liberal voters flock to the likes of Texas, Colorado, and New Hampshire, not only do they vote for Democrats who are more likely to instate tax hikes and restrictive corporate regulation, but these former blue staters also bring with them an alien set of values, which they attempt to shoehorn into their new states. As a result, it's not just the politics of these newly purple states that is changing. The liberal invasion of red state America has also caused *cultural* shifts.

The next morning, I texted my friend Rachel, asking if she wanted to meet up. She was an English teacher at my old high school, and she was my age, so we shared a similar perspective.

I suggested we take a drive up to downtown Hanover—the quaint little town fifteen minutes north of Grantham, where Dartmouth College sits. I use the term "downtown" loosely, because it wasn't more than two blocks of charming stores and a cross street, anchored by the First Congregational Church at one end and the quaint Hanover Inn at the other.

Rachel picked me up in her Jeep Wrangler and we made our way to Hanover.

"Let's go to Bagel Basement," I said. "I haven't been there in years. I miss their fresh-baked bagels and cream cheese. You can't find bagels like that in Texas."

"You're going to be in for a surprise," said Rachel as she swung the Jeep into a parking place on Main Street.

Was that good?

Getting out of the car, I scanned the storefronts where I expected to see Bagel Basement. "Where is it?" I asked.

"Right there," said Rachel, pointing to an all-too-familiar Starbucks logo over a front door.

"You've got to be kidding," I said. "I'm so sick of seeing Starbucks! Everywhere you go, there's another Starbucks. I had hoped that this area would be immune to this terrible contagion."

Suddenly the door flew open and two women emerged. They were dressed in expensive pseudo-rural clothes: pricey UGG shearling boots, designer jeans, Canada Goose parkas. It looked like a scene from Aspen. Steaming cups in hand, they blew right past us as if we were two mail-boxes. Then one of the women stopped and gave Rachel a perfunctory smile. "Oh—you're Ms. Swanson! From the school in Grantham! Nice to see you. Happy holidays!" Then she turned and walked away.

I watched Rachel watching the women get into a BMW. "That's Monica Fulbright and her daughter, Penelope. Monica works for an internet social media company—I forget which one."

"Where did they move here from?"

"Wellesley, Massachusetts."

Monica and Penelope are just the tip of the migrant iceberg. New Hampshire's population is among the most mobile in the nation.[11] Today, most Granite State residents weren't actually born in the state. Only a third of New Hampshire residents age twenty-five and older are natives. The largest source of new settlers to New Hampshire is the Boston metropolitan area, which is nearly the complete opposite of New Hampshire on just about every important cultural issue.

In New Hampshire, as in other red states being taken over by new-comers from blue states, voters can be placed in one of three categories: longtime residents, young residents now old enough to vote, and migrants who have recently moved to the state from another state. And as you might suspect, the younger voters tend to vote blue. But the migrants vote even bluer. Research has shown that 45 percent of young voters and 42 percent of migrant voters are likely to identify as Democrats.[12] Established voters show the lowest identification as Democrats.

It's no big surprise that young voters are typically more liberal than their parents or grandparents. That's the way it's been for decades. But they also vote at a much lower rate, which has shifted the actual voting power toward the older, more conservative voters who show up on Election Day in much higher numbers. But in states like New Hampshire, Colorado, and Virginia—and even Texas and Florida—the *combination* of young voters and migrants, both of whom tend to skew to the left, can make a real difference at the ballot box.

While the migrants have fled the high-tax states of New York, Connecticut, and Massachusetts for the simpler pleasures of central New Hampshire—or Colorado or Virginia—they may not be able to shake their addiction to all the services their pricy former states attempt to provide. They're addicts, viewing government as a source of largesse—a big fat cash cow dispensing creamy goodness for everyone.

All this ran through my head in a millisecond as Rachel and I walked into Starbucks. Coming through the gleaming new door and approaching the counter, with its piles of overpriced snacks and fancy coffee cups, I saw that this outpost of the Howard Schultz empire offered exactly the same trinkets as every other Starbucks I had ever seen. I could have been standing in a Starbucks in New York or San Francisco.

"At least we still have no sales tax," said Rachel as she paid for her cold foam cascara cold brew and a chocolate hazelnut croissant. "But the pressure's on. Just recently, the New Hampshire House had to leap into action to thwart other states from collecting sales tax in New Hampshire." In 2018, the Supreme Court ruled that states can require online retailers to collect sales taxes.[13] This means that when someone places an order from his or her home in tax-free New Hampshire, a store in New York could still collect sales tax on the purchase. The ruling has been seen as a victory for states that are losing tax revenues. But it's a kick in the gut to New Hampshire, which prides itself on having neither a sales nor an income tax.

The Live Free or Die State has been home to an independent spirit since the founding of the nation. Both delegates representing the state at the Constitutional Convention—Nicholas Gilman and John Langdon—were among the most passionate defenders of the Revolution.[14] Freedom from government has been a paramount New Hampshire value since the state's colonial constitution, which was written in 1776 at the beginning of the American Revolution. Its framers made the New Hampshire state government weak by design.[15] And Granite Staters have a constitutional aversion to taxes; they simply don't want to send more money to Concord, thereby giving state bureaucrats more power.

The Sixteenth Amendment, which allows the federal government to collect an income tax, was first proposed in 1911—and New Hampshire rejected it. And when the amendment finally did pass in 1913, the state was the last to ratify it. Soon afterwards, states began implementing their own income taxes...but New Hampshire never did. Even back in 1929, the *New York Times* noted, "New Hampshire manifests small enthusiasm for an income tax."[16]

New Hampshire still has a strong anti-tax attitude—but that may change as newcomers to the state change the political calculus. The forces of erosion are strong: the will to resist a broad-based tax may become weaker with changing demographics. In 2016, state representative Paul Henle—a Democrat representing Concord—proposed instituting an income tax and drafted a bill to that effect.[17] Thankfully the idea was eventually abandoned, but with the momentum on the Democrats' side, an income tax could become a reality in New Hampshire very soon.

It was time to move on to the next stop on my tour of bygone old glory days. Rachel and I took a ten-minute drive up I-89 to Lebanon, New Hampshire. I wanted to visit a charming store called Ye Olde Yankee Market. I tried to find it online but couldn't. Rachel told me not to worry—many of the old stores didn't have websites. But when we pulled up to the building where I expected to find Ye Olde Yankee Market, the sign over the front windows read instead, "Las Americas Deli Grocery." Standing on the sidewalk, which had been meticulously swept of snow, I peered into the big plate glass windows.

"This is a bodega," I said to Rachel.

I was starting to think Rachel was taking pleasure in seeing my reaction to the changes in our town.

We went inside. The store was crammed with a huge variety of delicious-looking food products. Still, I missed Ye Olde Yankee Market.

"Are there many Hispanics moving to New Hampshire?" I asked Rachel.

"Enough to make a difference," she replied. Peering at her phone, she said, "There's been a 23.1 percent increase in the Hispanic population in New Hampshire over the last eight years. Lebanon has one of the highest Hispanic populations of any city in the state."[18] It struck me as odd that Lebanon, which is located several hours north of the New Hampshire–Massachusetts border, deep in the heart of the state, would have such a significant Hispanic population.

Hispanic neighbors are welcome additions to the cities and towns of New Hampshire, but as voters they can make a difference in electoral outcomes. It's a demographic that almost always votes Democratic, regardless of what part of the nation they live in. Polls show 54 percent of Latino registered voters believe the Democratic Party has more concern for Latinos than the Republican Party, while only 11 percent say the Republican Party has more concern—a forty-three-point difference.[19] Add in the young voters and the domestic migrants from Massachusetts, and you've got a significant group of liberal voters changing the state. And the demographic trends keep going in their direction. (Of course, this wouldn't be a problem if the Republican Party figured out how to make these voters understand that GOP policies ultimately serve their best interests. That's a subject I'll address later in the book.)

"Lebanon is becoming rather trendy," Rachel continued.

She was right. And it only makes sense. Lebanon is the home of Dartmouth-Hitchcock Medical Center and Dartmouth Medical School, together comprising the largest medical facility between Boston, Massachusetts, and Burlington, Vermont. A number of medical and high-tech firms have located facilities near the medical center campus. Tele Atlas, a leading worldwide developer of mapping databases, has its North American headquarters in Lebanon. Novell and Microsoft also have major facilities there, as well as Novo Nordisk, a Danish multinational pharmaceutical company. When you build up tech centers in a rural-ish area, you're going to see the ideals and beliefs of those companies' workers follow along with them out of the big city.

"It won't be long before we've become a mini–Silicon Valley," I said. The snarky libertarian in me was kicking in. "People relocate here for the charming environment and low taxes, and before you know it, the charm is gone and the taxes are up."

Colorado: East California

After spending Christmas with Dad, I flew to Colorado to visit my college friend Tim. He lived in Firestone, a growing town of 13,000 people 30 miles due north of Denver. Actually, to say Firestone was "growing" is an understatement. The population boom in Firestone began at the turn of the twenty-first century, and more than 8,000 people moved there in a decade. This rapid growth was especially impressive considering that in the year 2000 the town's population was only 1,900 souls. By 2010, the town had a population of over 10,000, making it the fastest-growing Colorado community at the time.[20] New houses were being built as fast as the carpenters could pound the nails. Firestone was a town of opportunity in the Centennial State.

While the breakneck pace of growth had since slackened, Firestone continues to be one of the fastest-growing towns in Colorado. One driving force is the oil and gas industry that is bringing massive growth to the entire region.

Tim had an apartment with a spectacular view facing west toward the majestic Rocky Mountains.

"How much are you paying in rent?" I brazenly asked.

"Twelve hundred bucks a month. The apartment has a clubhouse with a twenty-four-hour fitness room and a multipurpose room for parties and events. Next to the clubhouse there's a large pool, spa, and a playground with an adjoining covered barbecue area. I've got my own little balcony, too."

"Hah! In New York or LA, twelve hundred dollars a month would get you the most disgusting, rat-infested studio apartment on a street where your life expectancy would be about five minutes. The only view would be of the addict shooting up in the alley outside your door."

Tim didn't say it, but I could see it in his eyes: *You have not changed.* We went into the kitchen, where, to my surprise, there were six marijuana plants under a grow light. "I didn't know you smoked, Tim."

He smiled. "Once in a while. I harvest from these Royal Mobys so I don't have to buy it from anyone. You might say it's a renewable resource."

"It's legal, right?"

"Of course!"

In 2012, Colorado made it legal to grow pot at home. Since then, the state's population has skyrocketed. Both marijuana entrepreneurs and young druggies packed their bags and moved to Colorado to partake in the drug industry.

On the one hand, the drug termed a "gateway drug" by some has turned out to be a gateway to a bunch of bad statistics that no one could have seen coming. Tourists aren't just buying weed now that it's legal—they're ending up in hospitals at far higher rates than residents. Since the legalization of pot, emergency room visits by out-of-staters have doubled.[21] But while Colorado has had to deal with some negative side effects, it seems indisputable that they are outweighed by the benefits of legal marijuana, which has been a major boon to the state economy.

An eye-popping report by Colorado State University–Pueblo's Institute of Cannabis Research revealed that the newly taxed and regulated marijuana industry contributed more than $58 million to Colorado's Pueblo County—a rural part of the state with just over 160,000 residents—alone. Pueblo County has made headlines for using cannabis excise taxes to fund local scholarships for hundreds of students each year. The rest of the nation could learn from Colorado when it comes to legalization: the firm New Frontier Data—a group that studies data and business intelligence in the cannabis industry—found that federal marijuana legalization would result in an additional $105.6 billion being injected into the U.S. economy between 2017 and 2025, and create jobs for at least 654,000 Americans.[22]

The doorbell rang. Tim went to answer it and greeted a woman at the door. She tried to get Tim to sign a petition. "We really need to take action to prevent the government from abolishing all traces of religion in our schools," said the woman, whose name tag said her name was Josephine. "We're gathering signatures for a ballot initiative. The courts are waging a war on religion."

Tim, who was determinedly nonpolitical, turned to me. "This is more up your alley. You talk to them."

Gladly!

The issue, as I learned, was that in 2015 the Colorado Supreme Court had struck down a voucher program in the state's third-largest school district as unconstitutional because it allowed public funds to be spent for tuition to religious schools. The ruling, which had reversed a decision by a state appeals court, meant the Douglas County School District could not administer its Choice Scholarship Pilot Program allowing parents to pay for a private school for their child, which could include a religious school.

There was a time when the focus was on where a child could get the best education and making it work, but now new people from outside the state had ideas on how this should all be done, making it impossible for lifetime Coloradans (like the one at Tim's door) to have their say in what they felt was best for the state.

"This issue is destined for the U.S. Supreme Court," said Josephine.

The Colorado high court's decision rested on a passage in the state's constitution prohibiting government aid to "any church or sectarian society, or for any sectarian purpose, or to help support or sustain any school…controlled by any church or sectarian denomination." At least thirty-seven states have similar language in their constitutions. They are known as "Blaine amendments," after a nineteenth-century speaker of the U.S. House of Representatives who proposed a constitutional amendment designed to prohibit states from funding religious educational institutions. The amendment was never adopted on the federal level, but individual states made it part of their laws. Most people, legislators included, don't even realize the Blaine amendment is in their state constitution until some group opposes tuition vouchers.

"But there's hope," said Josephine. "In 2017, the U.S. Supreme Court ordered the Colorado Supreme Court to re-examine the Douglas County school voucher program that the state court had struck down as unconstitutional."

The U.S. Supreme Court had struck down a similar policy in Missouri that prohibited public money from going to religious institutions. The high court ruled that the exclusion violated the First Amendment rights of churches, at least when the money was meant for nonreligious purposes.

Josephine finally left when I told her that, as an out-of-stater, I couldn't sign their Colorado initiative.

Tim and I went out to look at the mountains, clear and hard against the brilliant winter sky. "So what's happening with Colorado?" I asked him. "It wasn't so long ago that the Centennial State was reliably red."[23] Historically, reliably red Coloradans have picked the winner in eight out of the last ten presidential elections…until the generous five-point margin they gave Hillary in 2016. And when it comes to the state government, things have shifted significantly Democratic over the years. There's still a small majority for the Republicans, but it is just shy of fifty-fifty, and not trending in their favor.

Tim said the same liberal transformation was happening in other western states like Arizona and Nevada. The big political shift started in 2008 when Barack Obama won the state, a rare feat for a Democrat. He tapped into the fast-growing population of younger liberals flooding the "front range"—the eastern face of the Rocky Mountains, with Denver in the center. In a pretty short amount of time, it has become a mountainous version of San Francisco.

The six counties that make up the Denver metropolitan area—Adams, Arapahoe, Boulder, Broomfield, Denver, and Jefferson—account for about half of the votes in recent statewide elections. That's a powerful block of voters, and many of them are recent liberal arrivals from other states.

Party affiliations are shifting as these new left-wing residents flood the state. The Colorado secretary of state's office says there are now more registered Democratic voters in Colorado than registered Republicans. But a registered voter is not the same as a voter, and if you look only at *active* voters, there are about 8,400 more active registered Republican voters than active Democrats. But both parties are outnumbered by 1,284,407 unaffiliated voters, whose allegiances are up for grabs.[24] All it takes is one election for registered voters to become likely voters and flip the entire control of the state over to Democrats. Hello, progressive legislation. Just as in California and New York, there are pockets of Republicans in Colorado, but they don't live in the big cities—which skew the votes a lot.

Why the changes? Urbanization is one answer, as is Hispanic immigration. But the biggest reason is the nine-hundred-pound gorilla to the west: California.

Californians, who tend to be liberal, are emigrating out of the Golden State in massive numbers. They're fleeing the high taxes, high home prices, congestion, and overall craziness for greener pastures in neighboring states.

And many of them are moving to Colorado, bringing their blueness with them. We have already discussed two of the big resulting changes: Suddenly, marijuana is legal. And here are new restrictive regulations on guns, enough that gun manufacturers left the state, taking their jobs with them. But what's really sad is that the gun policies Colorado has adopted are not effective. Law-abiding Coloradans cannot protect themselves, but the legislators and the celebrities that ramble on…and on…and on about gun control all have security details that could take out anyone who threatened their precious selves in a second flat.

In addition, many new Coloradans are determined not to use the state's raw resources. They want to require Colorado citizens even in rural areas of the state to use alternative energy. Sounds pretty good, doesn't it? Well, it's also a job-killer and costly—plus, it is yet to be proven effective. And when you're in the middle of nowhere, you kind of need to have reliable energy.

No wonder Colorado has the awful nickname "East California."[25]

These cultural changes are not happening by random chance. They are happening because of the great migration out of California. A total of 142,932 people left California in 2016. They left for other states such as Texas, Arizona and Nevada, but Colorado was their top destination. So thousands of people are coming into the Centennial State from California. And simultaneously more people are *leaving* Colorado than ever before. Why? They don't like what it's becoming.

Native residents leaving as new residents flood in. Big cultural shift.

Now Colorado is facing a progressive brand of politics that pushes conservatives into more remote parts of the state—so much so that in 2013, eleven northeastern counties held a vote on secession. It all began when the Democratic-controlled Colorado General Assembly passed laws increasing reliance on renewable energy, as well as tighter gun control and livestock treatment laws. A law that would have put higher environmental standards on oil and gas production was narrowly defeated. During the debates over these laws, talk of secession began in the Eastern Plains area.

On the ballot on November 5, 2013, in eleven counties, the proposal to make "Northern Colorado" the fifty-first state received a split vote. But the effort underscored the real cultural divide between Colorado's urban centers and rural areas.

In California, meanwhile, polls reveal that most residents think the high cost of living, including housing, is the most important issue facing the state.[26] More than half of Californians want to repeal the state's new gas tax, which raised prices by 40 percent. And, as we have seen, the recent federal tax reform will only raise that high cost of living higher—not just for Californians, but for blue state residents in general, with the amount of their high blue state taxes that they can deduct on their federal returns now cut. Some conservative economists have predicted the new tax law could spur a mass exodus of wealth from New York and California over the following three years.[27]

The effective income tax rate (that is, what people actually pay) for high-income taxpayers in California could increase from 8.5 to 13 percent. Wealthy New Yorkers face a similar increase. Those increases would cause an exodus of thousands of residents from high-tax states, including Connecticut, New Jersey, and Minnesota, to states with low or no income tax.

The tsunami of migration from high-tax blue states will bring millions of people, thousands of businesses, and tens of billions of dollars of net income to what are now low-tax red states—and turn them purple with minimal effort, and blue with just a bit of commitment and pestering of the native population. And when you can't beat them, what do you do? If you're a Republican, you tend to join them.

Virginia: The Southernmost Northern State

Tim and I went out for dinner at a vaguely international restaurant called Injoy, a few miles down the road in Erie. We ate at the bar, which is more fun than sitting at a table. I had the lime chicken with safimoroccan spices, couscous, beans, and olives. I could have been eating at one of the best restaurants in New York or LA.

As it turned out, Tim knew our bartender. His name was Jerome, and he had grown up in Virginia before coming to Colorado for college. During a lull in the action, I asked him if he ever went home to visit.

"Sure I do. Every year I go back to see my parents in Chesterfield County. It's amazing how it's changing."

"Wasn't former House Speaker Eric Cantor from Virginia's Seventh Congressional District?" I asked.

"Yes," replied Jerome. "Solid red. The district went for McCain in 2008, Romney in 2012, and Trump in 2016. But that's changing. Now it's all about population growth in some areas and decline in other areas."

True. Remember, 150 years ago, Virginia was at the center of the Confederacy. The Virginia State Capitol on Capitol Square in Richmond served as the center of political power; it was the meeting place for the Virginia Convention of 1861 and wartime sessions of the General Assembly and the Confederate Congress. Robert E. Lee accepted command of

Virginia's armies there, and in 1862 President Jefferson Davis was inaugurated on Capitol Square.

Today, political experts say Virginia can be considered either the "northernmost southern state" or the "southernmost northern state." Shifting demographics favor the latter view. Until 1952, the Old Dominion had been a Democratic-leaning state. Then, as the Democratic Party turned left, Virginia began its shift into the red. Once President Johnson and the Democrats abandoned the cause of white supremacy and Richard Nixon invented his "Southern Strategy," the region became as solidly Republican as it had once been Democratic.

Virginia was a reliably Republican-leaning state until 2008, but demographic changes in densely populated counties in Northern Virginia close to Washington, D.C., have tilted those areas toward the Democratic Party once more. The shift has no doubt been accelerated by the fact that thousands of the D.C. bureaucratic elite live in Virginia, right outside the borders of the District itself. Nice, expensive houses and a wealthy pool of typically Democratic voters.

Also, recent population growth has been centered in traditionally Democratic areas, including Northern Virginia, just outside D.C.; the capital, Richmond; and Henrico County in the Richmond suburbs. And from 2000 to 2010, Virginia's Hispanic population, which tends to lean Democratic, increased by 92 percent, with two-thirds of that growth concentrated in Northern Virginia.[28]

Why are people leaving our nation's capital in droves, seeking a better life in Virginia?

Perhaps it's because D.C. is, as JFK so accurately described it, "a city of Southern efficiency and Northern charm." Or because it ranks as one of the most expensive cities in the United States. A recent report found you need to make $108,092 a year to live comfortably in D.C., and that's if you're just supporting yourself—no spouse or kids.

Then, to make matters worse, the D.C. metro area boasts some of the most horrific traffic in the nation and an abysmal public transportation system that makes New York's look like a dream come true. The area's heavy traffic will equal or often exceed gridlock found in California, Texas, New York, Chicagoland, or Atlanta.

And, of course, there are the insane taxes. When you pay taxes in D.C., your cash goes straight to the feds. Some crooked congressman from Illinois has more control over how your tax dollars are spent than the D.C. "city council." (I put that in quotes on purpose. It's basically a powerless lunch club.) The current license plates issued to all motor vehicles in the District are emblazoned with the slogan "End Taxation Without Representation" in big blue letters.

Let's go back to Virginia, where many of the escapees from Foggy Bottom are fleeing. Virginia was the only southern state to go to Hillary Clinton, who won it by more than Barack Obama had in 2012. In November 2017, Democratic gubernatorial candidate Ralph Northam defeated Republican Ed Gillespie by nine points, outperforming Clinton's five-point victory, while garnering a record number of votes for a gubernatorial candidate.

Meanwhile, Virginia Democrats have moved left. Party operatives on both sides have noted that during Mark Warner's successful 2001 run for governor, a popular local bluegrass band wrote ballads in support of his campaign. And in 2005, Tim Kaine won the governorship on a platform that included opposition to gay marriage, among other issues. But in 2008, Kaine stood in front of the Virginia Civil Rights Memorial at the state capitol in Richmond and declared, "Old Virginny is dead!"

Tim and I went back to his place, and I crashed in his spare bedroom. As I lay in bed I thought about my travels to New Hampshire and Colorado, and how much these states were changing—and how the same fate might be in store for many others, including not only Virginia but even the Lone Star State. And about how these transformations could be effectively opposed. You can't recover the past, but you can do your best to ensure the future is bright! And not only the heart of Texas…everywhere.

CHAPTER FIVE

The New City-States
How Red State Cities Explain Blue Victories

L ooking forward to the future of your small town being decided by the residents of the nearest metropolis—who vote in their own interests? Perhaps your house will be seized and bulldozed because it is within twenty miles of a potential water source for that big city. Or maybe the industry that fuels your town's economy will be regulated out of existence by environmentally woke city dwellers. Or longtime local traditions—from gun ownership to Christmas displays—could fall afoul of new state policies put in place by urban sophisticates who don't approve of your rural lifestyle. As cities that are taking in the most blue state refugees expand, their larger populations will drown out the voices of rural voters in the same state. This dynamic is already well established in the solidly blue states. And now the same process that made inland California, downstate Illinois, and Upstate New York subservient to the will of the major cities in their states is happening across the country in currently red states, whose cities are absorbing record numbers of blue state expats. Between 2016 and 2017, eight of the top eleven fastest-growing metro areas were in red states—with the cities gaining a far larger share of population than rural areas.[1] And seven of the top ten fastest-growing counties were red.[2] Red state urban centers such as

Atlanta, Nashville, Charlotte, and Dallas are growing so fast that they will soon be able to dictate many aspects of life in the rural parts of their states.

As Democrats flee blue states and relocate to cities in red states, places like Georgia and North Carolina will be pushed to the left. To see the potential effects of such changes, you just have to look at what happened in historically blue states when the most heavily populated urban areas were able to outvote their neighboring rural areas. For decades now, New York City, Chicago, and Los Angeles have determined how things go across New York State, Illinois, and California. Sparsely populated areas in those states effectively have no say at the ballot box—not only over politics at the state level, but even over their own rural communities—on, for example, control of their own water supply. And as big cities in those blue states became more liberal, residents of the rural parts of those states were subjected to the city dwellers' left-wing politics. Rural areas in states like North Carolina and Georgia are likely headed for a similar fate.

My followers on social media and the readers of my column at *The Hill* consistently tell me that their small communities are negatively affected by high taxes and government mandates passed by the liberal populations of their states' major cities. One email from a reader in rural Illinois really struck me. She described the major burdens that liberal politicians had put on local governments and schools around the state: mandates in aid of illegal immigrant students, restrictions on equipment and training for firefighters, and mandatory social justice training for municipal employees that has reduced effectiveness and increased local taxes. Illinois lawmakers elected by Chicagoans adopt left-wing policies that make them feel good—and pass the costs on to local governments across the state. Then cash-strapped towns, schools, and small cities, which can't afford to comply with all of these new mandates, pass the costs along to local taxpayers. Whether it's mandating LGBT history in the schools[3] or requiring municipalities to pay into the state's imploding pension system, more often than not, homeowners are stuck with the bill. Illinois governor Bruce Rauner estimated that the most egregious of the school mandates in his state cost taxpayers $200 million annually.[4]

"So how does the local government or school reduce these costs?" I responded to the email.

"They don't," she replied. "By this point it's way too late."

I guess I had already known that.

And there are plenty of other examples of liberal residents in major cities lording it over the people of the smaller cities and towns in their states—sometimes hundreds of miles of away.

The power that urban centers have over the rural parts of the blue states foreshadows the likely future in other states, as the great blue wave of newcomers to red states accelerates over the next decade. Almost all state-based policy in New York, California, and Illinois over the last thirty years has been dictated by New York City, Los Angeles and San Francisco, and Chicago, leaving the smaller population areas with little recourse. And over that time the areas of New York State, California, and Illinois outside those states' metropolitan centers have suffered catastrophic population losses. Cornell University estimates that Upstate New York will lose total population as a result of out-migration through 2035.[5] Eighty-nine of Illinois's 102 counties—all outside of Chicago's Cook County—lost population between 2010 and 2017.[6] Between 2016 and 2017, 37 of California's 58 counties suffered a domestic migration loss.[7] A hundred thousand Californians have left the state since 2010.[8]

Rural and suburban areas of blue states saw droves of their residents flee for greener pastures in the red states. While urban areas are losing people in higher numbers, nonurban areas are losing higher percentages of their total populations. And both sets of out-migrants from blue states are headed to red and purple states, hollowing out the red states' demographic cores. Hopefully readers in the small towns and rural areas of traditionally red states can learn from what happened to people in similar parts of the blue states.

The Future of the Extended City-State

The dense populations of the major cities of New York, California, and Illinois lean overwhelmingly to the left. And they dominate politics in their states, mandating policies that affect the population of the rest of their respective states. The enormous size of these cities allows them to dominate their states' politics, while they are insulated from many of the effects of those policies. And red state cities like Nashville, Charlotte, and Atlanta, which are some of the fastest growing in the country, could soon dominate their states in a similar fashion. Many Americans are leaving dense cities like New York City (over 530,000 in 2016 alone) and moving to midsize cities. The largest share of movers in 2016 moved to midsize cities and suburbs (351,000, while 171,000 went to larger cities and only 108,000 went to rural areas).[9]

And the longer this trend continues, the likelier that political life in the red states will replicate the urban dominance we already see in the blue states. New York City makes up over 43 percent of the population of New York State. Chicago is home to over 21 percent of Illinois's total population, and San Francisco and LA contain over 12 percent of Californians. Once cities reach a critical mass, they have the power to domineer over the rest of the state in their own interests. They can also treat rural areas and small towns as testing grounds for their progressive—and very expensive—agenda. The population surge in red state cities as a result of migration from blue states could import the same dynamic to states like North Carolina, Georgia, and Tennessee.

North Carolina's population has increased by about half since 1990, topping 10 million in 2017. Meanwhile, during the same time span, the population of Charlotte, its largest city, has doubled. Charlotte's population has also skyrocketed in terms of its share of the state's population. In 1990, the city's 430,000 residents represented 6.4 percent of the state; today's almost 860,000 residents represent 8.4 percent. At the same time, Raleigh has doubled in population and Durham is not far behind. These three largest cities were home to 12 percent of North Carolina residents in 1990—and almost 16 percent today.

While moving company United Van Lines ranked North Carolina the eighth most popular state to move to in 2016 and 2017, fifth in 2015, and third in 2014 and 2013,[10] Michael Walden, a North Carolina State University economics professor, has estimated that urban centers in the state will see their population increase 100 percent by 2050 while the populations of rural centers in the foothills and east of the state will actually decline during the same period.[11] According to the Carolina Population Center, urban areas will make up an astonishing two-thirds of the state's population by 2035, compared to just half today.[12]

Half of all registered voters in North Carolina were born out of state.[13] And 33 percent of these migrants are Democrats, compared to 30 percent Republicans. Among voters born outside of North Carolina, the largest share (14 percent) come from New York State. The former New Yorkers registered 39 percent for Democrats and 26 percent for Republicans. Among the 6 percent of the transplants who are from New Jersey, 36 percent registered Democratic and only 25 percent Republican.[14]

And registered voters originally born in other states are moving to cities at far higher rates than to other parts of North Carolina, increasing the cities' political power while also moving them leftward. Over half of the expatriates from New York, California, Ohio, New Jersey, and Michigan who moved to North Carolina lived in urban counties. Given the facts that urban voters are generally more likely to vote Democrat and these new city dwellers are from blue states, North Carolina is at serious risk of turning blue.

The cities most affected by this wave of new residents already made their presence felt in the 2018 election. In Raleigh's home county, Democrats had added three times as many new registered voters since 2010 as Republicans. And some of the largest increases in turnout in North Carolina between the off-year congressional elections in 2014 and 2018 were in the urban portions of the state. The urban triangle around Durham increased its voter turnout by a full 10 percent, which was 25 percent more than the state average.[15] In the Raleigh suburbs, Democrats defeated an astounding five incumbent Republican state legislators.[16] Sixteen-year-incumbent Wake County sheriff Donnie Harrison, a Republican, was defeated in 2018 by Democrat Gerald Baker with the help of $100,000 in ACLU campaign ad spending.[17] This was part of $25 million in campaign spending on left-wing causes by the group that year,[18] including over $1 million to oppose Brett Kavanaugh's nomination to the Supreme Court.[19] Lefty donations go through the ACLU to the next potential political battlegrounds—especially where Democrats can make new inroads.

Once elected, Baker proceeded to suspend the state's cooperation with ICE over deportation of illegal aliens with criminal records, making North Carolina a "sanctuary state" and safe harbor for criminal aliens.[20] Voters who think such major political changes will happen at some point in the future must realize that they're happening today.

A similar seismic shift is happening in Georgia because of new residents whose votes will likely lead to Democratic victories in the near future. In 2017 the state was the fifth-largest recipient of movers, adding over sixty-nine thousand net residents from other states. Fifty-seven thousand new residents came from New York, Illinois, Connecticut, California, and New Jersey combined.[21] While Trump won North Carolina in 2016 and the Democratic candidate failed to take the Governor's Mansion in 2018, the total vote difference in the gubernatorial contest between Republican Brian Kemp and Democrat Stacey Abrams was only fifty-five thousand votes—less than the number of migrants from the blue states listed above in one single year. New registrations from out-of-state residents will eventually flip the state.

Much of this change is in the greater Atlanta area, which voted heavily for Stacey Abrams. Though she didn't succeed, the Democrats did flip ten seats in the Georgia legislature—their biggest gain in twenty years.[22] Immigration is one cause for the shift: one out of ten Georgians was born in a different country.[23] But in-migration from northern states is another cause; just over half of Georgia's population was born in the state.[24] While far-left Democrat Stacey Abrams didn't win the governor's race in 2018, she is likely going to become governor or a senator if current demographic trends continue. Atlanta's Fulton and DeKalb counties in the Atlanta metropolitan area gave her a combined 568,000 votes. In 2014, they gave Democratic gubernatorial candidate Michelle Nunn 337,000 votes. That represents a *69 percent increase* in just one cycle!

As long as we're on the topic of red state cities pushing their states leftward, it would be remiss not to mention Tennessee. The state has taken in 178,000 new residents from 2010 to 2017, large numbers of whom hailed from blue states: 27,000 of the in-migrants in 2017 were from left-leaning states such as California, New York, Connecticut, Illinois, and New Jersey.[25]

But Tennessee's population growth has slowed in the last several years—with an interesting result. As migration from blue states slowed, so did the advance of liberal politics. Democrats seemed to have a chance of winning the growing suburban and urban districts surrounding Nashville, Tennessee's largest city, until the spigot of blue staters slowed to a trickle in recent years. In 2017 Nashville surpassed Memphis as the state's largest metro area, its population pushed higher by residents moving from other parts of the country. Between 2011 and 2015, the two single largest cities of origin outside of Tennessee for Nashville residents were Chicago and Los Angeles, with New York, Boston, Detroit, and San Diego not far behind.[26] Nashville's population has exploded over the last half-century. From 1960 to the present, its population has increased over 400 percent and absorbed several outlying suburbs. Since 1990 the population has surged at a faster rate than the national average, increasing over 35 percent to 690,000. The wider Nashville metro area has nearly doubled in population during this same time span, and now includes over 1.9 million people and 28 percent of the state's population (compared to 20 percent in 1990). While the city has grown dramatically, population loss in the traditionally Democratic city of Memphis seems to have muted the changes happening in Music City. In fact, Tennessee lost 2,000 residents in net migration in 2018.[27] The slowdown in migration from blue states seems to have stopped the left-wing political gains in Tennessee, allowing the state to remain red for the foreseeable future. Tennessee's population shifts seem to prove the overall rule. As population statewide has remained relatively flat over the last several years, there has *not* been the same leftward lurch as in other states.

But just as successful economies in Colorado and Texas are attracting new voters who are pushing those states into the purple column, the same thing could have happened in Tennessee. And Tennesseans should be grateful for their near escape. Just take a close look at how the voters in big blue cities have treated their rural neighbors in the past. It's a fate that would behoove the residents of small towns and rural counties in the red states to avoid.

If Bill de Blasio Was in Charge of the Sahara, It Would Run Out of Sand in Five Years

Make no mistake: as red state cities become populated with more liberal voters, they will force changes on the rural hinterlands. Lower-population areas of formerly Republican states will suffer a fate similar to that of the blue states' rural areas, which have seen their local independence eroded by imperial state capitals. Their economies have been crippled and their small towns destroyed. If it could happen there, why won't it happen to your corner of the world?

There is perhaps no better example of urbanites destroying the rural communities in their states than the century-long battle over water rights in California and New York. Major population centers like New York City and Los Angeles need tremendous quantities of water—and they have been happy to siphon it off from unwilling parts of their states, at the expense of their rural neighbors.

The natural splendor of Upstate New York has captured the imagination of the nation for centuries. But today the countryside that was the backdrop for both James Fenimore Cooper's Leatherstocking Tales and the real-life Industrial Revolution (think of the Erie Canal) has been devastated by the "needs" of New York City's residents. The region is now a sad sight, pockmarked with former industrial cities like Rochester and Utica. While Upstate New York has more in common, geographically and culturally, with its neighbors in rural Pennsylvania and the Rust Belt than with the residents of the five boroughs, political boundaries tie the area to the greater New York City metropolis. And the New Yorkers who live in the city tend to see Upstate New York as either their weekend playground or the home of unrefined rubes—on whom they are more than willing to force city-centric policies.

The best example is the forcible taking of water from the freshwater-rich region of the Catskills several hours north of the boroughs. Despite heavy ski and weekend traffic in the area, the counties of the Catskills still have a large majority of rural residents with decades' or centuries' roots. There is an existential conflict between Rip Van Winkle territory and the New York City Department of Environmental Protection (DEP). But it's only recognized as such in the "watershed"—the parts of New York State that supply New York City's drinking water. To the New York City residents who drink that water and to the politicians they elect, the whole thing is less than an afterthought.

Altogether, most of New York City's water supply comes from a total of nineteen reservoirs in two major watersheds—some over a hundred miles away from the city as the crow flies. The total watershed extends over a million acres, 130,000 of which the city has purchased, leased, or obtained easements in—most of it land surrounding the reservoirs.[28]

The city has a nearly inexhaustible wallet to fund such land grabs, allowing farmland and buildable lots to be purchased at full asking prices, often well above the actual market prices in the low-density region. There is no need to resort to eminent domain, as New York City dollars go a long way towards coerced sales among an aging and relatively poor population. But there is also the consistent implied threat that New York City can simply litigate any potential disagreements and bleed local budgets white in order to win.

This creates a number of hurdles for local residents. Their small counties with few resources are unable to maintain home rule over their own communities but have to serve at the whim of a city over a hundred miles away. As New York State's average population grows older, many residents see the utility in selling to the DEP rather than passing their property down to family members. Delaware County, which houses half of the watershed, has the oldest population of any county in the state. Residents can sell their land to the city before retiring to Florida, leaving the land "forever wild," never to be built on again. In other cases, farmers sign easements with the city with the catch that when the deed is transferred (usually through inheritance), large portions of arable land can never be farmed again.

As a result, much of this land is now off the table for development, as New York City buys up the land in swaths. Fertile farmland in floodplains and buildable land for homes or businesses near town centers are removed from the area's economic future. In 2018, during renegotiations of New York City's leasing agreements, the supervisor of Delhi, New York, said at a Delaware County Board meeting that the community is effectively boxed in from future expansion by watershed agreements, which prevent builders from expanding past borders controlled by the state. Nearby Margaretville, a village in the town of Middletown, which suffered traumatic flooding in 2011 from Hurricane Irene, has limitations on extending municipal water lines through DEP property. In fact, Middletown can only utilize 20 percent of its territory for development after factoring in hills and DEP landholdings.[29]

Part of the fierce rivalry between watershed communities and New York City is explained by the manner in which this system of reservoirs was constructed. By the early 1900s, the population of New York City had reached well over 4 million residents—subject to fires and cholera epidemics. The competition over Upstate New York water was fierce between New York City, New Jersey, and Philadelphia—with all three relying on the rich freshwater supplies of the Delaware basin in the meantime.[30] New York City utilized eminent domain to purchase substantial populated areas for the construction of dams for two of the reservoirs in the watershed. In another case, the village of Gilboa in Upstate New York was completely destroyed; it is now covered by the Schoharie Reservoir. New York's system of water control is far-reaching. Over 400 buildings, including over 350 people's homes, were destroyed to create it.[31] Eight communities were ruined and 2,000 people were displaced to build the Ashokan Reservoir alone.[32] A contemporary described the "barren waste, with only stone walls and gaping cellar holes," that was created as towns were dismantled. "Not a chimney was left standing."[33]

Local Upstate New York communities, often with populations smaller than a residential block in one of New York City's boroughs, have virtually no say over the operations and control of the watershed and its functions. This has caused a number of severe issues that many of these communities still deal with to this day:

- Boring through the Cannonsville Reservoir caused the release of muddy sediment into the nearby waterways and required the temporary draining of *the entire reservoir*.[34]

- Aging dams along the reservoirs pose a major danger to the people in the watershed area. By 2008, twenty-five of the thirty dams owned by New York City were deemed "high-hazard" by the National Inventory of Dams, the most famous of which was the Gilboa Dam at the Schoharie Reservoir. This particular dam posed a severe risk of catastrophic danger in case of a flood event. In response to local lobbying, the DEP agreed to a major series of repairs to the century-old dam right before the severe flooding of Irene in 2011—preventing a total dam collapse.[35]

- Corruption. The manager of Department of Environmental Protection contracts, Ifeanyi "Manny" Madu, was charged in 2018 with accepting improper gifts for the awarding of DEP contracts totaling $250 million. According to the Manhattan district attorney, Cyrus Vance, Madu accepted bribes from major engineering and construction firms in exchange for handing them early—and improper—information about the upcoming contracts for construction projects related to the watershed.[36]

- A significant increase in flooding surrounding NYC-owned dams over the last centuries, due to increased restriction of water flow. As a result, the area has suffered two "hundred-year" floods in the last twenty-five years.[37]
- Damage to fishing areas near the Gilboa Dam from sediment. A 1998 lawsuit by environmental groups claimed that New York City had violated the Clean Water Act, and the city lost the case and had to pay a $5 million fine.[38]
- Bureaucratic burdens on businesses. Local businesses are often unable to install or replace septic tanks without permission from New York City, over a hundred miles away. Towns and even county governments are under the control of a distant municipality without proper sovereignty over local property or municipalities. Local residents live under the looming threat of dam failure. New York City finally shelled out money for a system of emergency alarms, similar to air raid sirens, across the region only in 2007. The one time these sirens were activated, in 2011, they were knocked off-line—by severe flooding.[39] These communities could be destroyed with one catastrophic dam failure.

The overall effect on these small rural communities is a toxic mix of limited development, loss of local control, and loss of tax revenue. Since 1997, New York City has expanded its land acquisitions through a $300 million purchasing push.[40] The local residents who stay suffer, as the prices of remaining properties go up because of the high-dollar sales to New York City, jacking up property taxes for older homeowners and making it harder for young people to buy houses. And while New York City pays real estate taxes on the parcels it has purchased, the city can challenge the amount it pays after the residents leave the property. Land with houses or farms on it loses most of its taxable value, and municipalities are on the hook for the loss of these dollars. The property taxes on undeveloped rural property are far, far lower than needed to sustain municipal budgets.

Combined with the high-tax and mandate-happy state of New York, municipalities are stuck in an awful situation. Loss of property tax revenue requires dramatic tax increases for the remaining residents. And that's before you even take into account the high taxes and expensive mandates coming directly from the New York state legislature, which is dominated by legislators from New York City. And so these rural communities enter a downward spiral. Older people either take the city's money for their property or are driven out by the unaffordable higher taxes. Young people can't afford to buy homes. So taxes have to be raised even more—which makes it even harder for people to stay.

From 1997—when the large-scale land purchases by New York City began—until 2007, four of New York's five watershed counties saw a decline in the number of local farms. Delaware, Sullivan, and Schoharie Counties saw declines of over 10 percent (in Sullivan it was nearly 20 percent!). This precipitous rate was significantly worse than what their neighbors outside of the watershed saw. The number of new homes built in each county fell by at least 50 percent during the first full decade of the purchases.[41]

Several rural counties in Upstate New York also lost total population.[42] The population of Delaware County shrank by 5.12 percent, Schoharie lost 4.36 percent of its residents, and Greene lost 3.47 percent, ranking tenth. Nearby Columbia, also a watershed county, lost 3.33 percent. As a telling point of comparison, the population of Germany declined from 69 million to 66 million—a loss of just under 4 percent of the total—between 1939 and 1945, *during the most destructive war in history.*

The issues facing Upstate New York are especially ominous in light of the proposed "Green New Deal." The liberals in heavily populated coastal areas have political clout that will enable them to put their needs—and their political beliefs—ahead of the priorities, traditional lifestyles, and local autonomy of their more conservative fellow citizens in the heartland. If thousands could be displaced a century ago, and the remaining residents continue to see their self-government and way of life eroded out of concern about availability of drinking water for New York City, how many more will see their voices effectively drowned out by the threat of global climate change?

And Upstate New York is not the only example. Eastern California suffered a strikingly similar fate around the same time. The need for drinking water in Los Angeles destroyed nearby rural areas. As LA boomed, the need for water for a city built in a semiarid region became more pressing, and voters approved a series of bonds to create an elaborate system of aqueducts and reservoirs similar to those in New York.

The expansion of Los Angeles's water supply was a death sentence for the Owens Valley. At first locals were told that Los Angeles would need only any surplus water above and beyond what the locals needed. But the people of the Owens Valley and wider Inyo County were misled. Eventually the debate became so heated that it made it to the floor of Congress and required a decision by President Theodore Roosevelt.[43] The local residents were strong-armed and ended up selling tens of thousands of acres—which, without water, would be useless for agriculture—for much less than they had been promised. With the Los Angeles Aqueduct completed by 1913, the only thing left was to acquire the remainder of the watershed from the local residents.

The Owens River was rerouted to meet the water needs of the City of Angels, and by 1926 the former Owens Lake was a barren alkali flat that brings dust storms into the surrounding areas.

Insulted by the domineering actions of the city and government bureaucrats, some of the people of eastern California turned to violence. At one point, part of the aqueduct was destroyed by the locals to return water to the Owens River temporarily. Like New York City, Los Angeles challenged local property tax assessments, further straining the fragile rural area. By 1968, Los Angeles paid local residents zero local taxes on water transmission from their now-barren lands. Promises to keep the area alive through allowing some water flow never came to fruition. LA had seized 90 percent of the local water supply early in the process and went back for even more water in the 1970s. A second aqueduct and comprehensive groundwater seizures led to the further deterioration of the valley. The people of Inyo County sued the city for not complying with the California Environmental Quality Act, but despite rebukes from state courts, Los Angeles continued the pumping. As a result, the area is rapidly becoming a desert.[44]

But even that is far from the worst thing suffered by the rural residents. Project designers' lack of foresight wreaked catastrophic destruction. Not far from Santa Clarita, the water system's leaders constructed a large dam along the San Francisquito Canyon to provide ample fresh water for the metropolis. The St. Francis Dam, forty miles northwest of the city, opened in 1926. Unfortunately, three years later the dam—built with a poor foundation and an improper type of concrete—collapsed during flooding. The entire dam, including over 12 billion gallons of water, emptied in just over a minute. A wave over 140 feet tall crashed through populated areas, washing people and buildings out to sea. Over four hundred people were killed. Bodies of victims were still being found almost thirty years after the disaster. It was the deadliest dam failure in the United States in the twentieth century.[45]

Poor planning and the intentional siphoning of resources away from rural areas are still hallmarks of the water use issue in the Golden State today. As a result, much of inland California is drying up—both in terms of aquifers and in terms of lost population. But the war over water is now entering a new phase. It isn't just about Californians' need—or greed— for water anymore; it's also about the coastal elites' virtue signaling at the expense of their fellow citizens in more rural areas.

Overreach and Autonomy

The political power wielded by major urban centers has already destroyed rural communities in New York and California. As the great national population shift continues, we will see more of the same—across the country. Rural residents in states dominated by big cities often feel as if they are without political recourse to change the trajectory of their futures. As a result, these residents flee at high rates or turn to radical solutions. As the characters of red states are shifted by blue state expatriates, there is a chance that the remaining red areas of these states will go so far as attempted secession—as we have already seen in Colorado. There are serious movements in both New York and California to split the states into several pieces to allow rural residents more say over their own lives. Something similar may happen in Georgia or North Carolina if Atlanta and Charlotte double in size over the next generation.

Job growth in Upstate New York since 2010 is a *third* what it is in New York City.[46] In fact, in twenty-one upstate counties, employment has not recovered to the level it was before the Great Recession. If Upstate New York were ranked among all states, it would rank forty-seventh in the union in job creation since 2010. Five upstate counties have experienced negative GDP growth since the recession, while even the fastest-growing region north of NYC is growing at only half the rate of the national average.

This economic pain helps explain the serious push during the 2017 election cycle to split the state into three distinct regions. The New Amsterdam movement would have split the state into Upstate New York, New York City, and Long Island.[47] In an October 2017 interview, John Bergener, the head of the movement, cited state mandates and taxation and talked about establishing a "more representative form of government."[48]

In a similar movement in California, activists aimed to divide the state into multiple U.S. states, ranging from three to six. The plan gained enough signatures to make it onto the ballot in the 2018 election as Proposition 9. But then the California Supreme Court blocked Prop 9 from going before voters.[49] Tim Draper, the founder of the movement, which is called Cal 3, is a Silicon Valley billionaire who has spent over $5 million on two similar efforts and submitted over 400,000 signatures to the state.[50] Draper described the goal of his failed effort as "a protection from a government that was no longer representing its people."[51]

One reason for the push for autonomy in California, New York, and Colorado is the spiraling cost of unfunded mandates passed from the state to local governments. With the economies in rural parts of these states already withering, the higher tax rates are catastrophic. One list of total mandates for New York public schools exceeds fifty![52] New York also forces counties to pay a higher portion of Medicaid bills than any other state. In some cases, a county's Medicaid expenses represent *over half* of that county's property tax revenue.[53] This represents a $7.6 billion annual local tax burden, with $2.3 billion paid by counties outside of New York City.[54]

California's mandate albatross is its pension system. Illinois has faced similar issues. The city of Harvey, Illinois, laid off forty police and fire department employees due to $1.5 million redirected by the state to cover pension costs.[55] This came after a decision by the state's First District Appellate Court to raise local taxes to cover firefighter pensions. Now the city is talking bankruptcy. Up to two hundred (!) Illinois cities may see the state seize tax dollars to cover pension costs. Thanks to the Democrats in Illinois, the state's constitution does not allow for a reduction in pension costs. Harvey, a suburb of Chicago whose mall was featured in the movie *Blues Brothers*, has become a ghost of its former self. It has lost over five thousand of its thirty thousand residents since 1990, has a median income of half the national average, and even before the police layoffs was badly affected by crime.[56] But the Illinois legislature, dominated by politicians elected from heavily populated and very blue Chicago, has no pity on the rest of the state. In 2015 alone, Illinois legislators proposed an astonishing fifty-nine new unfunded mandates for local governments.[57]

Literally millions of people are leaving the rural parts of California, New York, and Illinois. As those red voters are driven out, the depressed incomes and home values in these regions allow waves of wealthy city folk to move in—bringing their blue politics with them. So at the same time that expatriates from blue states have a chance of flipping Texas and North Carolina to the Democratic column, other blue state citizens are moving from the cities to the suburbs and the countryside, moving them a few more ticks towards the Democratic Party. It's about as lose-lose as you can get. Will their new electoral clout allow these left-leaning voters to codify their preferred policies at the federal level? If so, red voters won't have any place left to pack up a U-Haul and move to.

CHAPTER SIX

Washington, D.C.
The Exception That Proves the Rule

Camel-colored trench coats, glossy pearl earrings, and the strong scents of Burberry perfume and soft leather bombarded my senses as I stepped off the train and into Union Station in the heart of Washington, D.C. I felt more like I was walking through an Ann Taylor ad than a train station as I made my way to the front doors to catch a cab outside. "Typical D.C.," I scoffed under my breath. "Land of preppy bureaucrats and congressional aides, all living off our hard-earned tax dollars." I suppose I was being a bit of a curmudgeon. I had come to "the swamp"—reluctantly, of course—to visit my dear old cousin Miriam, who worked an admin job for the Department of Health and Human Services. She's a staunch lefty, so naturally whenever we see each other (usually at our family holiday get-togethers) heated debates ensue. Yet over the years we've managed to maintain a close, cousinly friendship despite our extreme political differences.

As the taxi made its way through D.C., I couldn't help but notice how beautiful and pristine everything was. Not a leaf was out of place. The majestic sculptures and monuments gleamed in the sun; the parks were perfectly landscaped, with splendid fountains; high-end boutiques and cupcake shops lined the streets; young, attractive moms dressed in J. Crew from head to toe pushed baby strollers down the tree-lined streets. The nation's capital is a sharp contrast to New York City, where everything is hectic, dirty, and grimy unless you live on Fifth Avenue.

Finally, I arrived in Arlington, Virginia—a town just outside of the District—and pulled up outside of Miriam's three-story townhome in a lively neighborhood called Clarendon. She ran outside with a warm smile and arms outstretched to greet me. Once inside, I was reminded of how beautiful Miriam's townhome was; I hadn't been there to visit in years. The three-bedroom house had high ceilings, big windows, and gleaming hardwood floors.

After hours of catching up, jokes, and a few glasses of wine, I boldly asked Miriam how much she had paid for the townhouse. She didn't seem offended by my question. "I got this place for a steal!" she told me. "I only paid $250,000 for it when I moved to D.C. back in the early '90's. Today it's valued at well over $600,000."

My jaw dropped. She continued, "Real estate has increased in value significantly since I first came to the area. I'm lucky I bought this place when I did."

I guess I shouldn't have been too shocked by the steep increase in the value of Miriam's townhome. The federal government expanded vastly in size in the 1990s under the Bill Clinton administration; during his eight years in office the number of employees working for the federal government increased by over 10 percent.[1] Naturally, all of these government workers needed places to live. Many bought real estate in the District itself, while others moved to neighboring areas in Virginia and Maryland. As demand went through the roof, so did rents and real estate prices. From 1997 to 2000, the D.C. metropolitan area saw single-digit appreciation in its housing market year after year. Then, beginning in 2001, the area saw *double-digit increases* of 12–25 percent, until 2007.[2] When the national housing downturn hit, home values decreased almost everywhere in the U.S.—except for D.C.

We have seen how liberal areas—many of which have been destroyed by significant tax hikes, ballooning welfare systems, and failing public school systems—are losing residents in droves to conservative areas where companies are expanding and hiring at faster rates. The one exception to that rule would seem to be Washington, D.C. Washington is perhaps the only solidly blue part of the country immune to the detrimental effects of blue policies.

Gallup found that D.C. is the most liberal place in the nation; the percentage of people living there who call themselves liberal is significantly higher than the national percentage, and much higher than the percentage in any of the fifty states.[3] Since the 1961 adoption of the Twenty-Third Amendment, which gave D.C. three electoral votes, the District has voted for the Democratic candidate in every presidential election. The people who live and work around and in Washington, D.C., champion the same liberal policies that have led to out-migration and economic decay in blue states like New York, Illinois, and California. And yet, unlike those states, D.C. grows by leaps and bounds every year. The median household income in D.C. is $75,506, compared to the national median of $59,039.[4]

D.C. seems to be the exception to the rule—a liberal bastion that continues to prosper, even during economic downturns. Why? The reason is simple. The economy of the entire area is propped up by the one industry that never shrinks: the federal government, which is the D.C. area's largest single employer. (The second-biggest employer? Local government.)[5]

The U.S. capital was originally located in Philadelphia, beginning with the First Continental Congress. Our nation's first congressmen conducted business in a majestic building called Independence Hall, where both the Declaration of Independence and the U.S. Constitution were adopted. But in 1783, while the Continental Congress was meeting, a furious mob of soldiers swarmed Independence Hall and demanded payment for their service during the American Revolutionary War. The soldiers blocked the door and refused to allow the delegates to leave until their demands were met. The explosive protest came to be known as the Pennsylvania Mutiny. Members of Congress were frightened and urged John Dickinson, the governor of Pennsylvania at the time, to call up the militia to defend politicians from potential attacks by the angry group. But Dickinson sided with the soldiers and would not order their removal from Philadelphia.

After Dickinson refused to protect Congress with his militia, James Madison argued in *Federalist* no. 43 that the nation's capital needed to be distinct from the states in order to provide for its own maintenance and safety. Madison, Thomas Jefferson, and Alexander Hamilton chose a location on the Potomac River because it was situated neither deep in the north nor deep in the south—intentionally, to prevent bias in federal policymaking.

D.C. only has a nonvoting member of the House and, as I mentioned above, it didn't receive Electoral College representation until 1961, when the Twenty-Third Amendment was adopted. The nation's capital wasn't supposed to have political power of its own—much less to wield it in the interests of the federal bureaucracy. But today D.C. and its environs house an exploding population that benefits from government spending—and votes for ever more of it. Voters who live in and around the nation's capital vote for the higher taxes, spending, and regulation that is causing economic failure in and out-migration from the blue states. But instead of ruining the local economy, those blue policies make D.C. thrive.

And all that money is well spent, right?

The federal government spent $4.4 trillion in fiscal year 2019, much of it flagrantly wasteful. But all of it routes through or to Washington, and the effects—while disastrous for the country—are great for the District. Here's a taste of some of the worst spending of the last couple of years:

- $20,000 for an "adult summer camp" for artists and scientists to discuss communicating the effects of climate change followed by a two week "Art, Science, and the Cultural Terrain" session.[6] Whatever that is.

- A *billion dollars* to renovate 10.9 miles of a trolley in San Diego scheduled for completion in 2021 to serve fewer than 25,000 trips per day.[7]
- $152 million in funding to the National Endowment for the Arts. I could write an entire book about the waste involved in the Endowment, which seems to be operating on another planet. It spent $30,000 in 2017 for a dog-centric production of *Hamlet*, which, as the *Connecticut Post* reported, included "human actors shouting and chasing dogs and sheep in an open field in New Hampshire. The Endowment also granted a university $75,851 to scan fifteen puppets with a 3-D scanner in order to "enable viewers to control puppet functions and facial expressions."[8]
- Nearly half a million dollars to construct walls around a training facility in Afghanistan . . . that melted away when it rained. The walls were completely destroyed in four months.[9]
- $5 million on a project to find ways to convince hipsters to quit smoking (dear God). Part of the program included paying millennials $100 to quit and then blog about it.[10]
- A half million dollars on a project studying the effects of cocaine on the sexual habits of quails.
- $300,000 to inject hamsters with steroids and watch them fight.[11]

All of this cash is administered by an army of bureaucrats in offices in and around the capital. Filtered through the paychecks of pencil pushers, the cash has allowed the greater D.C. area to prosper as the rest of the country struggles.

Northern Virginia in particular has become a bedroom community for bureaucrats and lobbyists, who have changed the electoral calculus and economy of the state. Today, the greater Washington metropolitan area is the nation's sixth largest. The population of D.C. itself increased by an astonishing 21 percent between 2000 and 2017. And get this: the average income in the city is $75,000 per household, 27 percent higher than the national average.[12] Not surprisingly, the capital that relies heavily on federal largesse almost always votes for presidential candidates who advocate for bigger government. In 2016 Hillary Clinton garnered an improbable 90.9 percent of the vote, compared to Donald Trump's 4.1 percent.

The federal government funnels billions of taxpayer dollars to high-earning, unfireable bureaucrats who live in the suburbs. As the wave of people leaving states like California and New York grows, the direct effects of their blue politics will fall on the red states well before they ever hurt the District—if they ever do. The bluer the red states become, the more the federal government will grow, and the more prosperous and powerful the D.C. region will be. Washington is completely insulated from the problems that it causes.

Living in our new Imperial Capital comes with great perks. As the power of Washington has grown, so have the benefits of living there. D.C. politicians and bureaucrats don't have to deal with the negative effects of their own policies, and they enjoy privileges that private-sector workers can only dream of. Consider that members of Congress receive:

- A high-end Obamacare "gold" plan subsidized by taxpayers, which gives congressmen free healthcare and outpatient care.[13] The Obama administration also exempted member of Congress from paying taxes on their insurance plans, saving each member $12,000 a year.[14]
- The coveted federal pension, which is head and shoulders above private (and even state) plans. Members of Congress receive a lifelong taxpayer-funded pension benefit of up to $139,200 per year.[15]
- A loophole that allows them to benefit from insider trading. While stock trades using legislative information are

technically illegal, congressmen don't have to disclose their trades online because of a 2013 amendment to the STOCK Act. They can also use their political influence to get on corporate boards. There are reasons that members of Congress have historically done a lot better in the stock market than the average American household.[16]

- Death benefits of at least $174,000—almost double the benefit for a soldier killed in service. It's a guaranteed, built-in life insurance policy that the rest of us would have to pay into for years to receive.
- A schedule of just 138 workdays per year, on average—in 2012 it was just 126 days, including only *one full five-day week*. Despite the part-time schedule, congressmen each receive a $174,000 annual salary, more than three times the average salary for Americans who work full-time.[17]
- Over $4 million a year to spend on office equipment and supplies as well as $250,000 annually to spend on mass mailings.[18] This includes sending information similar to campaign advertisements to their constituents—essentially a campaign contribution with our tax dollars.
- Other goodies like free parking spaces and subsidized flights on most trips. In 2016 alone, these flights cost taxpayers about $1.5 million.[19]

The bureaucrats and government workers in D.C. also have a sweet deal. They receive:

- Wildly above-market compensation. Federal workers' pay is 17 percent higher than that of private-sector employees performing comparable work . . . for 12 percent fewer hours of work.[20] They work three fewer hours per week and are 50 percent more likely to take time off from work.[21] When you drill down further into the numbers, there is an even greater disparity between government and private sector compensation—a Princeton University study found that when "taking differences in employee characteristics into account," federal workers actually earn 34.2 percent more than comparable private-sector workers.[22]

- The "Cadillac" Federal Employees Health Benefits Program, 75 percent federally subsidized. These plans include health insurance plus vision and dental benefits. On top of that, federal retirees are eligible for health benefits at *fifty-seven* years old, a rare luxury in the private sector.
- Pension and Social Security benefits that are *three times higher* than private-sector employees' 401(k) and Social Security benefits.[23]
- Up to twenty-six paid days off plus ten paid holidays per year.
- A 0.2 percent chance of getting fired in a given year. That's more than forty-five times lower than their private-sector counterparts.[24] In some cases, it takes an effort from four different agencies to fire a federal employee, and the process can take years even in seemingly simple cases. This valuable shield protects public employees who are cited for malfeasance or incompetence. For example, it took nearly a year to fire a VA nurse who operated on a veteran while drunk.[25]

Meanwhile, a Brookings Institution study found that 65 percent of federal workers think job security is more important than helping the public, while only 30 percent think their organization does a good job disciplining poor performers.[26]

All of this isn't to demonize government workers, some of whom are undoubtedly hardworking and patriotic people. However, it is clear that D.C. is a bubble insulated from the poisonous effects of the left-wing policies that D.C. government bureaucrats vote for—the same left-wing policies that are destroying Democrat-controlled states and driving the great blue state exodus to red states.

The Habits of Bureaucrats

Miriam helped herself to another glass of sauvignon blanc. She was in rare form, happy to talk about her experiences since coming to the D.C. area. She works for the Department of Health, which is actually one of the more efficient federal agencies—but she has heard the *stories*. She told me about a guy who worked in a federal building down the street from her office, at the Environmental Protection Agency. He was making a $120,000 annual salary while he spent two to six hours *per day* watching porn at his desk.

"Well, obviously he was fired, right?" I asked.

Miriam laughed. "Well technically, yes. But it took eight months before he was formally let go—then he was put on paid leave for a year."

Guess I can't say I was shocked. Federal employees are largely protected from being fired by a combination of arcane employment rules, bureaucratic inertia, and extremely powerful public-sector unions. Even flagrant incompetence and theft often don't lead to government employees being let go. Miriam told me about some Health and Human Services employees who kept their jobs for months after formal written reprimands. In another case, a bureaucrat fought being fired for several years while collecting pay.

Still, Miriam seemed to think that the insane job security was something owed to federal workers.

"Could you imagine," she asked, "working for an employer that could just fire you on the spot? Like that?" She snapped her fingers.

Turns out most Americans can. But bureaucrats usually can't. In 2013, a mere 3,489 of the nation's 2.1 million federal employees were fired for cause.[27] And a large majority of those who were let go were new employees during their initial probationary periods. If you stick around for a while, the chance of getting fired is almost zilch. Once you've been there for several years, you're part of the inertia of the federal govern-ment—and don't worry, you're automatically doing a great job even if you're not producing tangible results. A Government Accountability Office audit found that in performance reviews, a full 99.5 percent of federal employees received a "fully successful" rating or higher from their supervisors. Only 0.1 percent received an "unacceptable" rating.[28]

For starters, it takes a long time to fire a federal employee. Once they've been there for a year, many employees receive a soft tenure that makes firing them a labyrinthine process. And even if an agency does fire an employee, the worker is allowed to appeal to the federal Merit Systems Protection Board (MSPB) to delay the process. In one case, employees of the Government Services Administration (GSA) were caught red-handed spending $822,000 for one conference in Las Vegas. One of the organizers, Jeff Neely, had trav-eled to Vegas at least six times on the taxpayer's dime in the months before the conference to "scout" locations (he got caught because he posted photos of himself partying on Facebook). The agency's administrator, Martha Johnson, stepped down because of the scandal—but it was discovered that she had paid Neely a $9,000 bonus while he was being investigated. Two GSA managers were fired over the debacle, but they appealed and had their firings overturned by the MSPB. Meanwhile, Neely was allowed to retire without punishment.[29]

Even worse for taxpayers is the fact that the worst employees are often not fired but instead placed in a strange, nonworking paid limbo. The federal government utilizes "administrative leave" for employees under investigations or for employees whom it would be too difficult to fire.[30] An audit found that the feds spend over $1 billion per year on administrative leave. From 2011 to 2013, 57,000 federal employees received at least a month's pay without work under the program, while 263 got at least a year off. You or I would be out the door on day one.

Miriam didn't show me her National Treasury Employees Union card, but it dangled on her lanyard with her ID. Federal employees are backed by some of the most powerful forces in organized labor. The American Federation of Government Employees is the largest, representing over

670,000 union employees. The organization benefits from the growth of the swamp and in turn helps it grow—by making it even harder to fire government workers. The public-sector union is funded in large part by tax dollars.

Miriam talked freely about retirement, which is a bit of a sore subject for most private sector employees counting their pennies for their golden years. Federal employees can retire at age fifty-seven, with some eligible at fifty-five. As if that wasn't good enough, if your agency changes its scope and you're let go as a result, you can apply for special early retirement at fifty (or forty-five, if you've worked for at least twenty-five years.)[31] Over 21,000 retired federal government employees receive federal pensions of over $100,000. The pensions represent a major burden on the budget—over $70 billion annually.[32]

Would you give up a high-paying job that allows you to retire at fifty-five and that you can't be fired from? Federal employees are three times less likely to quit their jobs than private-sector employees.[33] And yet a full quarter of federal employees are "non-essential"—by the government's own definition.[34]

Don't get me wrong, Miriam puts her heart and skills into her job. So do many of our federal workers. However, the system that Congress, successive presidents, and bureaucratic lethargy have combined to create is scandalous. Federal bureaucrats make life harder for the rest of the country by imposing oppressive, invasive, and expensive regulation, but D.C.'s population is immune to the ill effects of its own liberal ideology. Those who work for the federal government don't have to worry about being laid off or even fired for cause; they don't have to worry about their employer going out of business. The sheer size of the government, plus the volume of cash entering and leaving D.C., has allowed the city to prosper in spite of its left-wing policies—the same left-wing policies that have caused economic despair and incredible out-migration in blue states across the nation.

CHAPTER SEVEN

The New Exurbs
How Moving Vans and Rural Pushback Explain the Election of Donald Trump

"What a bunch of goddamn fools," the man ahead of me in line at Starbucks muttered angrily as he tossed the morning's edition of the *New York Times* into the trash before ordering his grande blonde roast latte. It was November 9, 2016, in New York City, less than twelve hours after Donald J. Trump beat all odds and was elected president of the United States. "TRUMP TRIUMPHS," the headline on the front page of the *Times* said that morning. "OUTSIDER MOGUL CAPTURES THE PRESIDENCY, STUNNING CLINTON IN BATTLEGROUND STATES." Almost everyone I saw in New York that day was shocked. They were angry. No...they were furious. Not at Trump, but at the people who had been stupid enough to show up at polling stations in droves to vote for him. The "goddamn fools" were the people Hillary had called the "deplorables"—rural and suburban working-class stiffs and hicks who simply weren't as smart as coastal elites.

How on earth could a bunch of overall-donning tractor drivers, stay-at-home mothers, laid-off factory workers, churchgoers, and Sunday football–watchers have taken down Hillary Clinton, the most well-funded and well-connected candidate in modern political history?

If you watched election night in your shoebox apartment in Manhattan or San Francisco, the results likely shocked you. But if you watched it on a CRT tube at your diner with the local callus-hands, you probably saw it coming.

This isn't a book about Trump. But the red victory in the 2016 election was, ironically, a major symptom of the blue invasion of red state America, which has been quietly playing out for many years now, reshaping the political map under our noses. White House terms last just four years. Demography is destiny.

The petty politics of the day—endless investigations, the border wall, and political food fights—are obscuring population changes that will have a profound and lasting effect on the fabric of our nation. But Trump's victory sheds light on the extent of the liberal takeover of traditionally red states, which has already altered the national political map for generations to come.

A May 2018 *New York Times* profile of Erie County, Pennsylvania, shed some light on the connection between Trump's election and the demographic changes we've examined in this book.[1] Erie, a former industrial center, is nestled between Appalachia, Ohio, Upstate New York, and the rest of the Rust Belt. It is now a microcosm of the transformation of America from the idealistic vision of 1950s factory workers coming home to their Cape Cods and families with two children to the industrial decline and social dislocation that characterize significant parts of our country today.

Here's what's revealing: Erie County provided one of the starkest surprises of the 2016 election. Barack Obama won the county 57–41 percent in 2012 and 59–39 percent in 2008. Reagan was its last great "R." (We're talking the Reagan sweep of 1984.) Then it turned to the "D."

But then in 2016 came Trump, flying in on a private jet and talking to everyone like they were real people. Smart people. It turns out lots of people liked that. Appreciated it, even. For decades Democrats took this nook of the Commonwealth for granted. They didn't sweat it when results became increasingly close in recent elections, and they were dumbfounded when they lost the county in 2016. The same thing happened across the former industrial heartland. Trump garnered over 60 percent of the vote in the vast majority of Pennsylvania's counties, including a blowout 84–13 percent victory in rural Fulton County. Trump was not only unpredicted; he was also unprecedented.

The victory was fueled by the resistance of smaller communities and populations outside of major urban centers to an increasing number of new residents. Former blue staters—primarily people from New York—who have relocated to Pennsylvania in record numbers during recent years have had a drastic impact on the state's economy and culture. New Yorkers fleeing the city's astronomical cost of living often find refuge in the much lower-cost Philadelphia and its suburban areas; in 2015 alone, more than twenty-five thousand people made the move.[2] And then—like the other blue state out-migrants we have seen—when these New York expats show up in Pennsylvania they often vote for the same blue state policies that caused them to move in the first place. Former New Yorkers are attempting to shoehorn their way of life into their new state, disrupting the lives of people who have lived in rural Pennsylvania for decades. For many working-class Pennsylvanians, a vote for Trump was a protest vote against the liberal newcomers who are taking over their state.

Piece after piece about the reasons behind Trump's win and the rural backlash against D.C. elites has been published by mainstream outlets. While there seems to be some superficial understanding of the resentment against Hillary Clinton, the nation's leading journalists fail to grasp the role demography played in 2016.

Consider the perspective of ordinary people enjoying their golden years in a state that is rapidly changing thanks to a growing population of newcomers. The societal change is disorienting. Concepts like "inclusion" have become cudgels in the culture war. Conservative folks who finally accepted the LGBT community must now grapple with the push to allow transgender individuals into single-sex elementary school bathrooms. Yes, many schools are actually implementing this idea, thanks to increasing pressure from growing left-wing populations in traditionally conservative states. These new voters are also jacking up the cost of living for the longtime residents: the recent transplants want higher taxes and more government services. And they're offended by community manger scenes—ones that have often been in place for a hundred years. Local community government meetings are now dominated by resolutions calling for small towns to be declared sanctuaries for illegal aliens, for a fifteen-dollar-per-hour minimum wage, or for slapping stiff taxes on bottles of soda.

It's just like in my own rural home state, New Hampshire, which, as we have already seen, is now dominated by Massachusetts transplants driving Priuses who want to force their worldview onto their new neighbors. Lyme—a small town in central New Hampshire that's considered a suburb of Hanover, where Dartmouth College is situated—has seen a population explosion during recent years. These newcomers were a key factor in the state's recent move to designate itself a "sanctuary town" for illegal immigrants.[3]

Residents who have lived in traditionally red states for decades are losing control over their own states and towns. The slow trickle of demographic change is flowing in only one direction—and to them it seems like it's all downhill. The higher cost of living caused by liberal policies is hard enough to manage, and the cultural changes add insult to injury. The message to longtime residents of the rural parts of the red states that are now turning blue? *You're the outcast. You're the past. America will be better when you're gone. Your country is no longer yours.*

Good people with strong roots are willing to fight for what's theirs, though.

Many of the liberal newcomers from blue states spend enormous amounts of energy on politics, as a sort of favorite hobby. While the longtime residents go about their ordinary lives, making a living and taking care of their families as they have always done, the refugees from the more woke blue states work day in and day out to turn their new communities into sanctuary cities, get plastic straws banned from restaurants, jack up taxes again and again to pay for all the government services they're used to, or work with the ACLU to shut down the traditional Christmas pageant. But presidential elections, which come around just once every four years, are a different story.

On November 8, 2016, in one rural county after another, rural and conservative voters banded together like Lilliputians and tied down the liberal Gullivers of the major urban centers. Dairy farmers and schoolteachers outweighed Madison, Detroit, Philadelphia, and Miami. People who hadn't turned out for decades or had never given a passing thought to a Republican presidential candidate (especially a billionaire from New York) voted—to paraphrase the 1968 Nixon campaign—like their whole world depended on it.

For them, it did.

The Big Move

There are many underlying reasons for the 2016 election results. The overarching political causes, campaign blunders, and masterstrokes will keep political scientists and historians hard at work for decades. But there is one other factor that they need to take into account—or they will be missing a major cause of those surprising results. Formerly red states are filling up with Democratic voters fleeing blue states. Years after these liberal voters built their own cities and states—places like San Francisco, New York City, and Chicago—on their own liberal principles, they decided to leave the mess that those principles had created. After they voted to raise taxes, increase welfare subsidies, and implement policies of "inclusion" because it was *the right thing to do*...they left. Their homes simply became too expensive, and good job opportunities were increasingly hard to come by.

These Democrats moved to red state America, where business-friendly policies have created robust job growth and a low cost of living. As a result, states like North Carolina, Colorado, New Hampshire, and Texas are now seeing a cultural divide open up between natives and new residents. The newcomers are like houseguests who overstay their welcome and start to change things around *your* house to bring them up to *their* standards.

One of the biggest influences on me growing up was *The Grapes of Wrath* by John Steinbeck. The book is set in the Great Depression and follows the Joads, a poor farming family forced from their Oklahoma home by a severe drought and economic hardship. Seeking opportunity and a brighter future, the family heads west. The story dramatizes life in the Great Depression and shows how it formed societal changes. The novel reflects Steinbeck's sympathy for Franklin Roosevelt and old-school liberal politics. But the yearning portrayed in the book is universal. Everyone longs for a basic level of economic and personal self-determination, and the resentment inspired by economic troubles still rings true today.

Today's great migration isn't the result of a natural disaster such as the Dust Bowl. It's caused by economic failure due to left-wing fiscal and political mismanagement. Substitute a man-made disaster for a natural one. The Democrats have wrecked the economies of the blue states, and now they're uprooting themselves to seek out greener pastures. Instead of the Great Depression overshadowing the whole nation, we have hundreds of smaller depressions crippling the regions traditionally administered by Democrats. Today's Joads are going in the opposite direction. They're leaving the Golden State for Oklahoma. What a difference eighty years makes. California boasts breathtaking natural beauty and a near-perfect climate. Geographically speaking, it's a land of sunshine and magic. But now the bright sun cannot hide the issues facing California—the state has lost a million residents over the last decade.[4]

Underlying the great move of the twenty-first century is a toxic mix of poor policy, fiscal disasters, and economic stagnation in America's blue states. Gone are the white picket fences and the possibility of supporting a family on a single income. It's not just California. On the east coast you have New York, which has also lost over a million residents since 2010. An additional eight hundred thousand are expected to leave those two blue states over the next two years alone.[5]

And then you have Illinois, the state with the highest out-migration rate. And it's not only Chicago that's being hollowed out. Eighty-nine percent of Illinois's counties have smaller populations than they did in 2010. Six hundred thousand people left the state over the last eight years.[6]

The migrants from blue to red states tend to come from three primary groups: young people crowded out by high costs of living, middle-class families struggling to make ends meet, and high-income residents (who trend older) looking to escape burdensome tax rates. Out-migration becomes more likely as families increase in size through births, a phenomenon that only further increases the population disparities between losing and gaining states.

While these population shifts—or at least the political developments resulting from them, with red state after red state turning to purple or even blue—have burst into the national consciousness in recent years, anyone paying attention to small differences in their close-knit neighborhoods and to voting patterns on the local level saw the massive changes coming. And demography isn't changing just the politics of the receiving states, but also the local culture. Kids' lemonade stands are being shut down (those pesky little entrepreneurs!) for not having the proper government permits. Bake sales are taboo, especially if they support a religious organization. The Boy Scouts changed its name to "Scouts BSA" to include girls. You read the headlines; you hardly believe it.

There was a time when newcomers brought some of their heritage along with them but accommodated themselves to the culture of their new states. There was a happy medium. A balance was reached. But ultimately Texas remained Texas, Colorado remained Colorado, and New Hampshire remained New Hampshire. Today, high numbers of domestic migrants to these states are overwhelming the traditional calculus. The changes extend far beyond the minor irritants that inspire the traditional bellyaching about damn Yankees. Lacking long-standing ties to and respect for the traditional culture of their new homes, many of the new residents don't see themselves becoming part of that culture. Instead, they see themselves as more enlightened than the rubes they're now living among. And so they act like colonizers who bring a superior culture along with them and feel justified in imposing it on the locals.

Put yourself in the shoes of a longtime resident of a town in rural New Hampshire with a population of eighty. Wouldn't this trend seem like a slow-motion invasion?

Most states affected by demographic decline are traditionally Democratic. Of the ten states projected to lose net population at any point between 2010 and 2040—Connecticut, Illinois, Maine, Michigan, Mississippi, New Hampshire, Ohio, Rhode Island, Vermont, and West Virginia—all but two are longtime Democratic strongholds. (Before you @ me, West Virginia has elected Republican governors twice since 1976, though the current governor Jim Justice flipped to the GOP last year.) The four fastest-growing states during that same time period? Texas, Colorado, Utah, and Florida. All traditionally red states.

Dig down into the numbers for American citizens transplanting themselves to other states, and the out-migration death spiral for blue states only looks worse. Between 2010 and 2017, blue states saw a demographic bloodbath. Looking at the sheer numbers of citizens finding new homes, one can see that Florida gained over a million new residents during that same time period. Texas gained 944,000, North Carolina 328,000, and Arizona 278,000.

Look at it as a percentage of the states' 2010 populations, and the figures are alarming:[7]

State	2010 Population	Total Internal Migration Change 2010–2017	Percentage Internal Migration Change
Connecticut	3,580,171	-153,276	-4.28%
Illinois	12,841,196	-642,821	-5.01%
Michigan	9,876,731	-225,302	-2.28%
New Jersey	8,803,708	-395,160	-4.49%
New York	19,405,185	-1,022,071	-5.27%
Vermont	625,842	-10,179	-1.63%
California	37,327,690	-556,710	-1.49%

These trends are simply unsustainable for the blue states losing residents in droves. They will eventually face economic despair and the collapse of pension plans and school systems as well-intentioned Democratic taxpayers flee the effects of the policies they put in place. Making matters worse, rather than attempting to solve the underlying issues by lowering tax burdens on individuals or businesses, the lefties in charge of blue states and cities often think the solution is to slap on a new tax. *Sure, that'll make things better. People will want to stay*!

This brings us back to the 2016 election. Why was the election of Donald Trump such a shock to urbanites and elites in both parties? Demography is a crucial part of the explanation.

How could a billionaire convince former steelworkers in Ohio that he was the choice for the restoration of American greatness? How could he sweep West Virginia coal workers off their feet (the very same voters who gave Bill Clinton a 13 percent victory in 1992)? The liberal invasion of red state America—or to put it more scientifically, demography—played as much of a role in 2016 as any other factor. Residents who felt their way of life was being transformed by coastal elites moving to their states and cities flocked to the MAGA banner. Trump's platform resonated with both the more populous regions and the hinterlands of the former industrial heartland. Candidates from both parties had made these same voters empty promises—peppered with condescending barbs—every election cycle: "They get bitter, they cling to guns or religion...." *Why thank you, yes, we will.*

The buildup to November 8, 2016, was a decade in the making, as blue state people migrated to red states. Conservative areas appealed to domestic migrants because of their tax climates, low cost of living, and job opportunities. And what didn't appeal to them—the local culture—was something that newcomers could slowly change, greatly to the chagrin of the longtime locals.

Take states with healthy histories of firearms ownership. Many of these places have seen their gun rights erode. We have seen how Colorado, historically known for its *laissez-faire* Western gun laws, is now home to some of the strictest gun laws in the nation.

Rural communities are paying a hell of a price for blue state expats' political and cultural influence. The traditions of small-town life are being erased by political correctness. A Christmas display was removed from a school door in Killeen, Texas, after complaints (and despite a 2013 state law allowing such decorations).[8] A lawsuit aimed to remove a Nativity scene—one of those scary, harmful, *Charlie Brown Christmas* scenes—from a mostly secular school play. When Trump said on the campaign trail, "When I started 18 months ago, I told my first crowd in Wisconsin that we are going to come back here some day and we are going to say 'Merry Christmas' again,"[9] that message resonated with red staters whose traditions are under attack from blue state in-migrants.

Perhaps the most startling example of the cultural changes being forced on small-town America by former blue state dwellers is the special privileges extended to the LGBT community. Some big shifts have happened on this issue over the past decade. In 2015, the *Obergefell* Supreme Court ruling gave gay couples the right to get married. This was undoubtedly a landmark victory for equal rights. But for many, it wasn't enough. North Carolina unknowingly painted a target on its fading red back with the passage of its 2016 Public Facilities Privacy & Security Act, which required people to use the restroom corresponding to the sex listed on their birth certificates. The public outcry, lawsuits, and boycotts became a nightmare for the state. All the good people of North Carolina wanted was for individuals to visit the bathroom of their born genders. It seemed logical, like common sense.

But the result was chaotic and costly: millions of dollars were spent on court cases challenging the law, Governor Pat McCrory lost his job that November, and the state was attacked from all angles, including by other states, companies, and even sports organizations. Vermont, New York, Washington, Connecticut, Minnesota, and California even banned state-funded travel to North Carolina over the issue.

Overall, the backlash against North Carolina's bathroom law cost the state economy $3.76 billion.[10] The best way to describe this massive retaliation is political bullying. Red state people don't bully blue state people on repressive gun control or economic rights issues in the blue states. The same cannot be claimed in reverse.

We have seen thousands of loud and destructive people march—or riot—in the streets to demand enormous cultural changes. Meanwhile, the average hardworking individual is forced to show up at work every day and pay his taxes, while being called an intolerant "deplorable" for not embracing every one of these cultural changes. The out-of-control left-wing social agenda is buoyed by Democrats from Connecticut, Illinois, New York, and California—many of whom have packed up and invaded red state America. The cultural changes washing over formerly red states across the nation felt to many voters like cresting floodwaters. These citizens believed they needed rescuing. So they demanded a *fighter*, instead of someone with traditional policy nuance. Red staters and other conservatives had an answer to the blue staters and other left-leaning cultural elites: Donald Trump. Electing him was their way of saying "enough."

The contrast in values and political views between native small-town voters and their new neighbors arriving from blue states, and the resentment building among many rural voters who feel they are losing control of their own communities, helps explain Trump's election.

The Rural Revolt

But not all rural areas are created equal. A solid rule of thumb is that the countryside is losing population, as rural areas suffer from the effects of intergenerational poverty. That trend has held for the last two generations. But things are beginning to change. While rural parts of city-dominated blue states such as Illinois, California, Connecticut, and New York continue to suffer bleak fates, many rural areas in red states like Indiana and Oklahoma are now growing in population.

Traditionally long-suffering areas of the South, including the Deep South, are now growing by leaps and bounds over their northeastern brethren. But, as we have seen repeatedly throughout this book, the natives of these areas fear that their traditional way of life—from their gun culture to their Christianity—is under assault. This cultural civil war began well before Trump arrived on the scene, and the conflict only appears to be accelerating.

Rural areas comprise 97 percent of America's landmass, but only 19.3 percent of its population.[11] The median age and the rates of military service are higher in rural areas than in urban ones, and rural residents are less likely to be poor—slightly lower incomes are offset by a lower cost of living, including more reasonable home prices.

Despite a relatively high standard of living, rural areas have been especially hard-hit by globalization and increased regulation. We've all seen the news stories about the major impact on a town or small city when a factory closes. In 2018, for example, General Motors announced plans to close three major plants and lay off some fourteen thousand factory workers in Middle America. Thousands of jobs that held communities together since the late nineteenth century are no longer. Politicians in D.C. and state capitals offer little help. Many elected officials and bureaucrats simply believed these sparsely populated areas are clinging to the past. They never consider that well-intentioned government policy may have blocked their way to the future.

Many of the policies created in the District of Columbia, Sacramento, Albany, and Springfield are put in place by and for city dwellers. Restrictions on manufacturing, raw materials, and transportation are often written by city rats—but they disproportionately affect country mice. State and federal legislators, who are overwhelmingly urban creatures, lack a basic understanding of the effects of their policies on the rural parts of the country. Rural areas in both red and blue states suffer major consequences from these poorly thought-out policies and from the elitist attitude that ensures they just keep coming.

Consider the inhabitants of coal country, who have had their lives upended by environmental regulation that has helped reduce the number of jobs in the coal industry to just a third of what it was in 1985. Blue state and former blue state voters tend to share the attitude toward coal that was behind the policies of the Obama administration. No wonder the decline of coal accelerated during the Obama years. When #44 took office there were over 152,000 coal jobs nationwide; by the time he left in 2016 there were only 69,000.[12] In 2008, Obama actually pledged to put coal plants out of business.[13] The Obama White House abjured clean coal and new coal plant production.

And if Hillary Clinton had been elected president, her administration would have continued down the same path. In 2016 she promised to put coal miners out of jobs.[14] Why would anyone in West Virginia vote for her? Hillary also endorsed heavy restrictions on fracking,[15] the practice that has brought the U.S. near–energy independence (with some help from our neighbors to the north). The states that benefited most from fracking—North Dakota, Wyoming, Ohio, Pennsylvania, and Texas—all voted against her. But fracking bans in states with large natural gas potential, including New York and California, have cut off an economic lifeline to some of the most economically destitute rural areas of the country. In state politics, the rural counties are outweighed by the voters in the cities. But many of these rural counties voted overwhelmingly for Trump. All he had to do was commit to putting coal miners back to work. And that was enough.

Regulation of nearly every kind—championed by former blue staters who have moved to red states that rely on farming—handicaps farmers at an already terrible time for their industry. Well-meaning subsidies and government schemes (think government cheese and ethanol) unwittingly distort markets and place farmers in a terrible renegotiated debt trap. These are near-catastrophic problems in rural areas dependent on agriculture. The struggles are real. Farmers have the highest suicide rate of any profession in America. Double that of veterans. This is a costly problem on all fronts—financial and emotional.

The problems of veterans too, though, are disproportionately felt in rural areas because rural states have disproportionately more military veterans. And the Obama years saw massive mismanagement of the VA system. When doctors who quit the VA are under investigation for medical malpractice or "raise reasonable concern for the safety of patients," the VA is supposed to report it to the national database, but it failed to report 90 percent of potentially dangerous doctors to the database. (In one incident, a VA hospital director failed to report a dangerous doctor who then went on to work at a private-sector hospital—where he potentially endangered hundreds of new patients. When you go to the hospital, you shouldn't have to worry that the doctor operating on you may intentionally harm you.) The VA also allowed scores of doctors with revoked licenses to practice. And the VA's insane wait times for treatment may have led to the deaths of 307,000 veterans. Arcane practices restricting treatment at non-VA facilities were especially insulting to rural veterans. Trump called the VA out on this and took veterans' worries to heart. He also carried these veterans by an almost 2–1 margin.

Big-city people simply don't understand the culture of rural areas. They make assumptions based on their own narrow perspectives. Meanwhile, rural people have no interest in dictating how city folks should live their lives. All they ask is to be left alone so they can earn a living.

Agriculture, forestry, fishing, hunting, and mining employ about 9.6 percent of the rural workforce. Manufacturing is still the big employer for most rural workers. Today it's at 12.1 percent, down from 20 percent in 1969 and 15 percent in 1999. American factory workers have faced fierce wage competition due to absurdly unfair trade practices. Nationwide, manufacturing employees represent 16 percent of all displaced workers—a total of almost half a million.[16]

Approximately half of all agricultural workers in America are illegal immigrants;[17] some estimates are as high as 70 percent.[18] Urban elites often characterize these as jobs that American citizens won't do. It's a convenient talking point for those who never even visit America's farming communities. But if you go to any rural area, you can see that is not the case. Young people are willing to work today, just as they were willing to work on their family farms a decade or two ago. I spent my summers picking berries at a local farm in New Hampshire while in high school, as did my parents.

It's true that some Americans won't work certain agricultural jobs because of very low pay. But a major cause of wage suppression is the abundance of illegal immigrant workers. An estimated 30 percent of the nation's foreign-born population are illegal immigrants; of the adult illegal immigrant population, well over 50 percent never completed high school, while an additional 24 percent only have a high school diploma. Because of the low education level of this population, coupled with the fact that they often lack English-language skills, the vast majority of employed illegal immigrants work in the low-skill sector. The result? About 7.4 million illegals are competing for jobs and income with 43 million Americans who legally work in the low-skilled labor force.[19] Numerous studies show that the large infusion of illegals has significantly depressed the wages of workers on the bottom rung of the economic ladder. A 10 percent increase in the number of workers in any industry lowers wages by at least 3 percent; some economists estimate that the earnings of low-skilled American workers drops by thousands of dollars per year thanks to the infusion of illegals into the workforce. Today many welfare programs pay better than low-paying jobs.

If fewer illegals were in the job market, wages would rise significantly. Yes, this would raise the cost of some goods—a head of lettuce would go up from $1.50 to $1.99. Is that moderate price increase worth it to save our country? You decide.

Once and Future Cities

Upper-middle-class and upper-class young people are remaking up-and-coming cities in traditionally conservative states—places like Denver, Austin, and Nashville—to their own cultural liking. The cost of this falls on the backs of local blue-collar workers and minority residents, both of whom are already struggling to pay increasing rents and other higher costs of living. The story of the waves of residents leaving blue states has been one of the most underreported of the last generation. It's time to start paying attention and take warning from what has happened to California, Illinois, and New York.

The 2016 election cycle was a harbinger for elections to come. Large population shifts—both internal and external—will continue to change the electoral landscape dramatically. The rapid movement of American citizens across state borders will also continue to radically transform the economy.

And yet there is no fiery rhetoric in our political discourse about internal mass migration as there is about immigration, both legal and illegal. However, migration within the United States amounts to a seismic demographic change with profound effects on our politics, culture, economy, and basic understanding of ourselves as Americans. As these changes continue, politics will get dirtier, meaner, and more visceral at every level. But not all is lost, dear reader. There are silver linings around these dark demographic clouds, I promise. We'll discuss those ahead.

CHAPTER EIGHT

More Divided Than Ever
How Echo Chambers Are Polarizing Our Politics—
and Our Nation

Hats, shirts, and stickers sporting Barack Obama's campaign slogan, "Hope and Change," were ubiquitous leading up to the 2008 presidential election. Donning Obama gear in major cities was more than just a political statement; it was a fashion statement that signaled to others you were one of *them*. You were enlightened and open-minded, and you had the intellectual superiority that one demonstrates by reading HuffPost.

Leading up to (and following) the 2016 presidential election, however, the same couldn't be said for Donald Trump garb. Sure, wearing the iconic cap in red state America was acceptable. But in a big city? The hat could put your life in danger. Just one week after Trump was elected president, a man riding the New York subway was pinned down and choked because he was wearing a MAGA cap. Nobody on the train did anything to help the victim as he was physically attacked.[1]

Publicly supporting Trump in the Big Apple makes you a target for harassment and violence. As a "social experiment" in March 2017, *New York Post* reporter Heather Hauswirth donned the signature Trump cap during a night out in Manhattan. Her first stop was The Happiest Hour, a hot-spot bar in the trendy West Village. Within ten minutes of her entering the watering hole, a manager demanded she remove the cap "immediately," citing a physical fight caused by MAGA hats a few days earlier. She took her hat off, but a few minutes later two men approached Hauswirth and asked to purchase the MAGA hat. She sold it to them, and one put it on his head. Within a few minutes the same bar manager and a bouncer approached the men and told them to take the hat off. When they refused, they were forcibly escorted out of the establishment.[2]

Conservatives are attacked on a regular basis in New York. Here are just a few recent examples:

- August 1, 2016: A left-wing mob violently ejected a conservative supporter from a New York City park because he was wearing a MAGA hat. As screaming leftists forced the young man from City Hall Park, police stood by and did nothing.[3]
- February 2, 2017: Unruly anti-Trump activists were arrested at NYU after disrupting a conservative speaker. When Trump supporter and *Vice* cofounder Gavin McInnes showed up to deliver his planned speech at the college, he couldn't even speak over the violent protesters yelling, "Shame! Shame! Shame!"[4]
- July 7, 2017: A Brooklyn man was viciously attacked by liberals with a broken bottle in a Manhattan bar because he was wearing a MAGA hat. The assault was so severe that the victim needed plastic surgery to reconstruct his face. The attackers were arrested but subsequently released without bail.[5]
- April 13, 2018: Two men mugged a teenaged tourist at knifepoint, accosting the eighteen-year-old from behind because he was wearing a red Trump cap. When the victim attempted to fight back, one of the attackers pulled a knife

on him, pointed at his hat, and asked, "What are you doing with that hat on?"[6]

- April 23, 2018: Trump supporter Milo Yiannopoulos was driven out of a New York bar by a liberal mob shouting at him, "Nazi scum get out!"[7]
- October 5, 2018: Pro-Trump *Fox & Friends* host Brian Kilmeade was stalked and harassed all day in Manhattan. The two men who followed Kilmeade around filmed themselves yelling at the television host and accusing him of being a racist on the subway. They encouraged strangers to harass Kilmeade, as well; people on the train began haranguing the host, with one yelling, "Stop grabbing pu**y!"[8]

New York liberals who claim to be inclusive and tolerant have shown themselves to be exclusive and intolerant when it comes to dealing with conservatives. The treatment of conservatives in the five boroughs speaks to how politically one-sided the city has become.

This is largely the result of people sorting themselves into cities, towns, and communities with like-minded people—as I'll explain in more detail later in this chapter. The end result is that liberal areas of the country, especially large cities, have become increasingly liberal while some rural areas have become increasingly conservative.

Nowadays, trying to find a true conservative in Manhattan is like trying to find Bigfoot in the Rocky Mountains. In an earlier, ancient era—like twenty years ago—New York City was home to many conservatives.[9] William F. Buckley was a Manhattanite. Ayn Rand lived in Manhattan, too, and her loyal follower and the future chairman of the Federal Reserve, Alan Greenspan, was born there. But call yourself a conservative there now, and you're likely to get chased by a mob. So what happened? Was it something in the rancid New York City drinking water that transformed every resident of the Big Rotten Apple into a liberal?

Blue state cities such as New York, Boston, and Chicago are getting bluer and more hostile to conservatives. In the 2016 election, nearly every large city in the nation rejected Donald Trump by an overwhelming margin.[10] This wasn't always the way things were. San Francisco was relatively red even after World War II, going Republican in 1952 and 1956. Philadelphia was solidly Republican until 1951.

Demographers generally agree that one of the biggest drivers of the ever-increasing liberalism of the nation's largest cities is the flight of tax-paying middle-class families. Not a huge surprise, as many urban centers—especially New York, Chicago, Los Angeles, and San Francisco—have become increasingly expensive and ridden with crime over the decades.[11] Some of these families relocate to surrounding suburban areas, but many pack up and head for low-tax red states like Texas, Tennessee, or New Hampshire. Many of these escapees are conservative—by the standards of the big blue cities they're escaping from. They object to the idea that their hard-earned wealth should be shared with anyone and everyone clever enough to sign up for public assistance but too lazy to actually get a job in the current booming economy.

But when these New York–style "conservatives" plant their L.L. Bean tent poles in North Carolina or Texas, and you compare them to the *real* conservatives who have lived in those red states for generations, the newcomers suddenly look like liberals. They want all the governmental bells and whistles they got back home, and their tolerance for taxes is way higher than the locals'. This phenomenon helps explain, for example, the recent push for an income tax in New Hampshire[12]—something that would have been laughable just a decade ago, before Massachusetts expats flooded the state.

So here's the situation: the people from blue cities like New York who are packing up the Range Rover and migrating inland are, in fact, ordinary liberals. They only *seemed* like conservatives in New York because everyone around them was *super liberal*. So these ordinary liberals who at home felt like conservatives arrive in North Carolina or Texas and suddenly *they're* the super liberals! Meanwhile, the rat-infested, pothole-filled, overtaxed neighborhoods of Manhattan are increasingly populated with the super liberals who have stayed behind. This group is mainly composed of two types: the poor people who can't afford to move and who have come to depend upon the largesse of taxpayer-funded government programs for their survival, and the super rich who like living in glitzy New York City and either don't care about paying high taxes or have high-priced accountants who can ensure they pay as little in taxes as possible.

New York City has more millionaires than any other city in the world.[13] But at the same time, the number of poor in the city has exploded during recent years. At the end of Mayor Bill de Blasio's first year in office, there were thirteen thousand more New Yorkers reliant on welfare than there had been the previous year.[14]

We have seen how red state cities are becoming increasingly liberal and even some rural areas in those states are being moved leftward by an influx of blue state expats. But meanwhile, other rural counties are staying as red and conservative as ever.

Nowhere is this more evident than in Texas.

In the 2018 U.S. Senate election between Beto O'Rourke and Ted Cruz, the liberal O'Rourke carried the *nouveau chic* urban counties, just as everyone expected. In Harris County, home to Houston, he beat the conservative incumbent by nearly 200,000 votes. O'Rourke won both his hometown of El Paso County and Bexar County, where San Antonio is located, by 100,000 votes; Dallas County by more than 230,000 votes; and Travis County, home to Austin, also by more than 230,000 votes. Cruz himself had predicted that O'Rourke would take Travis County, saying before the election that he believed the Hippie Hollow Park in Austin— where clothing is optional—would be empty on Election Day because "every one of those folks will be down there voting to turn Texas blue."[15]

Make no mistake—though it wasn't enough to give him the election, O'Rourke and his liberal agenda made significant inroads into Texas suburbs that had once been reliably conservative. In central Texas, O'Rourke grabbed votes in Hays and Williamson Counties, both rapidly growing bedroom communities that are absorbing new left-leaning residents from Austin. Hays County, southwest of Austin and home to Texas

State University, hadn't voted for Democrats at the top of the ticket since 1992. But the 2018 election results showed the county is turning blue, giving O'Rourke a 15.3-point margin there.[16] Hays County voters even gave a win to Governor Greg Abbott's Democratic challenger Lupe Valdez, despite the comfortable margin of victory Abbott had claimed over Democrat Wendy Davis in 2014.

But Texas is a very big state! In the two hundred plus rural counties of Texas, Beto ran into a solid red wall. If you look at the Texas map showing which counties supported each candidate, you'll see little specks of blue and lots of red. North, east, south, west, Cruz won county after county— some by massive margins. These consistent wins in rural counties gave him the victory.

The map also shows you how divided Texas—like many other states—has become. The danger for Republicans is that the polarization will end with a dedicated minority of conservatives facing a majority of big-tax, big-spend liberals.

Geographic Clustering Is Driving Polarization

The demographic changes sweeping the nation have deep roots in disparities of wealth, taxes, and social services across America.

At the very top of the economic ladder, many people with great wealth have so much money that they don't mind living in ultra-high-tax cities like New York. They can afford to live wherever they want! Immune to economic pressure, they're happy in their high-rise city condos and mansions in the suburbs.

But when you move down the ladder a few notches, you find that—in contrast to the ultra-wealthy—upper-middle-class people are *extremely* tax sensitive, and when the pressure grows too intense, they flee high-tax states for those with lower taxes. They leave Washington, D.C., for Northern Virginia, or Boston for New Hampshire, or San Francisco for Colorado. These new arrivals gentrify their neighborhoods and push longtime residents out.

Lower on the economic scale are working-class people who are self-supporting but can't always afford to move. They're most often found in red states, and that's where they stay unless the incoming rich folks drive up property values so much they have to pack up and move deeper into rural red country.

And at the bottom are the low-income people who benefit from the many social services provided by high-tax liberal cities and states. They remain firmly entrenched in their blue states and liberal big cities.

While these economic forces are powerful forces for polarization, the increasing division of America has other roots as well. Research shows that during recent decades the ideological gap separating Republicans and Democrats in Congress has grown increasingly wider.[17] This helps explain our elected officials' inability to compromise on significant policy initiatives. One driver of the dramatic increase in this polarization is the geographic clustering of Americans by political ideology. Author Bill Bishop laid out his theory of partisan geographic "sorting" in his book *The Big Sort*. Bishop found that since the early 1970s Americans have been organizing themselves into communities sharing similar values and beliefs—including political preferences. This clustering pattern has had significant political effects, helping contribute to the increasing divide in Congress, since like-minded communities elect like-minded politicians.[18]

The *Washington Post* conducted a study that backed Bishop's theory. The outlet looked at the presidential vote in congressional districts over the last sixty years. According to the *Post*, "During this period, the variance of district-level presidential voting has increased steadily, meaning that the degree to which most districts are different from the 'average' district has grown. This is consistent with Bishops' hypothesis of political clustering.... Our analysis suggests that something like 30 percent of the growth in House polarization may be attributable to geographic clustering of the electorate over time."[19]

This means that if you're a liberal, the chances are increasingly high that your neighbors will be liberal too; and if you're a conservative, your neighbors are likely to share your views. In the 2016 presidential election, more than 61 percent of voters cast their ballots in counties that gave either Trump or Clinton at least 60 percent of the major-party vote. That's up from 50 percent of voters who lived in such counties in 2012, and 39 percent in 1992. And during the same period—1992 to 2016—the number of "extreme landslide counties"—those decided by margins exceeding 50 percentage points—skyrocketed from just 93 to 1,196, or over a third of the nation's counties. What this means is that Americans are sorting themselves into two camps, not just in their minds and hearts but in where they actually live.[20]

None of this is surprising. People want to be around others who share their values, and they organize themselves into groups with others who are like-minded at nearly every level of society. This explains why most liberal-leaning blue state expats relocate to cities (rather than rural areas) within their new red state homes. As a result, cities in red states like Texas are becoming increasingly liberal while the rural areas have mostly remained bloodred. Tanya Santillan, a Mexican American attorney and self-described progressive from California, moved to Houston in 2016. She chose the Lone Star State's biggest city because it's known to be progressive. She told *The Guardian*, "Houston...is a bubble inside of Texas. People are a lot more progressive. I think maybe if I lived in a smaller town than Houston my experience would be completely different."[21]

Thus the urban–rural divide is sharply increasing as blue staters move to red states. *New York Times* columnist Ross Douthat noted that as large cities have become overwhelmingly liberal, they have also become the antithesis of egalitarian utopias. They are often dystopias divided between privilege and welfare. Douthat writes, "If cities are dynamic, they are also so rich—and so rigidly zoned—that the middle class can't afford to live there and fewer and fewer kids are born inside their gates. If they are fast-growing, it's often a growth intertwined with subsidies and 'too big to fail' protection.... We should treat liberal cities the way liberals treat corporate monopolies—not as growth-enhancing assets, but as trusts that concentrate wealth and power and conspire against the public good." As a solution, he proposed breaking up large cities by dispersing government offices to more rural areas of the nation. For example, the Department of Agriculture might fit in well in Nebraska or Oklahoma.[22]

As people continue to sort themselves into communities, cities, and states with others who have similar political leanings, there are negative consequences. When you rarely have to come in contact with others who have opposing opinions, your own views can easily become increasingly extreme. The art of compromise dies when we can all live in bubbles where our own views are constantly reflected back to us. And sadly, clustering isn't only happening at the community level; it's also happening on our televisions and computers.

Media Echo Chambers

Back in the late twentieth century, before the internet and widespread cable TV news, most Americans got their news from the same few sources. At the peak of his career in the 1970s, TV news anchorman Walter Cronkite had an average nightly audience of up to 29 million viewers on the *CBS Evening News*.[23] In 1985, the average home got just eighteen TV broadcast channels. A goal of any network was to capture as wide an audience as possible, which meant avoiding extremism on either side. Late-night TV host Johnny Carson attracted 10 million or more viewers at the peak of his career,[24] and a reported 55 million watched his final appearance on *The Tonight Show* in 1992.[25] A hallmark of his show was his avoidance of any pointed political commentary, with both parties receiving nothing more painful than a gentle ribbing.

By 2007, thanks to cable, the number of channels had jumped to more than 118, and now it's even higher. Today the viewership of evening news programs on CBS, NBC and ABC combined is smaller than that of CBS when Cronkite sat in the anchor's chair. And today's late-night hosts don't even come close to the audience Carson had, forcing them to scramble to entertain smaller—and more opinionated—audiences.

In competing for smaller audiences, broadcasters have found that it's profitable to cater to core interests. If you want music, you tune to MTV. If you want nature, you tune to National Geographic. If you want left-wing politics, MSNBC and CNN are your choices. For those on the right, it's Fox News. When you turn on the television today, you can choose to receive only the viewpoint that reinforces what you already believe about the political system. You can stay comfortably ensconced in your comfort zone, kicking back in your La-Z-Boy recliner, munching popcorn, and watching the politicians you hate get trashed. You never need to be challenged by an opposing viewpoint.

And that's just television. As an increasing number of families are cutting their cable cords, online news and streaming services have become king in the world of political news. A majority of Americans now get news from social media.[26] Our Facebook, Twitter, and Instagram accounts have become echo chambers, where we only come in contact with people and news sources that reflect our own opinions. Don't agree with *Mother Jones*'s left-wing stance? Simply don't follow its accounts. Find those right-wing Breitbart posts annoying? Simply block the outlet on Facebook and Twitter and you never have to see another article.

A few years ago, I noticed that an old friend had defriended me on Facebook. My heart dropped. Ours had been a genuine friendship, built on laughs and countless memories from the halcyon teenage years. When I messaged her to ask what had happened, her response was fast in coming. After months of seeing my reports on the immigration crisis in southern Texas—a focus of my journalism in 2014—enough was enough. She couldn't bear to read another line of the "offensive, disgusting" news from the border. In her words, "Republican filth."

I spent 2013 and 2014 writing on border issues as a reporter—not an opinion columnist. For any journalist in southern Texas during those years, nuance was in short supply. Thousands of migrants were flooding over a porous border daily and taking advantage of the diminished national readiness. All you had to do was park your car on high ground and watch it happen. The only "agenda" you could have there as a reporter was to pretend that a crisis wasn't happening. Which some did.

Deleting a friend on Facebook for reporting uncomfortable political information seems extreme. Yet it's also *extremely common.* This wasn't the first time, and probably won't be the last, that I've been defriended on account of politics. Chances are that it's happened to you too. What is going on?

According to a study from the University of Colorado, religion and politics are the two most common reasons people delete their friends on Facebook.[27] It turns out that we're even more likely to delete our closest friends than our casual acquaintances. The Pew Research Center found in another study that roughly 45 percent of "consistent liberals" have defriended or blocked a Facebook friend because they disagreed with his or her politics, while 31 percent of "consistent conservatives" have done the same to their liberal friends. But conservatives aren't off the hook: consistent conservatives are more likely than liberals to see political views similar to their own on Facebook.[28]

Add to the selectiveness of individuals the power of Facebook's and Twitter's behind-the-scenes algorithms that figure out what kinds of posts you like. If you consistently hit the "like" button on liberal posts, those kinds of posts will appear in your social media news feeds more often. Ditto for clicking "like" on conservative posts. Our social media accounts have become echo chambers where we hear only what we're most comfortable hearing.

The echo chamber phenomenon would be less troubling if Facebook weren't the biggest political news source for millennials.[29] The social media network has made us more politically plugged-in than ever, but it's also closing us off from new ideas, opposing viewpoints, and uncomfortable truths in ways we are just beginning to understand.

Echo chambers—both geographic and online—make extreme viewpoints mainstream by cutting out any dissenting opinion. Need proof?

Just turn on your television or browse your news feeds on social media, and you will be bombarded with polemics about the sky falling and credible threats of violence against political foes. You can read dim-witted threats any day on social media; take, for example, "comedienne" Sarah Silverman calling for a military coup,[30] or Madonna telling protesters she fantasizes about blowing up the White House, or Kathy Griffin proudly holding up the decapitated head of Trump in a disturbing video.

And this hyperpolarization online has led to real-life disturbing events. Violence seems to break out every time a conservative comes to speak at a college campus.[31] Furious mobs chased Ted Cruz, Sarah Sanders, and Kellyanne Conway out of restaurants as they attempted to dine peacefully with their families. House representative Steve Scalise was shot by an angry liberal trying to kill Republicans during their congressional baseball practice.

The Big Picture

All of these powerful forces—economic anxiety, the increasing liberalization of cities, rapid and disruptive technological change, and news outlets that are happy to tell you what they think you want to hear—are creating a society that's profoundly divided. But are things really as bad as we think? Has it ever been worse in the past? How can we make it better?

The first thing to remember is that if you look back over our nation's history of over three hundred years, there have been times when our internal divisions were *much* worse. There was the Civil War, that horrible period that still stands as the costliest conflict in our nation's history. From April 12, 1861, to May 9, 1865, an estimated 620,000 men— roughly 2 percent of the entire population—were killed.[32] If the same percentage of today's population were killed, the toll would have been roughly six million soldiers. In addition, tens of thousands more died from disease and in captivity.

Since the Civil War, our nation has had problems with homegrown hate groups. In the 1920s, the Ku Klux Klan waged a campaign of terror against African Americans in the South. On August 8, 1925, at the height of its power, 30,000 white-robed Klansmen marched down Pennsylvania Avenue in Washington, D.C. Forty-six trains had been chartered to transport the racists to the nation's capital from cities such as Cleveland, Toledo, Columbus, and Pittsburgh. The Klan spearheaded the gruesome post–Civil War practice of lynching. From its height in 1892 to the last recorded lynching in 1981—of Michael McDonald by several Klan members—over 4,700 people were so murdered.

The 1960s brought political assassinations and civil violence. We experienced rioting in our major cities, with the worst being the Detroit riots of July 1967. Those riots lasted five days and resulted in the deaths of 43—including 33 African Americans and 10 whites—1,189 injuries, over 7,200 arrests, and more than 2,000 buildings destroyed.[33]

The early 1970s saw the scourge of left-wing terrorism. Between August and November 1969, the first bombing campaign, the work of a group of New York City leftist radicals led by a militant named Sam Melville, featured attacks on a dozen buildings around Manhattan.[34] Despite Melville's quick arrest, the floodgates opened. According to FBI statistics, the United States experienced more than 2,500 domestic bombings in just eighteen months in 1971 and 1972, with virtually no solved crimes and few significant prosecutions.[35] Terror bombings in America were commonplace, especially in cities such as New York, Chicago, and San Francisco. Nearly a dozen left-wing radical underground groups, including the Weather Underground, the New World Liberation Front, and the Symbionese Liberation Army, set off so many bombs during that tumultuous decade that people all but accepted them as a part of daily life.

Throughout our nation's history, we've overcome division and come together during trying times. But the rise of echo chambers presents new challenges by allowing us to avoid debate altogether. No one can deny that healthy, even contentious, public debate is a good thing. And the growing divide between red state and blue state America is a cause for concern.

As a nation, we face real external threats—Islamic extremism, Russian militarism, and the growing power of China's economy coupled with its desire to play a bigger role on the world stage. And our success in facing future challenges will depend greatly on our ability to respond and move ahead as one people.

The good news is that crises can bring positive change. From the horrors of the Second World War emerged NATO and the most durable peacetime alliance in history. From the ashes of Watergate and the resignation of Richard Nixon came the presidency of Ronald Reagan and the collapse of the Soviet Union. Sometimes it takes a harrowing experience to remind us of what we share—and of the fact that united we will stand, just as divided we will surely fall. At some point, we will make the conscious effort to de-escalate confrontations and rein in aggressive attitudes toward those who don't share our worldviews. We'll open ourselves to rational discourse and strive to see the legitimate ideas presented by all sides. As Dr. Martin Luther King Jr. said, "Returning violence for violence multiplies violence, adding deeper darkness to a night already devoid of stars. Darkness cannot drive out darkness; only light can do that. Hate cannot drive out hate; only love can do that."

CHAPTER NINE

Reading the Tea Leaves
A Look into the Not-Too-Distant Future

Behold, for your own edification, a glimpse at what the country might look like in ten years. Below we show the state of our nation in 2029 if the blue state invasion continues to wash over the purplish and red states, turning them blue by the end of the 2020s. It goes well beyond just Texas and Florida, as much of the Rocky Mountain West and Deep South may be pulling the lever for the Democrats before too long. This is the potential worst-case scenario, one I feel obligated to share.

There would be a strong possibility that a traditional Republican could not win the White House for decades if critical swing states moved into the solid blue category. The dynamic in national politics would shift from right vs. left to progressive vs. socialist. If these scenarios from my diary of the future start coming true, I'll be frightened—and trying to figure out if I can predict lottery numbers, too.

Diary Entry, January 20, 2029

I didn't vote for our new president, Kamala Harris. A little grayer than when she ran against Trump in 2020, but no smarter, she swept last November's elections on her "For the Many" platform. We escaped the prospect of Alexandria Ocasio-Cortez as vice president, but she'll be Treasury secretary if confirmed by Congress. Andrew Gillum, chosen in order to peel off Florida's electoral votes, will be vice president. The Harris-Gillum ticket did carry the Sunshine State, but it turns out that it wasn't needed for victory...not by a long shot.

Republican president Mike Pence didn't carry the states that he and Donald Trump had won in 2016—or the ones he had won in 2024, not even with help from libertarian voters coming out for Vice President Rand Paul. It was a disappointment, but not completely unexpected. Most of the swing states needed for victory went by large margins to new president Kamala Harris. (It's going to take a while for me to get used to writing that.) Increased electoral vote totals for a number of traditionally red states simply weren't enough to stop the Democrats' juggernaut.

Despite a relatively close popular vote, the political calculus was in the Democrats' favor. Pence won Indiana, Ohio, even Pennsylvania. But Virginia, North Carolina, and Georgia flipped to the Democratic column. Florida remained too close to call for much of the night. But then at 9:00 p.m. the eighty-year-old Wolf Blitzer shocked CNN viewers with a stunning announcement:

"Texas is too close to call."

I can't say I was shocked. After all, as they say, demography is destiny. Texas was the state that sent Senator Beto O'Rourke to Washington over Ted Cruz in 2024. The tight Senate race that election cycle was one sign that the new demographic profile of cities like Austin was playing directly into the Democrats' hands.

As the night went on, the news grew more and more glum. By less than a half million votes, both Texas and Florida went to the Harris-Gillum ticket. A Democratic victory was a fait accompli by this point. Colorado, Nevada, and California (with 74 percent of the vote in) put the final nails in the coffin. It was over.

Back to the present: President Harris was in rare form making her inaugural address today.

"As the first woman as our nation's leader—and first woman of color," she said in the freezing rain, "it is time for the nation to consider fairness as our top goal in all federal and state decision-making. To begin, I will be appointing three new justices to the Supreme Court beyond our existing nine to begin our transformation into the nation I know America can be." The monstrous crowd erupted in applause.

"Towards a Fairer Union," read the banners. A Soviet-style image of Harris—something like those Alexandria Ocasio-Cortez campaign posters from 2018—looked down on the crowd from hundreds of placards. The faux-Russian letters underneath Harris's face were a nice touch, if a bit over the top.

I watched television and shook my head at every mention of our "unfair economy" and the need to override state policies in order to tackle inequality and climate change. Harris read off a laundry list of new taxes and regulations and a plan to freeze all new fossil fuel production.

I didn't vote for this agenda, but 56 percent of Americans did. And now they have a shot at making it reality. Most right-leaning analysts simply couldn't fathom how so many formerly red states could vote for a candidate who called socialism "a legitimate alternative to our for-profit system" during the campaign.

So I've decided to start this journal as an "as-it-happened" record of the last gasp of limited government. I'll be watching as the Democrats take the same liberal policies that have ruined the economies of the blue states—driving liberal voters into formerly red states and thus, ironically, making possible this blue wave victory—and impose them on the whole country. It's not going to end well. In the words of the famous Ron Paul meme, "You should have listened."

Diary Entry, January 27, 2029

I had C-SPAN on in the background, airing the ongoing debate in Congress over President Harris's cabinet appointees. Some were surprisingly uncontroversial, but most of them were a train wreck waiting to happen. The president didn't have to compromise, thanks to the simple fact that Democrats now had sixty-one senators—on top of a 270–165 advantage in the House. There was only so much that the determined Republican minority could do.

Senator Rick Scott of Florida acted as the lead questioner, trying to pry more than talking points and vague non-answers from the nominees.

"What, in your opinion, is the top challenge to the United States military in the next four years?" Scott asked Defense secretary–nominee Tim Kaine.

Kaine said firmly, "Well, first it has to be climate change. Then, of course, it is gender equality in the service."

Scott followed up, "By equality, you mean extending Selective Service to women?"

Kaine was ready. "Not that kind of equality."

This continued through most of the day, with most nominees saying they would make the "national emergency" of climate change (already declared by President Harris) their major goal.

Senator Scott also had a chance to question proposed Energy secretary (and billionaire Democratic activist) Tom Steyer. Steyer had been one of the top financial backers of the Harris campaign; he and his companies had donated over $100 million to her cause. These hearings finally put him in front of the national audience he had vainly hoped to find with his attempts to impeach Trump; Steyer acted like he had been waiting for years for this moment at the podium. Instead of answering Scott's first question, he went on a twenty-minute John Galt–style rant explaining his ideology and overarching goals. For the sake of brevity, I include only a bit of it here (and omit altogether his hand-waving and smug chuckling to himself).

"You see, Senator." Steyer paused. "Senators. America's changed. Our young people have grown up with the proper education to understand how income inequality and the concentration of wealth has created our current climate crisis. That is why the Green New Deal will rebuild this nation while phasing out the fossil fuels that are destroying our only planet. Top scientists predict that if we don't do anything in the next ten years, the effects of climate change could be irreversible."

Senator Lindsey Graham, who had won his latest re-election bid by the skin of his teeth, piped up, "What about the constitutionality of what you're proposing?"

Steyer briefly deviated from his pre-written comments. "This is a global crisis. It requires actions that match it. And when the confirmations of the new Supreme Court justices Obama, Booker, and Newsom are complete, there will not be an issue with a single one of these programs."

The shock of the election had hit many conservatives and libertarians hard. They didn't march and contest the results like Hillary and her fans did back in 2016, but they realized the economic and cultural future of the nation was grim. GOP campaign strategy over the last decade had focused on immigration from foreign nations—while domestic migration had been reshaping the political map right under the Republicans' noses. Liberals had flocked to red states in record numbers, accomplishing with their U-Hauls a change in the electoral calculus that any political strategist would have killed for.

Diary Entry, February 22, 2029

The fights over cabinet appointees are mostly over. Almost all of the president's nominees were confirmed by large majorities in the Senate—and most didn't receive a single Republican vote. It was a bit of a depressing spectacle, with only Steyer being bounced—after a Daily Caller exposé revealed that he had cheated on his taxes for decades. Former Illinois governor and also-billionaire J. B. Pritzker took his place and was confirmed with fifty-seven votes.

Because of the changing demography of the country and a few lucky breaks, the Democrats have a filibuster-proof supermajority in the Senate. But now comes the really radical part of the new administration's program: getting President Harris's three additional justices confirmed to expand the Supreme Court.

"After all," she said in a speech right before her inauguration, "it's only fair to bring balance back to the Supreme Court. Small-government extremists stole the seats for Justices Kavanaugh and Gorsuch. Instead of subjecting the country to a lengthy and painful impeachment process, it will be much easier to cancel their vote out through appointments."

Court-packing has only been tried once before, under President Franklin Roosevelt in 1937. Roosevelt wanted to add six more justices to the Court to obtain favorable rulings on New Deal legislation that the Court had previously ruled unconstitutional. But even with a substantial Democratic majority in the Senate and the pressures of the Depression, FDR was unable to execute his plan.

Roosevelt also wanted to implement a mandatory judicial retirement age of seventy.[1] President Kamala Harris is in favor of that "reform" as well, as it would force Justices John Roberts, Clarence Thomas, and Samuel Alito from the bench, leaving only four conservatives—Pence appointee Thomas Hardiman, along with Neil Gorsuch, Brett Kavanaugh, and Amy Coney Barrett, all appointed by Trump—on the Court. The collateral damage would be the forced retirement of Justice Sotomayor—but she would no doubt be replaced with a forty-five-year-old hardcore liberal ready to serve for decades. This would represent a complete remaking of the Court—and of the American constitutional order. And Congress is ready to push it through. Another domino is about to fall.

The court-packing plan and mandatory retirement proposal are just the tip of the iceberg. The White House and prominent left-wing journalists are promoting what they're calling "the Federal Override." As blue states continue to rack up tremendous debt, their public financing is becoming unsustainable. Back in 2013, Detroit filed bankruptcy and union leaders called on Congress and President Obama to give the city a federal bailout. Detroit's $20 billion debt was the result of fiscal mismanagement and liberal tax-and-spend schemes. Now the same fiscal crisis has been replicated in cities around the nation.

With recessions plaguing the Northeast states as well as Illinois, Michigan, and California, there are no easy answers. Major companies like Boeing and Microsoft have either pulled up stakes completely or kept just a shell of their former corporate headquarters in the blue states and cities. Politically radical cities like Seattle and Chicago have seen their economies implode.

Thankfully, traditional red state economies continue chugging along, bolstered by sound fiscal policy, appropriate regulation, and energy extraction. The Override is a plan to "level the playing field." While only the most radical Democrats are willing to argue for punishing the more economically successful states (most of which happen to be conservative), it's clear that's what the Override amounts to. The freeze on new fossil fuel production, already being discussed amongst House Democrats, would cripple states like Texas, West Virginia, Wyoming, and Alaska. Even worse, they want to use federal power to supersede state and local laws, giving the federal government power over decisions on minimum wage, energy production, safety regulations, and much more. Local autonomy is going to be a thing of the past.

It's wrong—it's unconstitutional—but, in the name of "fairness" and rescuing the blue states, it looks like it's going to happen.

Diary Entry, April 16, 2029

It worked. All of it. Despite every delay and procedural gambit that the Republicans in Congress attempted, President Harris and the Democrats have a bulletproof 8–4 Supreme Court majority.

Supported by blue state governments and their representatives in Congress, the Democrats are also well on their way to achieving federal bailouts for their failing states—despite the fact that under the fiscal year 2029 budget, the nation will hit an incredible $2 trillion deficit, mostly due to the exploding costs of Medicare and Social Security. And this is before President Harris's planned expansion of Medicare into a single-payer system ("Medicare for All"). Despite this unsustainable largesse, the blue states are demanding a series of bailouts for the financial disasters within their borders.

The rescue package proposed for the blue states is a convoluted system of artificially low interest rates for their accumulated debt, the assumption of state pension obligations by the federal government, and direct cash infusions to the states paid for with a sharp increase in capital gains taxes—the so-called "Robin Hood tax."

This sort of bailout will only reward bad behavior. The combined pension liabilities of Illinois, New York, and California reach into the trillions, while each of those states ranks in the bottom ten in road quality and high school graduation rates. Governor Andrew Cuomo, now in his fifth term after three failed presidential bids, has already made a promise to divert bailout funds into higher salaries for public union officials.

Today, with the debate over the Federal Override winding to a close and the package headed for passage in Congress, I went out for a stroll. What I saw on my walk illuminates why the GOP lost the election and is losing the debate—and what domestic migration in America has wrought.

The economic boom that major cities like Houston saw in the 2010s and 2020s is now fading. Storefronts that previously offered boutique items like custom cupcakes, beard balm, and organic free-trade kombucha are now shuttered. I walked into one with a "Closing Sale" sign out front. What just five years earlier had been a popular site for twenty- and thirty-somethings was almost empty. A balding man in his early forties decked out in flannel and suspenders greeted me from behind the counter.

"What happened here?" I asked, looking at shelves that had recently held South American alpaca hats and thick-framed designer glasses.

"The fat cats have put me out," the gentleman said. "It's a shame, too. I was just about to turn a profit before my trust fund ran out."

"How did this happen? What did they do?" I asked.

"The city couldn't afford my grant anymore." The store—The Gentleman's Mustache—had been receiving money from federal grants to the city of Houston intended to support the arts. Through some creative grant writing and a subsidy from his family, the proprietor of The Gentleman's Mustache had been able to pay his rent after the boom years and his hipster customer base declined. "*They* have so much, and working-class people like me just can't make ends meet. It wasn't like this in Brooklyn."

I guess it wasn't. I exchanged a few more pleasantries and ducked out the door, wondering how the rest of the country is doing.

Diary Entry, April 20, 2029

Yesterday I flew to Washington, D.C., and hopped in an Uber to my cousin Miriam's house in Arlington, Virginia. Miriam is no longer working, having taken early retirement from her government job. I'm crashing at her townhome while I attend a major meeting in D.C. on the GOP election postmortem.

Miriam is as pleasant and accommodating as ever. Her house has seen several major upgrades and is as sleek and modern as any I've ever been in. In fact, her only complaint is that the city council has rejected her application to build an extension onto the house because of a new raft of byzantine zoning and building restrictions. Still, she's in good spirits.

"How's retirement treating you?" I asked her, putting down my bags.

"Frankly," she said, smiling, "it's been wonderful. I'm glad that my pension is guaranteed from Washington. I couldn't imagine what those poor California state employees went through, not sure that they would get their pensions until Kamala stepped in."

On my way to the conference center this morning, I noticed that the greater Alexandria and Fairfax area is absolutely gleaming. The roads here are well kept, and there seem to be cranes everywhere, reflecting the recent decision to expand federal agencies by 50 percent to keep up with the pace of the Override. Unemployment here remains low, even as it is shooting up across the country. Foreign luxury cars keep pace with taxis as men and women in pressed clothes head to work. Clearly, D.C. has remained the exception to the rule; the Imperial Capital is flourishing, even as cities like Los Angeles and Philadelphia consider bankruptcies or federal bailouts.

Finally I made it to the conference, where representatives from the Heritage Foundation, the Cato Institute, and other conservative and libertarian think tanks were in attendance. The faces were forlorn; this event had the pall of an unexpected funeral.

Taking our seats, we twenty participants discussed some recent developments under the Kamala administration. The new Supreme Court had overturned an Indiana law restricting increases in local school funding to the rate of inflation, and Chief Justice Obama wrote in the majority decision that the state—and all states—"had a minimum responsibility to meet the obligations of the other 49 in regards to health, education, and other social welfare spending to preserve a more perfect union." We agreed: it's like something out of *The Road to Serfdom.*

Meanwhile, on a silent monitor playing C-SPAN in the corner of the room, we could see the Senate debate on the latest part of the Federal Override. Vice President Gillum was sitting with Senate majority leader Schumer in case he had to break a tie. Then the scene switched to the House, where we saw Democrats manage to pass a bill to significantly expand the state and local taxes tax exemption. Now the wealthy residents of high-tax states will receive almost full credit for the state and local taxes they pay, offset by a "small" increase in the corporate tax rate. The bill is popular with the public despite most of the tax credits going to wealthy homeowners in big cities.

As one of my fellow attendees at the conference put it, "The Democrats were able to effectively create a coalition of the poor and the upper-middle class. All of them believe that they can pin the bill on the villain of the day: red state governments, the rich, and offshore corporate profits."

I did a little back-of-the-envelope math and pointed out that the $5 trillion annual proposed cost of the Override and universal healthcare plans was more than the profit of all of the Fortune 500 companies combined last year.

Then we talked about some delayed quarter 1 GDP figures that were released today. Not only has the United States' economy shrunk for the first time in years, but the sharpest declines were in red states. The unique state-level policies that had kept their economic engines running are now being snuffed out by the Federal Override. The cost of gasoline has increased by 50 percent. It's "nothing to worry about" though, according to eighty-nine-year-old House Speaker Nancy Pelosi—the government should simply give tax credits for expensive electric cars.

Meanwhile, rural states are really feeling the pain. Aggressive EPA mandates have banned new woodstoves because of their emissions. Farmers can't use diesel to run their machinery anymore. At a recent photo op at a heavily subsidized electric tractor factory, President Harris told the assembled workers, "I've heard that one of these babies can go a full six hours without needing another charge." Oh boy.

A raft of "fair housing" programs is cropping up across the nation as part of a $400 billion "housing equity" program. New apartment complexes are intended to drive down rents through subsidies and rent control, but the new higher, federally mandated wages are causing housing prices to spike across the country. Meanwhile, now that the student loan guarantee maximum has been doubled, there has been an unprecedented surge in tuition at colleges across the nation. A newly decreed $30-per-hour minimum wage is dragging down the economies of the formerly low-wage states, especially in the countryside.

Conservative states have passed laws allowing natural resource extraction, and their minimum wages were commensurate with their local circumstances. But the EPA, Department of Commerce, and the Supreme Court—applying a liberal (heh) interpretation of the Commerce

Clause—keep shutting them down. If the red states are suffering, the blue states are in even worse shape. Tech and finance companies are shuddering mightily under the weight of the new federal regulations. More than a handful have moved their headquarters to Canadian cities just over the border. Some even went to Havana to set up shop under the new democracy there. Major corporate hubs like New York City are shedding workers at a rapid pace.

And yet the Harris administration's far-left program is still exceedingly popular in the big cities, which are benefiting in some ways. Federal offices are popping up in metropolises across the country to police the raft of fresh federal mandates and oversee the new federal spending. In many major cities there are now rich, mini D.C.s, flush with federal money and surrounded by Michelin-rated restaurants and trendy businesses catering to the government employees. Meanwhile, the only booming economic activity in the surrounding rural areas seems to be plywood companies bringing in supplies to board up businesses and foreclosed homes.

Diary Entry, June 10, 2029

Just like that, the city of Denver, previously one of the most fiscally sound in the nation, has declared bankruptcy. It turns out city officials have been cooking the books over the last several years to hide the runaway costs of the overgenerous state pension program. With the collapse of the craft beer industry and demise of the fracking boom, there wasn't enough money to pay the bills.

The millennials who flocked to Denver a decade ago would seem to have reached the end of the road. At this point there aren't any more booming red states for them to move to. Even with the massive expansion of government, there are only so many federal jobs to go around, and the red states are being deliberately "leveled" to the same state of failure as the blue ones. There go the last pockets of the country with low costs and booming economies. The "will work for quinoa" and "three Gender Studies degrees, no job" signs pretty much say it all.

And Colorado is in no fiscal shape to bail out Denver.

I actually visited Denver a few weeks ago to see a friend. And that visit paradoxically left me feeling hopeful rather than depressed. The former hipsters who had been able to skate by on other people's money now seemed to be clueing in to the realities of the market. You can only ignore the laws of economics for so long. Some of the invaders who had turned Colorado from red to blue were going in the opposite direction themselves, opting for a more traditionally conservative lifestyle, settling down, buying foreclosures and fixing them up, getting married, and even having kids before their biological clocks ran out. Some of them had come to the realization that the world still needs carpenters, plumbers, electricians—more than it needs exotic tea shops—and that no diktat from Washington can mandate away a leaky toilet (although I'm sure they'll try). Most of the storefronts were still empty, but one at a time, some lights were starting to come back on.

I noticed that these former hipsters and delayed adults were into politics—but differently than before. Precious few were willing to admit to having become conservatives or libertarians, but there was a serious effort to bring some semblance of fiscal conservatism to the city council. I had a chance to interview one of the candidates, a thirty-nine-year-old recently married woman, April. She had studied political science at a private school back east on scholarship and was clearly quite bright. She was clear about why she and her running mates were seeking the council seats.

"We just need some changes," she said. She ticked off a number of creeping fees that had really added up over the years: fuel taxes, business taxes, and cell phone fees. It had all hurt the city's economy—going into expanded bureaucracy instead of paying off debts. A spate of building restrictions had made it nearly impossible to build nonsubsidized apartment complexes and single-family homes. The high local minimum wage had reduced employment.

"The next Paul Ryan," I said, scribbling notes.

"I wouldn't go that far," April said, "But I just never realized how *expensive* everything was. I guess most people don't until it's too late."

Diary Entry, November 15, 2030

More than a year has passed since I last wrote in this diary. In that time, Republicans won big in a number of red and purple states in the midterm elections on the platform of rolling back the Override. They fell short of winning back either house of Congress, but it was a step in the right direction. The dramatic demographic shifts of the last twenty years had short-circuited American federalism and our Constitution's limits on the size and power of government. Washington has grown ever wealthier with the implementation of each crazy campaign promise by the Democrats put into office by blue votes from former red states. So it's cheering to see that trends may finally be turning in the opposite direction.

Also in that time, circumstances took me back to Denver for a story on the new city council. April's group had pulled off an old-fashioned victory over the Democratic machine. Through knocking on doors and persistence they now had a handful of seats at the table. Some of the blue state transplants weren't quite ready to vote Republican, but for the first time they were willing not to vote Democrat.

Things were still tenuous in Denver, but I noticed several new shopping centers and restaurants on my way into the city. Republicans had almost won the state senate back. It was a loss, but it was the closest the GOP had been in several cycles. I felt as if, after a long decade, the overwhelming blue wave was beginning to recede.

New families were sprouting up around the city, and I realized that the young people growing up during this recession and era of political radicalism might bend the other way and become more conservative than their parents.

"How did you know that we would win?" April asked me. This time she was talking to me in her city council office, smiling and chatty.

"I really didn't," I replied. But I had known that somewhere, sometime, somehow things had to start becoming sane again.

"It's strange" April said, "how Colorado and the country changed so much, so quickly."

I nodded.

April continued, "Did anyone see this coming?"

All I could do was crack a grin.

"Well, *someone* must have."

CHAPTER TEN

The Case for Optimism

Even Hipsters Can Help Make America Great Again

I know what you must be doing by now, nine chapters in—you're reaching for the bourbon. You're asking yourself whether the country can survive the massive demographic changes I've broken down in this book.

The U.S. has undergone significant demographic transformations in the past, and we have heard pronouncements of political and cultural gloom and doom before. America saw mass migrations around the time of the Civil War and again in the early twentieth century. Those waves of immigrants sparked panic and led to nativist movements—but despite those fears, they didn't spell the end of the American republic. Instead, the United States always endured, always lived on. Our founders intentionally put limits on government power. Democrats (and some Republicans) have eroded these safeguards over time, but for the most part they still remain strong; we have powerful checks on government abuse and political radicalism. So fear not! America isn't over yet. There is hope for the areas invaded en masse by new liberal residents. Neither socialist rabble-rousers nor the right-wing groups that spring up in reaction to them will gain long-term control of our country, even if Democrats ruin selective states within it.

Yes—over the next generation there *will* be a plethora of economic, social, and political problems caused by the demographic changes I have reported in this book, but there is also hope for the nation's future. For starters, the high likelihood of a political "snapback" against Democratic Party radicalism means that the middle of the twenty-first century could see the rise of a Reagan-like figure who would restore major fundamental principles of our constitutional government. The pendulum swings; it swings back. This possibility, in combination with some more optimistic population trends, means that conservatives have a fighting chance. If Republicans stick to their small-government roots, they will have the power to pull the electorate to the right.

Here's a positive trend: while the blue state refugees are turning Republican states more purple, this will paradoxically increase the political weight of these new swing states—which could still swing in the red direction, especially in presidential election years. Every ten years, all 435 seats in the House of Representatives are reapportioned according to state population. Not only does this add to or subtract from the voting power of each state in Congress, but it also determines the number of votes each state gets in the Electoral College. In the aftermath of the 2010 census, Arizona, Georgia, Florida, Nevada, South Carolina, Texas, Utah, and Washington gained a net eleven House seats—and electoral votes. Ten of those are in states that the GOP can conceivably consistently win. Meanwhile, reliably Democratic Michigan, Massachusetts, New York, and Illinois lost a total of five House seats because of out-migration.

The 2020 census data isn't available yet, but Election Data Services, a firm that uses estimates of state-by-state changes in the electorate, predicts the following gains and losses in the number of electoral votes:

- Texas will gain three
- Florida will gain two
- Arizona will gain one
- Colorado will gain one
- Montana will gain one

- North Carolina will gain one
- Oregon will gain one[1]

Democratic states such as Michigan, New York, Illinois, Minnesota, and Rhode Island will likely shed six more electors. And for the first time in history, California may lose one as well. There could be a swing of more than thirty electors away from Obama's 2008 numbers. If the Republicans can keep the red states that they have traditionally won in their column, demography could end up working in their favor in the next decade—despite the liberal invasion.

There are some other reasons for small-government conservatives to hope, even amidst the oncoming blue wave. There is the potential for cultural assimilation. Blue state voters enjoying the benefits of red state policies could start voting in support of those policies—slowing or even stopping the deluge of coastal refugees' politics.

History teaches that assimilation like this has a much better chance of reversing the effects of demography than does overt government policy wielded as a cudgel. Consider a prominent example from the nineteenth century.

Otto von Bismarck was the preeminent diplomat of the Western world in the second half of the nineteenth century. He deftly manipulated Europe's balance-of-power politics to the advantage of his domestic political allies and shrewdly used political and military tactics to forge Germany into a unified country and a great power. He served for twenty-eight years as prime minister and foreign minister and is remembered as the "Iron Chancellor." He nevertheless made memorable errors in his domestic policy. As political power in America shifts to states that are gaining population—mostly traditionally red states being flooded with migrants from blue states—perhaps we can learn from his mistakes.

Bismarck feared the influence of the Catholic Church because, though Germany was mostly Protestant, the Catholic minority was large and growing. So the Iron Chancellor closed down Catholic churches and even imprisoned priests as part of his *Kulturkampf*, or culture war. He attempted to fight demographic realities with government policy instead of winning on the battleground of ideas—and failed miserably. Instead of curtailing the power of the Church, the *Kulturkampf* drove many German Catholics, who felt persecuted, into the arms of the Church. In a rare political defeat, Bismarck was forced to back down.

But if government repression of your political opponents doesn't work, neither does attempting to co-opt their agenda. Bismarck, a traditional conservative German aristocrat loyal to the kaiser, also detested and feared the socialists. The Iron Chancellor was afraid that the recently formed German Empire could become a hotbed for radical politics. In the 1870s he used his power to promulgate laws against them, banning the Social Democratic Party, their meetings, and their newspapers; he even empowered the state to arrest party members and try them in special police courts. But though the Social Democrats were not allowed to field candidates under their party, individual members ran as independents and won an increasing number of seats in parliament.

By the early 1880s, Bismarck, in his anxiety about the Social Democrats' growing influence, made a different miscalculation. He decided to implement many of their policies, thereby co-opting their political agenda and stripping them of public support. The resulting system of "State Socialism" instituted by Bismarck's conservative government included pensions, unemployment insurance, disability coverage, and the forerunner to universal healthcare. But instead of neutering the Social Democratic Party as Bismarck had hoped, these programs became astonishingly popular, and they were eventually expanded well beyond Bismarck's original framework. They significantly boosted the Social Democrats' popularity among the common people. As the government's scope and breadth grew, so did the bureaucratic infrastructure necessary to carry out its programs—which the socialists inevitably infiltrated to push for further changes.

From the time of the "reforms" until Bismarck's forced retirement in 1890, the socialists tripled the number of seats they held in the German parliament, and that year they garnered the most votes of any party. It was an instance of the classic "if you give a mouse a cookie" paradox. Instead of being satisfied with his feast, he now needs milk to go with his cookie, and a glass to put his milk in, and so on.

And that's an object lesson for us in twenty-first-century America. Today there is a significant faction within the Republican Party seeking to find common ground with the Left. Many Republicans are ready to compromise with left-wing economic initiatives by expanding social spending or raising taxes. Take the recent expansion of Medicaid under Obamacare. Some Republicans who should know better, like John Kasich of Ohio, supported the expansion of Medicaid. Apparently, they felt they were playing with other people's money, and they feared the wrath of the voters who looked forward to benefiting from the expanded benefits.

And yet—surprise!—the Medicaid expansion turned out to be far more expensive than was estimated at the time the Republicans decided to compromise on it. In fact, it's the very kind of reckless government spending that Republicans are elected to oppose. In case after case, standing firm with conservative ideas results in more effective governance and actually wins votes for Republicans. Former Wisconsin governor Scott Walker stuck to his guns on critical issues, such as allowing employees to choose whether they wish to join unions. Such strategies may not always win the next election, but they do produce results, and those results often turn liberal voters into conservative voters. Actual results are more effective than any campaign slogan or political talking point. Today, thanks to Walker's staunch conservatism, most Wisconsinites enjoy lower property taxes than they did before he took office. They can also thank him, in large part, for the Supreme Court's 2018 decision in *Janus v. American Federation of State, County, and Municipal Employees*, which allowed Wisconsin to become a "right-to-work" state; workers in the state are no longer forced to unionize. Given that 93 percent of unions' political donations go to Democrats, it's no wonder that many workers find it utterly unfair to be forced to pay union dues.

Walker made policy compromises at times, but he never gave in on core principles. Wisconsin has trended significantly redder as a result. In his bid for reelection in 2018, Walker lost to Democrat Tony Evers by just over 1 percent. That year was a good cycle for Democrats, but Wisconsin is trending red in presidential elections; the Republicans went from losing the state by fourteen points in the 2008 presidential race to winning the state in 2016. Even in purple states, competent governance will win over new conservatives and reduce the ill effects of migration from the blue states.

Of course, compromise is a defining feature of American politics, and it is necessary for a functioning republic. But moving toward the squishy middle when it's not absolutely necessary will only backfire on Republicans. Expanding programs like Obamacare is not the answer to conservatives' electoral problems in states that are becoming purple. Under Mike Pence, Indiana refused to expand Medicaid and instead got a federal waiver to create a system of health flex accounts that individuals pay into to receive better coverage.[2] As a result, the state saw the number of uninsured citizens fall, while holding overall costs down. The system worked so well that the Trump administration implemented a national waiver system for states, dubbed Section 1115—with seventy-one waivers implemented or pending to date.[3] The system isn't perfect, but it puts more control in the hands of states rather than the federal bureaucracy, and sixteen states have implemented (or will soon) work requirements for the program.

Remember, Bismarck thought he could contain the influence of the socialists by legally repressing them as he repressed the Catholics in the culture war, and it didn't work. But neither did adopting their agenda in a vain attempt to steal their thunder. Ironically, today the arch-monarchist and staunch conservative "Iron Chancellor" is remembered as the founder of the modern welfare state. He gave the proverbial mouse a cookie, and his people got to pay for the glass of milk.

The Counter-Colonizers

While many families pack their bags in blue states and head for Texas or Wisconsin just for a lower cost of living and a lighter tax burden, there are also people who leave states like California or New York specifically because they recognize the devastation of their states' progressive economic policies. And in addition to these folks moving to red states to embrace their conservatism, there are also larger efforts afoot to preserve the unique characteristics of conservative states through intentional mass migration.

As NPR (yes, *that* NPR) reported in 2017, many conservative Californians who feel their state has slipped away are making the trek to Texas. Interestingly, one of the individuals profiled in the NPR article moved with the help of a new company called Conservative Move, formed by Dr. Paul Chabot.[4] Chabot is a lieutenant commander in the Navy Reserve and an Iraq War veteran who was nearly elected to Congress from California's Thirty-First District in 2014. Chabot, who himself moved to Texas from the Golden State in 2016, told NPR, "I jokingly say North Texas out here reminds me of Orange County, California, in the 1980s."[5]

Put simply, not all blue state residents who flee are unaware that liberal policies have slowed economic growth and made opportunities stagnant in their home states; some have a thorough understanding of the reasons they had to leave their former Democratic homes. In some cases, voters who came from California made their new homes even *more* conservative. According to a study by Quartz, right-leaning migrants from California tend to move to conservative locations in Texas, while those who are left-leaning tend to move to progressive locations like Austin.[6] As a result, a portion of the effect of blue state refugees is muted. There is a possibility that at least some of the effects of the waves of ignorant Massachusetts and New York expats will be mitigated by people who vote to maintain the sound policies and conservative traditions of their new homes.

In some parts of the country, we're even seeing a Republican revival as recent arrivals with conservative leanings get involved in local and state politics. A memorable recent example is former Massachusetts senator Scott Brown, who moved to New Hampshire and sought the Senate seat there in 2014; he lost narrowly to Democrat Jeanne Shaheen but likely has a bright political future in the Granite State. Even in Texas, many prominent House members came to the state after adulthood. Texas lieutenant governor Dan Patrick was born and studied in Maryland. Former Florida governor Rick Scott, now representing the Sunshine State in the Senate, was born in Illinois and raised in Missouri before coming to Florida well into his business career. New residents are able to punch above their weight if they take concrete actions to push their new homes in a more conservative direction—motivated by knowledge of what they're escaping from.

Some Sunshine in an Otherwise Cloudy Forecast

While the big story is blue state refugees turning red states purple and even blue, some states are being pushed in the opposite direction by an influx of new conservative-leaning residents. A key swing state—perhaps *the* key swing state—Florida, is home to massive waves of new residents each year. In fact, the state has the second-lowest percentage of residents born in the state; only 64 percent of Floridians were actually born there.[7]

Every year, Florida gains a considerable number of new residents from Puerto Rico. Since Hurricane Maria ravaged the island in 2017, over seventy-five thousand Puerto Ricans have relocated to Florida, where they enjoy full voting rights. The number of Hispanic registered voters in the state has grown at a rate three times faster than the overall number of registered voters there since 2016. Cuban Americans, who have traditionally been Republicans, and half of whom voted for Trump in 2016, have historically dominated the Hispanic vote in Florida elections. But today, Puerto Ricans make up 31 percent of eligible Hispanic voters in Florida—the exact same fraction as Cubans in the state. Although left-wing policies have helped destroy the economy in Puerto Rico, where 40 percent of residents rely on food stamps and the labor participation rate is a pitiful 40 percent, Puerto Ricans have voted for Democrats in overwhelming numbers in Florida elections. In 2016 Hillary Clinton won 72 percent of the Puerto Rican vote.

And still, in spite of the waves of Democratic Puerto Ricans moving to Florida in recent years, the state hasn't veered sharply to the left. In fact, in some ways it has actually moved to the right. That's because there is a high enough number of other new residents who lean conservative moving to Florida every year, and they help mitigate the political effects of left-leaning Puerto Rican voters. Every one of Florida's last six governor's races was won by a Republican (yes, that counts Charlie Crist before his party-reassignment surgery). The state has two Republican senators for the first time since Trump won Florida's electoral votes in 2016—narrowly, though the 116,000-vote margin was significantly larger than George W. Bush's 537-vote lead in 2000. At the statehouse level, Florida's Republican Party is strong. Despite losing seats in the 2018 election, the GOP holds more seats in the state senate (23–17) and house (73–47) than the Democrats. It was just a few decades ago that the Florida state senate was split down the middle 20–20, and the Democrats held a 71–49 margin in the house as recently as 1993. In January 2019, *Politico* reported that the Sunshine State is shifting further red and called it "Trump's state to lose."[8]

There is a strong correlation between retirees moving to Florida and the state's rightward shift. Florida has the highest percentage of residents sixty-five and older in the nation: 19.1 percent. Some local figures are much more dramatic. Sumter County—home of the "Villages" retirement community you've seen commercials for on TV Land—is an astonishing 52.9 percent senior. Four of the top ten counties with the oldest demographics in the nation are in Florida. Number two is Charlotte County, which is almost 38 percent sixty-five and older. Fifty-three of Florida's sixty-seven counties have more seniors than the national average. The statewide percentage of senior citizens is almost 50 percent higher than the national mean.

In the 2018 midterm elections, overall turnout across Florida was 62.6 percent, but it was higher in areas dominated by white retirees, many of whom were originally from other states. In Sumter County, for example, the turnout for white Republican men was an astonishing 80 percent.

And between 2010 and 2030, the share of Florida's population made up of elderly residents is projected to double, reaching nearly five million.[9] As the number of retirees flocking to the state balloons, so does the number of GOP voters in Florida. In 2000, registered Democrats outnumbered Republicans by 373,000.[10] With the sharp increase of retirees entering the state, that Democratic advantage shrank to 228,000 by 2018. People move to Florida mainly to retire, not to escape failing Democratic states in search of work. As a result, the new residents come from all over the country instead of mainly from the coasts and Illinois. A 2017 Census Bureau survey estimated that of the 566,000 new residents the state had gained over the previous year, only about 5 percent (30,000) came from California. More than that were from neighboring Georgia and Texas.[11] That geographic diversity is a real contrast to the throngs of Democrats packing up for Oregon, Colorado, North Carolina, and Texas—and it shows in election results.

An Ounce of Prevention...

There are also movements to try and reduce the negative effects of the invasion of the blue state refugees. Some of these are organized efforts; others, more diffused.

Novelist Wesley Rawles proposed the "American Redoubt": parts of the Mountain West, including Idaho, Montana, and Wyoming, would act as a last-resort colony for libertarian leaners with a prepper vibe. Rawles describes it as effort to "move to completely virgin territory and start afresh" as "pistol-packing Amish."[12] The Redoubt idea has strong undertones of being a refuge in case of economic collapse or even war. The concept was endorsed by the libertarian Constitution Party presidential nominee Chuck Baldwin, who put his money where his mouth was and moved to Montana. While Rawles and Baldwin count the number of Redoubters to be in the four figures, an exact number is hard to pin down. They have been able to elect officials in their libertarian mold—in already deep-red Idaho.

Perhaps the largest effort to move small-government advocates to one condensed area is the Free State Project, which aims to get as many libertarians as possible to move to a single state by providing strong financial incentives. In 2003 the members chose New Hampshire as their destination. Anyone who desires to be part of the project vows to move to the Granite State within five years of the date on which it reached its numerical goal of twenty thousand, and by 2016 that many people had pledged to make the move to New Hampshire thanks to the group's efforts. Ultimately, the Free State Project is attempting to shift the state's politics. Eighteen of its members were elected to the New Hampshire House of Representatives in 2014. The Free State Project has been endorsed by Ron Paul himself[13] and derided on *The Colbert Report*.[14]

A Democratic member of New Hampshire's house, Cynthia Chase, called the Free State Project the "single biggest threat the state is facing today." (Whenever a lefty calls your efforts a "threat," you know you're doing something right.) She added, alarmingly, "What we can do is to make the environment here so unwelcoming that some will choose not to come, and some may actually leave. One way is to pass measures that will restrict the 'freedoms' that they think they will find here." Chase expressed her true feelings, adding that the new residents are not welcome to "steal our state."[15]

Another candidate for the New Hampshire house, Democrat Lucy Edwards, told her supporters a story about a friend who had had a room for rent. Upon learning that one potential tenant was planning to come from Texas to support the Free State Project, the friend lied and said that that the room had already been rented. The friend added, "I didn't appreciate him coming here to change our state government, it was an insult to me. That if he wanted to make change to start self-examining his own life in a mindful way and stay in Texas to make the changes he wants, not come here. And not contact me again."[16] So much hate for twenty thousand libertarians looking for a new home. And this movement really isn't even looking to make New Hampshire a new political landscape, but instead to preserve its legacy. The Free Staters don't want to transform the Live Free or Die state but to keep New Hampshire true to its freedom-loving character. They are essentially just serving as a counterbalance to the thousands of new residents coming to the state from Massachusetts each year. Nevertheless, the Democrats are not taking it well. In response to the wave of small-government "extremists," the Concord Police Department applied for over a quarter million dollars in federal Homeland Security funding for an armored car, claiming that, among other groups, "Free Staters...are active and present daily challenges"[17]

The leftist magazine *Mother Jones* encapsulated this sentiment in its exposé of the Free State Project's "plot" to "take over New Hampshire." Among the nefarious schemes of this small band of emigrants? Getting elected to the local school board and using tax dollars for school vouchers for eligible students, installing ATMs that accept Bitcoin, protesting against a ban on Uber rideshare services, and supporting marijuana legalization.[18] These ideas might not align with the political beliefs of every person in New Hampshire, but they surely fit the state's ethos as the "Live Free or Die" state.

The libertarians of the Free State Project intuited this book's thesis before it hit the shelves. Massachusetts residents moving to New Hampshire make up the largest share of domestic migrants coming to the Granite State.[19] That trend is so significant that NPR gave New Hampshire the nickname "low-cost Massachusetts."[20]

Even if the Free State Project fully succeeds in its goal, the libertarian in-migrants will represent something like 2 percent of the state's adult population. Still, considering that the 2016 presidential election outcome in New Hampshire was decided by just under four thousand votes (0.37 percent), it's easy to understand why the state's Democratic leaders are panicking. If you want to know "What can I do?" to stop the blue wave sweeping the nation, you could do a lot worse than looking up real estate values in Nashua or Keene.

Our Secret Weapon: The Melting Pot

One of the most powerful tools to save states—and thus the fate of the nation as a whole—from colonization by our blue state betters is actually already in our hands. There's ample evidence that millennials and the following Generation Z will increasingly begin to vote conservative as they come of age. Forces similar to those that turned so many of the former hippies and poseurs of the 1960s into Reaganites less than two decades later will shift many of these liberals into moderates or conservatives. A combination of maturing millennials and immigrants turning towards the GOP may blunt some of the demographic changes of the twenty-first century.

Some patterns have dominated American politics for the last fifty years and will continue into the future. The steps traditionally associated with passage into adulthood shift voters significantly to the right: having children, getting married, and owning a house. As most millennials check one or all of these boxes, they will very likely follow the same trend.

The nation's 73 million millennials will soon outnumber the baby boomers.[21] Members of this young generation have delayed adult responsibilities, and they vote like it. A full 59 percent of millennials are single and have never been married, and 60 percent do not have any children.[22] The average age of marriage has shifted towards the late twenties for both men and women, and one in six married couples now has no children. These trends have significant political effects: in the 2016 election, Donald Trump carried 52 percent of married voters, compared to Hillary Clinton's 44 percent. Among unmarried voters, it was the opposite—55 percent for Clinton and only 37 percent for Trump. Add in the "gender gap," and you see an even more striking contrast: married men supported Trump by a 56–37 percent difference, while unmarried men went for Clinton 51–41—a 29 percent difference. Both married and unmarried women backed Hillary, but at 53–41 and 65–28 percent respectively—a 15 percent difference.[23]

Unmarried women made up an astonishing 34 million voters—or 26 percent—of the 2016 electorate.[24] If even *half* of the unmarried millennials marry and start voting like their currently married fellow citizens,

Democrats will be in deep trouble. Millennial women's votes would go from 22.1 million for Clinton and 9.5 million for Trump (a formidable 12.6 million advantage) to 20 million for Democrats and 11.7 million for Republicans (a significantly smaller 8.3 million–vote advantage). This one *likely* change would *completely wipe out Hillary's popular vote victory.* Of course, all of this assumes nothing shifts among men or other demographic groups.

The blue wave rests on a once-in-a-generation moment; the Democrats are benefiting from the fact that the millennials have reached voting age but haven't yet taken on many of the responsibilities of adulthood. Similarly, LBJ's massive victory in 1964 can be partially attributed to the fact that it was the first presidential election the baby boomers could vote in; the Democrats went on to lose five of the next six presidential elections.

Millennials are already voting Republican in increasing numbers. While the majority of young people still vote Democrat, there is reduced support for the party with each successive election. A Reuters-Ipsos poll found that only 46 percent of millennials supported the Democratic Party in 2018, down from 55 percent in 2016.[25] Interestingly, despite the media narrative after the Parkland shooting, young people are actually the generation least likely to support gun control. A 2015 Pew poll showed that while 57 percent of American adults supported banning all "assault weapons," only 49 percent of adults ages 18–29 did (compared to 63 percent of people over sixty-five).[26] A Gallup survey the same year found that while 56 percent of Americans believed concealed-carry rights made the country safer, a whopping 66 percent of young people agreed—by far the highest of any age bracket.[27] Furthermore, young people are more likely to self-identify as moderates or conservatives than members of Generation X or the baby boomers were at the same age.[28]

While after Watergate the Democrats seemed to be poised to sweep out the Republicans, there were zero leftist presidents from 1968 to 2008. Why didn't the great Democratic wave continue after 1964? The short answer is that the baby boomers grew up. Millennials may be a different breed, but they are likely to follow in the footsteps of previous generations, as twenty-two-year-old baristas and out-of-work graphic designers become adults with the full trappings of engaged citizens.

So the Democrats' assumption that they have a permanent lock on the millennial vote could be a big mistake. And another could be taking the votes of immigrants for granted. In fact, Democrats and Republicans could both be wrong about the political implications of immigration.

Large waves of immigration from foreign nations have Republicans lamenting that the new immigrants will vote for Democrats ad infinitum, but history shows that that is not always the case.

In the late nineteenth and early twentieth centuries, for example, many feared that Irish and Italian immigrants would skew American culture and politics. These migrants were often poorer than other immigrant groups and overwhelmingly Roman Catholic—in a mostly Protestant nation. Anti-immigrant sentiment obscured the fact that these families, in search of a better life for their children and grandchildren, were eager to adapt to American ways. No *Kulturkampf*, like the one Bismarck tried, was necessary to bring these new Americans into the wider national culture—the melting pot did it instead.

The first generations of Irish and Italians voted overwhelmingly for the Democratic Party. Then, as now, the Democrats had a strong hold on large cities like Boston and New York—the very places that many immigrants were moving to. And with their iron grip on the segregated South, Democrats appeared likely to triumph for the foreseeable future. Immigrants and their children helped elect FDR and Truman in five consecutive presidential elections.

There was a significant worry that Irish and Italian Americans would continue to vote for Democrats. But these fears turned out to be misplaced. A different country of origin and a different religion from those of the majority of the population were of little consequence several generations in. States that had been dominated by the newcomers, like Massachusetts and New York, started trending Republican. Between 1952 and 1970, Republicans won five of six governor's races in New York and six of nine in Massachusetts (the state had a two-year gubernatorial term for part of this period). When the immigrants assimilated and their children and grandchildren moved out of the major cities, they became more conservative.

Republicans need to throw out the notion that immigrants, especially those from Latin America, will automatically vote for Democrats forever. Today, Latin Americans may not vote for Republicans in the high percentages that Cubans fleeing Fidel Castro's regime did in the 1950s and 1960s. But the fact that about 40 percent of Texans of Mexican descent vote GOP and that Puerto Rican voters put Rick Scott over the top in 2018 is nothing to scoff at. Add in the new diaspora of Venezuelans fleeing socialism, and it's easy to see that these fears are exaggerated.

Assimilation won't solve every issue—there will, of course, always be migrants (both domestic and foreign) who don't see the irony of voting for the very policies they fled. Case in point: many new Austinites don't want oil drilling in the state of Texas—even though a drilling ban amounts to biting the hand that feeds. Similarly, there are waves of new Coloradans who don't care about marginal tax rates as long as the ski slopes stay open. Many upper-middle- and upper-class blue staters moving to Texas or Georgia will simply keep voting to raise taxes or restrict oil drilling because they do not see the widespread effects of these policies. These folks ought to do some thinking about the reasons they left behind their original blue state homes and moved to red states in the first place. But we have to accept that many of these true believers will not change their minds.

But don't lose hope—there is good reason to think that future generations and new immigrants will self-integrate into the wider political center and right. This outcome will likely take some time (and perhaps be too late to keep Texas red). But there is a light at the end of the tunnel, and it's not just an oncoming train.

The Movers Who Made the Reagan Majority

Despite the distressing near-term effects of our continuing domestic migration, it is worth remembering that the last similar wave in

American history eventually gave rise to the Reagan Revolution. Although it is by no means assured, it is likely that electoral results over the next several cycles will resemble the post–World War II political roller coaster.

The voters of the Greatest Generation were far less conservative than their parents, and there was a real possibility that their votes would maintain the Democrats' stranglehold indefinitely. After all, many of these veterans were union workers and had voted for Roosevelt and Truman. But a shot at the American dream created a core of these voters who would reliably elect conservatives for the next two generations.

The exodus from urban areas, which was massive and continued well into the next generation, was highly significant in electoral politics. A variety of factors contributed to the move. Saved-up military and industrial salaries from during the war, when families had been unable to spend this accumulated wealth because of rationing and service, were a major factor. Furthermore, the G.I. Bill offered a host of incentives for homeownership and education. Many of these families moved from major urban centers and industrial cities like New York and Chicago either to suburbs within driving distance of the cities or to new pastures in Western states, especially California. Cash savings and the G.I. Bill, lack of restrictions on housing construction, and new prefab construction techniques caused a housing boom in the millions (think the cookie-cutter homes in Levittown). The number of suburbanites tripled, to over 37 percent of the nation's population.[29]

One clear winner of the postwar flight from the big cities was California. The Golden State's population increased by an astonishing 53 percent from 1940 to 1950; between 1940 and 1980 it quadrupled to 23 million. During this era California became the trendsetter of the nation. It surpassed New York in population as the nation's largest state. It also became a key GOP bastion. Except for 1964, California voted for Republican presidential candidates every year from 1952 to 1988, and it brought Ronald Reagan and Richard Nixon to the national stage.

The baby boom generation took a radical leftward turn, but conservatives remained ascendant in the postwar years. There were several key reasons:

- Increased homeownership correlates closely with voting for right-wing candidates. Between 1945 and the 1960s, the number of homeowners increased by 50 percent nationwide.
- The leftward drift of the Democratic Party starting in the 1960s and the radicalism of young people pushed many traditional Democrats into the Republican camp, as I'll outline below.
- The Republicans, in contrast, won the electorate over with effective state governance. In California, for example, with the exceptions of father and son Pat and Jerry Brown, Republicans won every governor's race between 1942 and 1994.
- The material prosperity of the nation, beginning with the postwar boom, tracked closely with Republican success in presidential elections. The GOP won seven of ten races between 1952 and 1988.
- As voters moved from the cities to the suburbs, they lost enthusiasm for the Democratic Party and stopped voting like city dwellers. Suburban politics are typically red. Take Orange County, California—*all* of whose Republican members of Congress lost in 2018. Not so long ago, it was the most conservative large county in the state, and one of the most conservative in the nation. In 1966 Orange County voted 72 percent for Reagan for governor and went for the Republicans in all but one of the gubernatorial races during the Cold War period.

So there's a saving grace in the fact that many young people—more than are headed to concentrated urban centers like Brooklyn and San

Francisco—are migrating to decentralized, sprawling areas. As the greater San Antonio and Denver areas see large population increases, former frustrated renters in high-price cities will now be homeowners who vote more conservatively.

The Reagan Revolution was due to a number of factors beyond simple demography. But the shift of moving feet in the preceding decades was a necessary condition for Reagan's victory in 1980. Many returning World War II veterans had cast their first ballots for Franklin Roosevelt—just like Reagan himself. But as they settled in their new Cape Cods with white picket fences, they realized their stake in the traditional American republic. And while at one point it seemed inevitable that their kids—the dreaded baby boomers—would push our nation leftward, they too got married, had kids, bought homes in the suburbs, and continued to elect conservative presidents.

Thank God. And thank the Greatest Generation.

Still the Shining City on the Hill

The waves of people leaving blue states will be a distinct political, economic, and social challenge not just for the receiving states and rural areas but for the nation's politics as a whole. Most likely, the coming debates about bailing out states that are up to their eyeballs in pension debt will be among the most vicious in the nation's history.

But the blue diaspora is a major challenge that you can help solve. The very fact that you're interested enough in the topic of demographic destiny to pick up this book is a step in the right direction.

The clue to the solution lies in our not-too-distant political past.

Consider the political trajectory of the 1960s and 1970s. Law-and-order candidate Richard Nixon followed nearly a decade of Democratic ascendancy and liberal attempts to remake the social order. Donald Trump's legacy is far from written, but in many ways his presidency has tracked closely with Nixon's—in all of the *good* ways. Both men were elected on similar platforms in similar circumstances. In both instances, there was hunger for a staunch conservative in the White House after years of a liberal administration pushing its radical agenda down the throats of rural America.

The Democratic Party went from landslide victory in the 1964 election to increasing irrelevance—almost falling apart in the process. At one point in the '60s a coalition of anti-war protesters, feminists, and environmental radicals appeared to be nearly unstoppable, but the long-term result was twelve years of Reagan-Bush and the triangulating, quasi-centrist Bill Clinton.

Since then, national politics has trended back in the opposite direction. Since Barack Obama was first elected in 2008, his Democratic Party has moved ever leftward. But while the Democrats tend to make every issue a national issue and an ideological litmus test, the Republicans have the edge in local politics. GOP candidates tend to be better than Democrats at tailoring their messages and goals to the specific district in question. GOP politicians often gear their messages towards local concerns and needs, which blends well with their fiscal conservatism at the national level.

The Democrats have become a party of enclaves—the big cities, the "Left Coast," and the Mid-Atlantic region, which benefits so heavily from the federal government. If out-migrants from those enclaves can turn red states like Georgia and Texas blue—and we have seen how close they are coming—the Democrats will win on the national stage for the foreseeable future.

It will benefit the Democratic Party greatly if they nominate candidates who appeal to the spirit and character of their states; they stand a real chance in even the most conservative places. We have seen how Beto O'Rourke's 2018 Senate run was a left-wing campaign with a genuine Texas twist—which came very close to succeeding. Exit poll data show that while Cruz lived there for over ten years and won Texas by a convincing 63–36 percent margin, O'Rourke actually led 51–48 percent among native-born Texans.[30] If Democrats return to a more local-based strategy across the fifty states, they have a chance of winning among both expats and from-birth residents. Buyer beware: the O'Rourke example may actually translate quite well into other conservative states. Call it the reverse Scott Brown effect.

Now think back to the legislative massacre that happened during Obama's presidency. Republican commentators loved to point out that from the Democrats' 2009 peak until the end of the Obama White House, the Democrats lost over a thousand legislative seats at the state and federal level. This is because Democrats mostly nationalized those races, while the GOP ran impressive state-by-state campaigns.

That's how the GOP is able to win consistently at the state level, with all of the ancillary perks this brings: setting state-level economic policies, controlling redistricting, and preventing budget crises. Scott Walker may have lost in 2018, but he had already been able to transform Wisconsin into a leaner, more competitive Midwest economy. Rinse and repeat across most of the country. But continued Republican success on these lines depends on Democrats not learning from their mistakes. And even the Democrats learned not to renominate Michael Dukakis again. If they have learned from O'Rourke's success to run candidates with local appeal, and if the GOP in traditionally red states doesn't adapt to the coming waves of migrants from blue ones, the electoral map will shift in the Democrats' favor.

On the other hand, the Democrats' ideological inflexibility will likely lead the party further and further to the left. Two congressional and thirty-eight state and local candidates endorsed by Democratic Socialist Party (DSA) chapters won in the 2018 midterms.[31] This represented a majority of the DSA-endorsed candidates (of which there were seventy in total) and included two high-profile House races: Alexandria Ocasio-Cortez in New York and Rashida Tlaib in Michigan. Others included state representatives in New York, Pennsylvania, Maine, and Maryland. A full Democratic Socialist takeover of the Democratic Party may not be in the cards, but the insurgent campaign of socialist Bernie Sanders, not to mention the avowed socialists sent to Congress from major cities, shows that this is a real possibility. Still, as of 2018, only 37 percent of

Americans view socialism positively (that number is actually down slightly from 2012)[32]—meaning that a hard lurch to the left is still incompatible with the broader American electorate.

Democratic politicians will likely face increasingly withering purity tests that will drive candidates well out of the American mainstream. Fifty-seven percent of Democrats view socialism positively (just 47 percent say the same about capitalism). And the centralized organization of the Democratic Party will likely mean that candidates for local office will be far to the left of their constituents—and that outside of wave elections, Democrats will have trouble capturing the laboratories of democracy, even if they capture the White House or Congress.

Cognitive dissonance will eventually push the party to a breaking point—perhaps not a great schism or even a series of pitched presidential primaries, but instead a pullback like the one after Reagan-Bush, when Bill Clinton became the first Democrat in a generation to win the presidency by running as a moderate conservative. Many Americans are fiscal conservatives and social liberals. These citizens will likely not vote for the crazy ideas that dominate today's college campuses. They will not support a party with no plan to pay for Social Security or Medicare benefits after their respective trust funds dry up. They're not going to be eager to bail out the blue states and blue cities whose economies have been wrecked by liberal policies—and by mid-century there will likely be a moment of clarity when Americans see fiscal collapses or bailouts for Democrat-dominated states and prosperity for states in Republican hands.

Conscious political choices were to blame for the fact that the Left never had its shining moment in the 1970s and 1980s. The Democrats made a sharp and disastrous turn to the left in 1972 with George McGovern—and they look set to make a similar mistake in 2020. Left-wing incompetence and repeated purity tests—as in the 1980 Kennedy-Carter primary—tore the party apart. And the media were astonished when the libertarian-leaning conservative Ronald Reagan won the presidency. The Democratic Party's increasingly extreme leftism was a bridge too far for most Americans, and the Democrats were left in the political wilderness for a dozen years.

But there are no permanent majorities in American politics. Even three consecutive terms of single-party control of the presidency happened just three times in the twentieth century. The seismic shift of Democrats moving to purple and red states will likely lead to painful surprises for Republicans—including the likelihood that Texas and Georgia will be swing states in the 2020s or 2030s.

This book is a warning. And many of the projections I have laid out are already coming to pass. The 2020 election will see many of the factors we have discussed in play. Fundamental shifts from red to purple and possibly to blue are already taking place in Virginia, North Carolina, Colorado, and elsewhere. But conservatism isn't on its deathbed. Far from it. Government overreach and blue state bankruptcies will lead many voters to see the Democrats as the party of financial irresponsibility. The nation currently has a large bubble of young people who will moderate their views just as their parents and grandparents did.

We're in for a bumpy ride, and there is a chance that the 2020s and 2030s will take the country substantially to the left. But remember, New York City finally elected a Giuliani and the country finally elected a Reagan. Many blue state refugees left their former homes when they saw that living in their original homes just wasn't working, given the realities of dollars and cents. But they brought their political leanings with them. When, however, this population realizes that high-tax regimes hurt their bottom line or that environmental regulations threaten their new state's economic lifeblood or that restrictions on new construction make housing unaffordable, the light bulb will turn on.

Save your time arguing with your millennial cousin at the Thanksgiving table. Use it instead to volunteer in a local campaign. Help a Republican or libertarian candidate explain to your new Prius-driving neighbors why they decided to call Colorado or North Carolina home.

It's all of our jobs to make sure that our homes remain the great places they have been and to protect their culture and economic vitality for the next generations. More than fifty years ago now, during his famous "A Time for Choosing" speech in 1964, Ronald Reagan told the assembled crowd that there is no place else for us to go if freedom is overrun in our homes. Thus, it falls on our shoulders to preserve what we can while rolling back the excesses of the irresponsible and destructive Left.

What can you do? Readying your 401(k) or pension plan for your golden years? Not only do Florida and Texas have warm weather and no income taxes, you'll be going to the front lines of the battle that could decide our country's future. Tired of your local town, city, or county raising taxes? Consider a run for office. If your small business is being crushed by California's economic climate, ask yourself why you haven't packed up and moved to Tennessee or Utah. Lend this book to a friend or neighbor. Drop an extra copy off at the library or recommend it to your book club. Every one of these actions will help move your town, your city, and, heck, even your country in the right direction.

Just as the individual raindrop never sees itself as the flood, many blue state refugees just don't realize what they're doing to their new states. But you have the power right now to be one of the drops that turns the tide in the other direction.

Giving in is a choice. Decline is a choice. Abandoning your state's traditions and history is a distinct and dangerous choice that will only accelerate the political damage from the demographic changes. *You* are the one leaving a legacy for the future of your hometown and state, from taxes to policy to culture. *You* are the biggest obstacle to radical change. *You* can be that Goldwater delegate watching with your mouth agape as Reagan gives his speech—and hopping on board for the wild ride from political decimation to conservative triumph in just twelve years.

This is your Time for Choosing.

Acknowledgments

I would like to thank Ronald Goldfarb for steadfast support and advocacy over the years. James Finkelstein and my editors at *The Hill*, Frank Craig and Anjelica Tan, have encouraged my research interests and provided me with a platform to engage in national debates on vital matters. Several arguments first developed in my column for *The Hill* served as foundations for parts of this book. I wish to thank Cliff Maloney and Sean Themea for involving me in the Young Americans for Liberty family. Their work is creating a freer and more prosperous future for our country. M.W.A., a gifted researcher, contributed insights and analysis for this book. I must also express my gratitude to Thomas Cooper, whose long-standing mentorship and friendship I hold dear. Kevin McCullough has been a constant ally and source of valuable advice in the right-of-center media space. The extraordinary team at Regnery Publishing provided me with a special opportunity to investigate and develop the important topics covered in this book. Elizabeth Kantor of Regnery deployed exceptional editing skills to sharpen the work's message. I am eternally grateful to my parents for their ongoing support.

Notes

Chapter One: The Decline and Fall of the Blue States

1. "10 Most Expensive Cities in America," CBS News, https://www.cbsnews.com/pictures/10-most-expensive-cities-in-america/2/.
2. Eric Goldschein, "The Most Dangerous Neighborhoods in New York," Business Insider, September 8, 2011, https://www.businessinsider.com/most-dangerous-neighborhoods-in-new-york-2011-9.
3. Tom Wilson, "20 Years of Cleaning Up NYC Pissed Away," *New York Post*, July 10, 2015, https://nypost.com/2015/07/10/apparently-its-now-ok-to-pee-on-the-streets-of-new-york-city/.
4. Rebecca Klein, "Reports of the 'Worst School' in NYC Will Make You Very, Very Depressed (Update)," HuffPost, updated January 25, 2014, https://www.huffingtonpost.com/2014/01/13/ps-106-worst-school_n_4591569.html.
5. Johnny Knocke, "The MTA Loses Six Billion Dollars a Year and Nobody Cares," Medium, July 6, 2016, https://medium.com/@johnnyknocke/the-mta-loses-six-billion-dollars-a-year-and-nobody-cares-d0d23093b2d8.
6. Aaron Short, "People Are Fleeing New York at an Alarming Rate," *New York Post*, April 1, 2017, https://nypost.com/2017/04/01/people-are-fleeing-new-york-at-an-alarming-rate/.
7. Jonathan Williams, "Americans Continue Their March to Low-Tax States," *The Hill*, February 12, 2019, https://thehill.com/opinion/finance/429623-americans-continue-their-march-to-low-tax-states.
8. Carl Campanile, "New York's Economy Is Sputtering," *New York Post*, May 11, 2017, https://nypost.com/2017/05/11/new-yorks-economy-is-sputtering/.
9. Williams, "Americans Continue Their March."
10. Luis Gomez, "Leaving California: Here's Who's Moving Out, Who's Moving In," *San Diego Union-Tribune*, February 22, 2018, https://www.sandiegouniontribune.com/opinion/the-conversation/sd-california-losing-low-income-people-gaining-wealthy-people-per-report-20180221-htmlstory.html.
11. Dom Calicchio, "Texas, Florida See Big Population Gains, While New York, Illinois See Big Losses, Census Bureau Data Show," Fox News, January 2, 2019, https://www.foxnews.com/us/texas-florida-see-big-population-gains-while-new-york-illinois-see-big-losses-census-bureau-data-show.
12. Gordon Dickson, "Texas Adds the Equivalent of Another Arlington to Its Population," *Fort Worth Star-Telegram*, December 20, 2017, https://www.star-telegram.com/news/business/growth/article190750684.html.

13. Chuck DeVore, "New Yorkers and Californians Can't Stop Moving to Texas," *Washington Examiner*, May 30, 2018, https://www.washingtonexaminer.com/opinion/new-yorkers-and-californians-cant-stop-moving-to-texas.

14. Simone Foxman, Patrick Clark, and Sridhar Natarajan, "Tax-Hike Fears Trigger Talk of Exodus from Manhattan and Greenwich," Bloomberg, November 27, 2017, https://www.bloomberg.com/news/articles/2017-11-27/in-greenwich-and-manhattan-tax-hike-fears-fuel-talk-of-exodus.

15. Walter Hamilton, "One in Every 25 New Yorkers Is a Millionaire, Study Says," *Los Angeles Times*, July 22, 2014, https://www.latimes.com/business/la-fi-one-in-every-25-new-yorkers-is-a-millionaire-study-says-20140722-story.html.

16. Julie Satow, "Minimizing the Pain of Trump's Tax Law," *New York Times*, August 24, 2018, https://www.nytimes.com/2018/08/24/realestate/minimizing-the-pain-of-trumps-tax-law.html.

17. John Nolte, "Nolte: Andrew Cuomo Now Blames Florida for $2.3B Budget Shortfall," Breitbart, February 13, 2019, https://www.breitbart.com/politics/2019/02/13/andrew-cuomo-blames-florida-2-3b-budget-shortfall/.

18. Foxman, Clark, and Natarajan, "Tax-Hike Fears."

19. Charles Lane, "A Democrat Is Proposing a Dubious Tax Idea—And It's Not Alexandria Ocasio-Cortez," *Washington Post*, January 7, 2019, https://www.washingtonpost.com/opinions/alexandria-ocasio-cortezs-tax-idea-is-big-and-bold—but-not-that-radical/2019/01/07/1c01dce2-1299-11e9-803c-4ef28312c8b9_story.html.

20. "T18-0140–Repeal $10,000 Limit on Deductible State and Local Taxes; Baseline: Current Law; Distribution of Federal Tax Change by Expanded Cash Income Percentile, 2018," Tax Policy Center, Urban Institute & Brookings Institution, September 24, 2018, https://www.taxpolicycenter.org/model-estimates/repeal-10000-state-and-local-tax-salt-deduction-limitation-sep-2018/t18-0140-repeal.

21. Adam Ashton, "Wealthy Exodus to Escape New Tax Rules Worries California Democrats," *Sacramento Bee*, January 18, 2018, https://www.sacbee.com/news/politics-government/capitol-alert/article195405279.html.

22. Andy Kiersz, "Here's How Each US State's Population Changed between 2016 and 2017 Because of People Moving In and Out," Business Insider, January 12, 2018, https://www.businessinsider.com/state-domestic-migration-map-2016-to-2017-2018-1.

23. Bob Woods, "Another Fleeing Corporate Giant: Connecticut Is Facing a Business Migration Crisis," America's Top States for Business, CNBC, July 11, 2017, https://www.cnbc.com/2017/07/11/connecticut-is-facing-a-corporate-migration-crisis.html.

24. Woods, "Another Fleeing Corporate Giant."

25. James Freeman, "'My Clients Are Fleeing NJ Like It's on Fire,'" *Wall Street Journal*, May 2, 2018, https://www.wsj.com/articles/my-clients-are-fleeing-nj-like-its-on-fire-1525289556.

26. Robert Frank, "One Top Taxpayer Moved, and New Jersey Shuddered," *New York Times*, April 30, 2016, https://www.nytimes.com/2016/05/01/business/one-top-taxpayer-moved-and-new-jersey-shuddered.html.

27. Travis H. Brown, "New Jersey's Revenue Instability Exposed by David Tepper's Move to Florida," *Forbes*, April 18, 2016, https://www.forbes.com/sites/travisbrown/2016/04/18/new-jerseys-revenue-instability-exposed-by-david-teppers-move-to-florida/.

28. Noah Cohen, "N.J.'s Richest Man until He Fled for Lower Taxes, Trump Critic David Tepper Buying Panthers," NJ.com, May 16, 2018, https://www.nj.com/essex/2018/05/njs_richest_man_until_he_fled_for_lower_taxes_trump_critic_david_tepper_buying_panthers.html.

29. Ashlea Ebeling, "New Jersey Hikes Taxes on High Earners and Curbs Loophole," *Forbes*, July 13, 2018, https://www.forbes.com/sites/ashleaebeling/2018/07/13/new-jersey-hikes-taxes-on-high-earners-and-curbs-loophole/.

30. Richard Florida, "Do Taxes Really Cause the Rich to Move?" CityLab, June 29, 2016, https://www.citylab.com/equity/2016/06/do-taxes-really-cause-the-rich-to-move/487835/.

31. Jim Miller, "Almost Half of California 2014 Income Taxes Paid by Top 1 Percent," *Sacramento Bee*, April 27, 2016, https://www.sacbee.com/news/politics-government/capitol-alert/article74271532.html.

32. George Skelton, "When It Comes to Paying Taxes, California Is Bernie Sanders' Kind of State," *Los Angeles Times*, May 2, 2016, https://www.latimes.com/politics/la-pol-sac-skelton-bernie-sanders-tax-revenue-20160502-story.html.

33. John Myers and Liam Dillon, "Gov. Jerry Brown Offers Part of a Historic Budget Bonanza to Help Ease California's Homelessness Crisis," *Los Angeles Times*, May 11, 2018, https://www.latimes.com/politics/la-pol-ca-jerry-brown-may-budget-proposal-20180511-story.html.

34. "Announcement: Moody's: Fiscal Test of Most Populous States Show Texas Best Prepared for Next Recession, California Least Ready," Moody's Investors Service, April 21, 2016, https://www.moodys.com/research/Moodys-Fiscal-test-of-most-populous-states-show-Texas-best--PR_347649.

35. Joel B. Pollak, "Majority of California Residents Want to Leave: Poll," Breitbart, February 14, 2019, https://www.breitbart.com/politics/2019/02/14/majority-of-california-residents-want-to-leave-poll/.

36. "States with Most Government Employees: Totals and Per Capita Rates," Governing.com, February 15, 2019, www.governing.com/gov-data/public-workforce-salaries/states-most-government-workers-public-employees-by-job-type.html.

37. Kimberly Leonard, "California Democrats Plan to Extend Medicaid to Illegal Immigrants," *Washington Examiner*, December 3, 2018, https://www.washingtonexaminer.com/policy/healthcare/california-democrats-plan-to-extend-medicaid-to-illegal-immigrants.

38. David Crane, "Government Debt Growth in California," Medium, June 27, 2018, https://medium.com/@DavidGCrane/government-debt-growth-in-california-5896f939051b.

39. Jeff Desjardins, "How Each US State's Economy Measures Up to Countries around the World," Business Insider, June 2, 2018, https://www.businessinsider.com/how-each-us-states-economy-measures-up-to-countries-around-the-world-2018-5.

40. "California's State Budget: The Governor's Proposal," Public Policy Institute of California, 2019, https://www.ppic.org/publication/californias-state-budget/.

41. Laura Waxmann, "SF Voters Approve Parcel Tax Upping Teacher Pay," *San Francisco Examiner*, June 6, 2018, http://www.sfexaminer.com/sf-voters-approve-parcel-tax-upping-teacher-pay/.

42. Jerry Nickelsburg, "The Unintended Consequences of Extending Proposition 30: The Initiative that Helped Solve California's Budget Crisis Could Now Create a New One," Zocalo Public Square, November 18, 2015, http://www.zocalopublicsquare.org/2015/11/18/the-unintended-consequences-of-extending-proposition-30/ideas/nexus/.

43. Brian Overstreet, "California to Hit Startup Founders with Big Retroactive Tax Bills," Xconomy, January 15, 2013, https://xconomy.com/san-francisco/2013/01/15/california-to-hit-startup-founders-with-big-retroactive-tax-bills/.

44. Wendy McElroy, "California: Remember the Taxes You Didn't Owe? Surprise!" Explore Freedom, The Future of Freedom Foundation, February 27, 2013, https://www.fff.org/explore-freedom/article/california-remember-the-taxes-you-didnt-owe-surprise/.

45. Robert W. Wood, "IRS Can Audit 3 or 6 Years, but California Can Audit Forever," *Forbes*, October 18, 2016, https://www.forbes.com/sites/robertwood/2016/10/18/irs-can-audit-3-or-6-years-but-california-can-audit-forever/.

46. Wade Roush, "The Surreal, Ironic Story Behind California's Retroactive Tax on Small Business Investors," Xconomy, January 24, 2013, https://xconomy.com/san-francisco/2013/01/24/the-surreal-ironic-story-behind-californias-retroactive-tax-on-investors/.

47. "Editorial: Connecticut's Money Is Moving Out," *Hartford Courant*, January 3, 2018, https://www.courant.com/opinion/editorials/hc-ed-tax-migration-0102-20180102-story.html.

48. Joe Cutter, "Study Finds Residents Leaving NJ—And Taking Their Money with Them," New Jersey 101.5, October 19, 2016, http://nj1015.com/study-finds-residents-leaving-nj-and-taking-their-money-with-them/.

49. Seth Augenstein, "Millionaire Households Fleeing N.J. by the Thousands, Study Says," NJ.com, January 21, 2015, https://www.nj.com/news/index.ssf/2015/01/10000_millionaire_households_fled_nj_last_year_study_says.html.

50. Michael Lucci, "IRS Migration Data Show Wealth and Youth Are Fleeing Illinois," Illinois Policy, November 3, 2016, https://www.illinoispolicy.org/new-2014-irs-migration-data-show-wealth-and-youth-are-fleeing-illinois/.

51. Jeffrey J. Selingo, "States' Decision to Reduce Support for Higher Education Comes at a Cost," *Grade Point* (blog), *Washington Post*, September 8, 2018, https://www.washingtonpost.com/education/2018/09/08/states-decision-reduce-support-higher-education-comes-cost/.

52. California Health Care Foundation, *California Health Care Almanac: Medi-Cal Facts and Figures*, September 2009, https://www.chcf.org/wp-content/uploads/2017/12/PDF-MediCalFactsAndFigures2009.pdf.

53. California Health Care Foundation, "Medi-Cal Facts and Figures: California Health Care Almanac Quick Reference Guide," December 2017, https://www. chcf.org/wp-content/uploads/2013/05/MediCalFactsFigures2017.pdf.

54. Sammy Caiola, "Emergency Room Visits, Wait Times on the Rise in California," Capital Public Radio, August 9, 2018, http://www.capradio.org/articles/2018/08/09/emergency-room-visits-wait-times-on-the-rise-in-california/.

55. Benjamin Elisha Sawe, "US States by Medicaid Enrollment," WorldAtlas, updated August 1, 2017, https://www.worldatlas.com/articles/us-states-by-medicaid-enrollment.html.

56. "Medicaid's Share of State Budgets," Medicaid and CHIP Payment and Access Commission, https://www.macpac.gov/subtopic/medicaids-share-of-state-budgets/.

57. National Association of State Budget Officers, *State Expenditure Report: Examining Fiscal 2015–2017 State Spending*, 2017, https://higherlogic download.s3.amazonaws.com/NASBO/9d2d2db1-c943-4f1b-b750-0fca152d64c2/UploadedImages/SER%20Archive/State_Expenditure_Report__Fiscal_2015-2017_-S.pdf.

58. Myers and Dillon, "Gov. Jerry Brown."

59. Jack Dolan, "UC Is Handing out Generous Pensions, and Students Are Paying the Price with Higher Tuition," *Los Angeles Times*, September 24, 2017, https://www.latimes.com/local/lanow/la-me-uc-pensions-20170924-story.html.

60. Marc Joffe, "UC Compensation Is out of Control," *Record Searchlight*, May 3, 2017, https://www.redding.com/story/opinion/columnists/2017/05/03/uc-compensation-out-control/101247370/.

61. Marc Joffe, "25 UC Retirees Receive Annual Pensions Exceeding $300,000," California Policy Center, May 3, 2017, https://californiapolicycenter. org/25-uc-retirees-receive-annual-pensions-exceeding-300000/.

62. Marc Joffe, "Convicted or Not, L.A. Sheriff Baca Will Collect a Big Pension," California Policy Center, January 17, 2017, https://californiapolicycenter.org/convicted-not-l-sheriff-baca-will-collect-big-pension/.

63. Caitlin Chen, "California Unions Win Another Pension Lawsuit. Will Their Streak Continue?" *The State Worker* (blog), *Sacramento Bee*, August 7, 2018, https://www.sacbee.com/news/politics-government/the-state-worker/article216237135.html.

64. Lisa Snell, "California's Pension Crisis Hits Disadvantaged Students the Hardest," *Orange County Register*, September 8, 2018, https://www.ocregister. com/2018/09/08/californias-pension-crisis-hits-disadvantaged-students-the-hardest/.

65. Tami Abdollah, "Prop. 30 Fact Check: Schools Are a Mess, So Why Should We Pay More?," *Pass / Fail* (blog), 89.3KPCC, November 2, 2012, https://www. scpr.org/blogs/education/2012/11/02/10846/prop-30-fact-check-schools-are-mess-so-why-should-/.

66. Geoff Mulvihill, "Many State Pension Systems Have Huge Funding Gaps, Liabilities, Pew Report Claims," *USA Today*, April 12, 2018, https://www. usatoday.com/story/money/economy/2018/04/12/many-state-pension-systems-huge-funding-gaps-report/511159002/.

67. Mark J. Perry, "Putting America's Enormous $19.4T Economy into Perspective by Comparing US State GDPs to Entire Countries," *Carpe Diem* (blog), American Enterprise Institute, May 8, 2018, https://www.aei.org/publication/putting-americas-enormous-19-4t-economy-into-perspective-by-comparing-us-state-gdps-to-entire-countries/.

68. Andy Kiersz, "Mapped: The Sorry State of America's Roads," Business Insider, April 5, 2018, https://www.businessinsider.com/map-road-quality-in-each-state-according-to-us-news-2018-4.

69. YoGov Wizards, "The 21 California DMV's with the Longest Appointment Wait Times," *YoGov* (blog), May 1, 2017, https://yogov.org/blog/21-california-dmvs-longest-appointment-wait-times/.

70. *Investigations of Improper Activities by State Agencies and Employees: Misuse of State Time, Economically Wasteful Activities, and Misuse of State Property,* "Summary," California State Auditor, July 2018, http://www.auditor.ca.gov/reports/I2018-1/summary.html.

71. Don Sweeney, "Wish You Could Hire Someone to Wait in Line at the DMV? Now Some Californians Can," *Sacramento Bee,* August 6, 2018, https://www.sacbee.com/news/state/california/article216190495.html.

72. "CT Ranks High in DMV Wait Times," *Hartford Business Journal,* February 20, 2014, http://www.hartfordbusiness.com/article/20140220/NEWS01/140229998/ct-ranks-high-in-dmv-wait-times.

73. Heidi Wallis, "Speeding Tickets: Where Does Your State Rank?" *Esurance On* (blog), https://blog.esurance.com/speeding-tickets-where-does-your-state-rank/.

74. Sarah Kliff and Soo Oh, "America's 4,150 Traffic Cameras, in One Map," Vox, October 16, 2015, https://www.vox.com/a/red-light-speed-cameras.

75. Daniel C. Vock, "Why Cities Hit the Brakes on Red Light Cameras," *Governing,* March 2015, http://www.governing.com/topics/public-justice-safety/gov-cities-hit-brakes-red-light-cameras.html.

76. David Kidwell and Alex Richards, "Tribune Study: Chicago Red Light Cameras Provide Few Safety Benefits," *Chicago Tribune,* December 19, 2014, https://www.chicagotribune.com/ct-red-light-camera-safety-met-20141219-story.html.

77. Maggie Clark, "Red-Light Cameras Generate Revenue, Controversy," *USA Today,* October 15, 2013, https://www.usatoday.com/story/news/nation/2013/10/15/stateline-red-light-cameras/2986577/.

78. "Is Your City Next? Chicago Area Red Light Cameras Rake in Revenue," K40 Electronics, https://www.k40.com/is-your-city-next-chicago-area-red-light-cameras-rake-in-revenue/.

79. Brendan Bakala, "390,000 Drivers Set to Receive Refunds for Red-Light and Speed Camera Tickets," Illinois Policy, January 30, 2018, https://www.illinoispolicy.org/390000-drivers-set-to-receive-refunds-for-red-light-and-speed-camera-tickets/.

80. Katherine Loughead, "State Gasoline Tax Rates as of July 2018," Tax Foundation, August 8, 2018, https://taxfoundation.org/state-gas-tax-rates-july-2018/.

81. Eugene Kim, "All the Crazy Things Happening Because of San Francisco's Ridiculous Housing Prices," Business Insider, April 10, 2016, https://www.businessinsider.com/crazy-things-people-do-to-survive-san-franciscos-housing-prices-2016-4.

82. Kim, "All the Crazy Things."

83. Erika D. Smith, "The Legislature Did Its Part to Fix Sacramento's Housing Crisis. Now It's Your Turn, Bay Area Refugees," *Sacramento Bee*, September 19, 2017, https://www.sacbee.com/opinion/opn-columns-blogs/erika-d-smith/article174139716.html.

84. Kevin Fagan, "California's Homelessness Crisis Expands to Country," *San Francisco Chronicle*, September 8, 2017, https://www.sfchronicle.com/news/article/California-s-homelessness-crisis-moves-to-the-12182026.php.

85. Wikipedia, s.v. "State Bankruptcies in the 1840s," last modified October 20, 2018, 14:51, https://en.wikipedia.org/wiki/State_bankruptcies_in_the_1840s.

86. Stephen Eide, "City Bankruptcies Should Be a State Responsibility," *Orange County Register*, January 28, 2017, https://www.ocregister.com/2017/01/28/city-bankruptcies-should-be-a-state-responsibility/.

87. Annie Ropeik, "Kuster, Pappas Join Progressives in Calls for 'Green New Deal,'" New Hampshire Public Radio, December 11, 2018, https://www.nhpr.org/post/kuster-pappas-join-progressives-calls-green-new-deal#stream/0.

Chapter Two: The New Economic Reality

1. Brandon Bruce, "Meet Four High-Tech Knoxville Startups that Could Shake up Their Industries," *Knoxville Mercury*, June 7, 2017, http://www.knoxmercury.com/2017/06/07/meet-four-high-tech-knoxville-startups-that-could-shake-industries/.

2. "Best Places to Live in Knoxville, Tennessee," BestPlaces, https://www.bestplaces.net/city/tennessee/knoxville.

3. "Rent Trend Data in Knoxville, Tennessee," Rent Jungle, https://www.rentjungle.com/average-rent-in-knoxville-rent-trends/.

4. "Rent Trend Data in New York, New York," Rent Jungle, https://www.rentjungle.com/average-rent-in-new-york-rent-trends/.

5. "Rent Trend Data in San Francisco, California," Rent Jungle, https://www.rentjungle.com/average-rent-in-san-francisco-rent-trends/.

6. "Rent Trend Data in Los Angeles, California," Rent Jungle, https://www.rentjungle.com/average-rent-in-los-angeles-rent-trends/.

7. Rebecca Elliot, "Democrats Turn Harris County a Darker Shade of Blue," *Houston Chronicle*, November 9, 2016, https://www.chron.com/news/politics/houston/article/Democrats-turn-Harris-County-a-darker-shade-of-10603042.php.

8. Brian Rogers, "Republican Judges Swept Out by Voters in Harris County Election," *Houston Chronicle*, November 10, 2018, https://www.chron.com/news/houston-texas/houston/article/GOP-Free-Zone-Republican-judges-swept-out-by-13376806.php.

9. Michael Theis and Olivia Pulsinelli, "Report shows where new Houstonians originate—and where Texans like to relocate," *Houston Business Journal*, January 9, 2017, https://www.bizjournals.com/houston/news/2017/01/09/report-shows-where-new-houstonians-originate-and.html.

10. Mike Morris, "Houston City Council Adopts Tiny Tax Rate Increase," *Houston Chronicle*, October 10, 2018, https://www.chron.com/news/houston-texas/houston/article/Houston-City-Council-adopts-tiny-tax-rate-increase-13296154.php.

11. Dave Fehling, "'Good Regulation' Won't Hurt Texas Oil and Gas," Houston Public Media, August 10, 2016, https://www.houstonpublicmedia.org/articles/news/energy-environment/2016/08/10/163682/good-regulation-wont-hurt-texas-oil-and-gas/.

12. Justin Wise, "Denver Considers Plastics Ban," *The Hill*, December 10, 2018, https://thehill.com/blogs/blog-briefing-room/news/420695-denver-considers-plastics-ban.

13. Andrew Kenney, "Denver Mayor Declares Victory Over Jeff Sessions' DOJ after 'Sanctuary City' Funding Fight," *Denver Post*, October 12, 2018, https://www.denverpost.com/2018/10/12/denver-sanctuary-city-funding-fight-victory/.

14. Joshua Rothman, "New York City Crime in the Nineties," *New Yorker*, December 5, 2012, https://www.newyorker.com/books/double-take/new-york-city-crime-in-the-nineties.

15. Wikipedia, s.v. "Demographic History of New York City," last modified December 1, 2018, 04:01, https://en.wikipedia.org/wiki/Demographic_history_of_New_York_City.

16. Dean Meminger, "NYPD Ups Patrols Underground to Curb Rise in Subway Muggings," Spectrum News NY1, May 9, 2018, https://www.ny1.com/nyc/all-boroughs/news/2018/05/09/nypd-ups-patrols-underground-to-curb-rise-in-subway-muggings.

17. Katie Honan, "Cost of Housing Homeless in Shelters Keeps Rising in New York City," *Wall Street Journal*, September 19, 2018, https://www.wsj.com/articles/cost-of-housing-homeless-in-shelters-keeps-rising-in-new-york-city-1537377091.

18. Travis Loose, "Portland Ranked #1 Best Foodie Scene in America: WalletHub.com," Patch, October 9, 2018, https://patch.com/oregon/portland/portland-ranked-1-best-foodie-scene-america-wallethub-com.

19. Dustin Nelson, "This Beer Train Takes You into the Mountains on a Day-Long Beer Adventure," Thrillist, September 18, 2018, https://www.thrillist.com/news/nation/durango-brew-train-beer-vacation.

20. Jonathan Shikes, "The Flatirons Food Film Fest Turns the Camera on Brewing and Craft Beer," *Westword*, October 8, 2018, https://www.westword.com/restaurants/the-flatirons-food-film-festival-will-show-craft-beer-movie-beermaster-10878378.

21. Mark Harden, "Census Bureau Toasts Colorado Jobs from Beer and Breweries," *Gazette* (Colorado Springs), October 5, 2018, https://gazette.com/premium/

census-bureau-toasts-colorado-jobs-from-beer-and-breweries/article_1bb8be28-c8f1-11e8-9011-f3edf12b678b.html.

22. "Great American Beer Festival," Great American Beer Festival, https://www.greatamericanbeerfestival.com/.

23. Sara Bernard, "Portland and Seattle Parks Make Them Top-Ranked Cities," *Oregon Public Broadcasting*, May 19, 2015, https://www.opb.org/news/article/portland-and-seattle-parks-make-them-top-ranked-cities/.

24. "2017 November General: Official Results; Results by Locality," Virginia Department of Elections, updated December 8, 2017, https://results.elections.virginia.gov/vaelections/2017%20November%20General/Site/Locality/FAIRFAX%20COUNTY/Governor.html.

25. Chesapeake, Va., Code § 46-8(a) (1970); "Halloween Safety Tips & Hours," City of Chesapeake Virginia, http://www.cityofchesapeake.net/government/City-Departments/Departments/Police-Department/crime_prevention/halloween.htm.

26. "State and Local Tax Burdens, 1977–2012," Tax Foundation, January 20, 2016, https://taxfoundation.org/state-and-local-tax-burdens-historic-data/.

27. Jared Walczak, "Washington Voters to Consider a Carbon Tax—Again," Tax Foundation, September 13, 2018, https://taxfoundation.org/washington-consider-carbon-tax/.

28. "Cigarette Smuggling Makes WA Tax Revenue Go up in Smoke," *Seattle Business*, https://www.seattlebusinessmag.com/blog/cigarette-smuggling-makes-wa-tax-revenue-go-smoke.

29. Katherine Loughead, "State Gasoline Tax Rates as of July 2018," Tax Foundation, August 8, 2018, https://taxfoundation.org/state-gas-tax-rates-july-2018/.

30. Jason Torchinsky, "Proposed Oregon Bill Would Tax People with Cars 20 Years or Older for No Good Reason (Updated)," Jalopnik, February 10, 2017, https://jalopnik.com/proposed-oregon-bill-would-tax-people-with-cars-20-year-1792227249.

31. Nate Hanson, "Oregon Workers to Pay New Transportation Tax Beginning July 1," KGW8, June 26, 2018, https://www.kgw.com/article/money/oregon-workers-to-pay-new-transportation-tax-beginning-july-1/283-567914495.

32. Lisa Brown, "Construction Completed on Boeing's First St. Louis Commercial Airplanes Facility," *St. Louis Post-Dispatch*, October 13, 2016, https://www.stltoday.com/business/local/construction-completed-on-boeing-s-first-st-louis-commercial-airplanes/article_7de07ca0-a976-5760-b5b6-30a47fd2cf80.html.

33. Chuck Raasch, "Boeing Jet Deal Means Big Boost for St. Louis Jobs," *St. Louis Post-Dispatch*, September 28, 2016, https://www.stltoday.com/business/local/boeing-jet-deal-means-big-boost-for-st-louis-jobs/article_30fea475-4246-569b-8ede-1ade79d571c8.html.

34. David B. Larter, "Skilled Worker, Parts Shortages Still Hurting Hornet and Growler Maintenance, Government Watchdog Finds," *Defense News*,

September 15, 2018, https://www.defensenews.com/naval/2018/09/15/ skilled-worker-parts-shortages-still-hurting-hornet-and-growler-maintenance-government-watchdog-finds/.

35. Drew Atkins, "Q&A: Councilmember Sawant on Public Broadband and a Socialist Microsoft," Crosscut, September 2, 2015, https://crosscut. com/2015/09/ qa-councilmember-sawant-on-public-broadband-and-a-socialist-microsoft.

36. Gene Balk, "Seattle Taxes Ranked Most Unfair in Washington—a State among the Harshest on the Poor Nationwide," *Seattle Times*, April 13, 2018, https:// www.seattletimes.com/seattle-news/data/seattle-taxes-ranked-most-unfair-in-washington-a-state-among-the-harshest-on-the-poor-nationwide/.

37. Daniel Beekman, "Seattle Soda Tax Brings in More Than $10M in First Six Months," *Seattle Times*, August 8, 2018, https://www.seattletimes.com/seattle-news/politics/seattle-soda-tax-brings-in-more-than-10m-in-first-six-months/.

38. Minda Zetlin, "Here's How Much You Need to Live Comfortably in America's 10 Most Expensive Cities," *Inc.*, April 5, 2018, https://www.inc.com/minda-zetlin/cost-of-living-san-francisco-new-york-boston-most-expensive-cities.html.

39. City of Seattle, *Race and Social Justice Initiatives in the Budget*, 2018, https:// www.seattle.gov/financedepartment/18proposedbudget/documents/RSJI.pdf.

40. Sean Kennedy, "In Seattle, Compost Your Food Scraps—or Else," CNN Politics, updated October 3, 2014, https://www.cnn.com/2014/09/24/politics/ seattle-composting-law/index.html.

41. Printus LeBlanc, "Smug Seattle Keeps Throwing Money after Streetcar, Bike Lane Fiasco That's Totally off the Rails," Fox News, July 31, 2018, https:// www.foxnews.com/opinion/smug-seattle-keeps-throwing-money-after-streetcar-bike-lane-fiasco-thats-totally-off-the-rails.

42. Alex Cordell, "'Democracy Vouchers' Are a Sham," *Washington Examiner*, October 19, 2017, https://www.washingtonexaminer.com/ democracy-vouchers-are-a-sham.

43. Alana Semuels, "How Amazon Helped Kill a Seattle Tax on Business," *The Atlantic*, June 13, 2018, https://www.theatlantic.com/technology/ archive/2018/06/how-amazon-helped-kill-a-seattle-tax-on-business/562736/.

44. Mary Bowerman, "Seattle's $15 Minimum Wage May Be Hurting Workers, Report Finds," *USA Today*, June 27, 2017, https://www.usatoday.com/story/ money/nation-now/2017/06/27/ report-finds-seattles-15-minimum-wage-may-hurting-workers/431424001/.

45. The Seattle Minimum Wage Study Team, *Report on the Impact of Seattle's Minimum Wage Ordinance on Wages, Workers, Jobs, and Establishments through 2015* (Seattle: University of Washington, 2015), https://evans.uw.edu/ sites/default/files/MinWageReport-July2016_Final.pdf.

46. Bethany Jean Clement, "The End of 2017 Brought More Seattle-Area Restaurant Closures," *Seattle Times*, January 10, 2018, https://www. seattletimes.com/life/food-drink/ the-end-of-2017-brought-lots-more-seattle-area-restaurant-closures/.

47. Scott Greenstone, "Is Seattle's Homeless Crisis the Worst in the Country?" *Seattle Times*, January 16, 2018, https://www.seattletimes.com/seattle-news/homeless/is-seattles-homeless-crisis-the-worst-in-the-country/.

48. Hallie Golden, "In a Growing Crisis, Seattle Uses City Hall as a Homeless Shelter," CityLab, August 23, 2018, https://www.citylab.com/equity/2018/08/seattle-city-hall-homelessness-emergency/568234/.

49. Hanna Scott, "Seattle City Council Debates Erecting Giant Tents for the Homeless," MyNorthwest (KIRO-FM), October 8, 2018, mynorthwest.com/1137911/seattle-debates-giant-tents-homeless/.

50. Sarah Anne Lloyd, "Seattle's High-Poverty Neighborhoods Have More Than Doubled since 2000, Report Says," *Curbed Seattle* (blog), July 14, 2017, https://seattle.curbed.com/2017/7/14/15974712/high-poverty-neighborhood-density-report.

51. Nigel Jaquiss, "Opponents of Portland Clean Energy Measure: Tax Haul Could Double City's Estimate," *Willamette Week*, October 9, 2018, https://www.wweek.com/news/2018/10/09/opponents-of-portland-clean-energy-measure-tax-haul-could-double-citys-estimate/.

52. Noel K. Gallagher, "Portland Voters Easily Approve School Budget," *Portland Press Herald*, June 12, 2018, https://www.pressherald.com/2018/06/12/portland-voters-decide-school-budget/.

53. Noel K. Gallagher, "With State School Funding Drying Up, Portland Studying Possible School Closures, Redistricting," *Portland Press Herald*, September 3, 2018, https://www.pressherald.com/2018/09/03/with-state-school-funding-drying-up-portland-studying-possible-school-closures-redistricting/.

54. Gordon R. Friedman, "Mayor Ted Wheeler in Talks to Raise Portland Business Taxes," *The Oregonian*, April 17, 2018, https://www.oregonlive.com/portland/2018/04/mayor_ted_wheeler_in_talks_to.html.

55. Gordon R. Friedman, "Portland Businesses on Track to Dodge Millions in City Taxes Owed," *The Oregonian*, April 17, 2018, https://www.oregonlive.com/portland/2018/04/portland_businesses_on_track_t.html.

56. Art Edwards, "Portland Couple Demands Arts Tax Refund," KGW8, March 6, 2016, https://www.kgw.com/article/news/local/portland-couple-demands-arts-tax-refund/70718631.

57. Brad Schmidt, "Portland's Leaf-Removal Fee Puzzles, Angers Residents," *Oregonian*, October 29, 2010, https://www.oregonlive.com/portland/2010/10/portlands_leaf-removal_fee_puz.html.

58. Elise Herron, "The City of Portland Is No Longer Charging Fees for Leaf Pickup," *Willamette Week*, October 2, 2018, https://www.wweek.com/news/2018/10/02/the-city-of-portland-is-no-longer-charging-fees-for-leaf-pickup/.

59. Jonathan Maus, "Oregon's New Bike Tax: $77,000 in Receipts and $47,000 to Collect Them," Bike Portland, May 21, 2018, https://bikeportland.org/2018/05/21/oregons-new-bike-tax-has-netted-just-30000-so-far-this-year-281802.

60. Mike Ludwig, "Under Activist Pressure, Portland Agrees to End All Corporate Investments," Truthout, April 11, 2017, https://truthout.org/articles/under-activist-pressure-portland-agrees-to-end-all-corporate-investments/.

61. City of Portland, Oregon, *Multnomah County: Sign, Awning Permit and Registration Fee Schedule*, 2014, https://www.portlandoregon.gov/bds/article/355013.

62. Jessica Floum, "Portland Finances Get an 'F' Grade for Hidden Debt; City Officials Disagree," *Oregonian*, January 24, 2018, https://www.oregonlive.com/politics/2018/01/portland_finances_get_an_f_gra.html.

63. Gordon R. Friedman, "Oregon Runs a Government Waste Hotline. It Wastes Money," *Oregonian*, September 2017, https://www.oregonlive.com/politics/2017/09/oregon_runs_a_government_waste.html.

64. Nigel Jaquiss, "Blue Bins Used to Save Portlanders Money. Now They Are Costing Us," *Willamette Week*, June 8, 2018, https://www.wweek.com/news/2018/06/08/blue-bins-used-to-save-portlanders-money-now-they-are-costing-us/.

65. Paris Achen, "Survey: Inefficient Spending Equals Government Waste," *Portland Tribune*, May 9, 2018, https://portlandtribune.com/pt/9-news/394997-288272-survey-inefficient-spending-equals-government-waste.

66. "New Mexico Report – 2018," Talk Poverty, accessed February 16, 2019, https://talkpoverty.org/state-year-report/new-mexico-2018-report/.

67. Rachel Sapin, "Rural NM Has the Highest Poverty Rate Among All States' Rural Areas," *Albuquerque Business First*, December 9, 2016, https://www.bizjournals.com/albuquerque/news/2016/12/09/rural-nm-has-the-highest-poverty-rate-among-all.html.

68. Dennis Domrzalski, "Nearly a Third of NM's Native Americans Live below Poverty Level," *Albuquerque Business First*, February 20, 2013, https://www.bizjournals.com/albuquerque/news/2013/02/20/nm-native-americans-below-poverty-level.html.

69. "Poverty Rate by Race/Ethnicity," Henry J. Kaiser Family Foundation, accessed February 16, 2019, https://www.kff.org/other/state-indicator/poverty-rate-by-raceethnicity/?currentTimeframe=0&sortModel=%7B%22colId%22:%22Location%22,%22sort%22:%22asc%22%7D.

70. Justina Grant and Cayla Montoya-Manzo, "New Mexico Ranked Worst in the Nation for Child Poverty," *New Mexico News Port*, December 5, 2017, http://www.newmexiconewsport.com/new-mexico-ranked-worst-nation-child-poverty/.

71. J. Scott Moody, "New Mexico Has the Fifth Highest Tax Burden in the Nation for 2015," Key Policy Data, May 24, 2017, https://keypolicydata.com/blog-archives/2017/05/new-mexico-has-fifth-highest-tax-burden-nation-2015/.

72. Susan Montoya Bryan, "New Mexico Moves Up in Oil and Gas Rankings," *U.S. News & World Report*, January 3, 2018, https://www.usnews.com/news/best-states/new-mexico/articles/2018-01-03/new-mexico-moves-up-in-oil-and-gas-rankings.

73. Chris White, "Colorado's Fracking War Heats Up as Polls Show Citizens Leaning Toward a Gas Ban," The Daily Caller, September 10, 2018, https://dailycaller.com/2018/09/10/colorado-fracking-election/.

74. Julie Turkewitz, "In Colorado, a Fracking Boom and a Population Explosion Collide," New York Times, May 31, 2018, https://www.nytimes.com/2018/05/31/us/colorado-fracking-debates.html.

75. Rhodes Cook, "Registering by Party: Where the Democrats and Republicans Are Ahead," Rasmussen Reports, July 12, 2018, http://www.rasmussenreports.com/public_content/political_commentary/commentary_by_rhodes_cook/registering_by_party_where_the_democrats_and_republicans_are_ahead.

76. Greg Avery, "Colorado Small Businesses Start and Fail More, Study Finds (9News Video)," Denver Business Journal, August 26, 2013, https://www.bizjournals.com/denver/blog/boosters_bits/2013/08/colorado-small-business-start-and-fail.html.

77. Kim Monson, "In Response: We Don't Need a Tax Hike to Fix Colorado's Highways," Colorado Politics, August 14, 2018, https://www.coloradopolitics.com/opinion/in-response-we-don-t-need-a-tax-hike-to/article_e6067721-3b7f-5552-9025-9a3a993be2fc.html.

78. Jason Blevins, "Plan to Quadruple Property Tax Rates for Colorado's Short-Term Rentals Is Nixed," Colorado Sun, October 4, 2018, https://coloradosun.com/2018/10/04/property-tax-short-term-rentals-colorado/.

79. Monica Vendituoli, "Marijuana Businesses Threaten to Leave Colorado After Governor's Vetoes," Denver Business Journal, June 8, 2018, https://www.bizjournals.com/denver/news/2018/06/08/marijuana-businesses-threaten-to-leave-colorado.html.

80. Colorado Health Institute, ColoradoCare: An Independent Analysis—Finances, August 2016, https://www.coloradohealthinstitute.org/sites/default/files/migrated/postfiles/Financial_Analysis_Report_FINAL.pdf.

81. Linda Gorman, "Single-Payer Health Care: The More Coloradans Knew, the Less They Liked It," The Daily Signal, August 29, 2018, https://www.dailysignal.com/2018/08/29/single-payer-health-care-the-more-coloradans-knew-the-less-they-liked-it/.

82. Jennifer Haberkorn, "Single-Payer, Once Shunned, Makes a Comeback in Colorado Governor's Race," Politico, August 3, 2018, https://www.politico.com/story/2018/08/03/single-payer-once-shunned-makes-a-comeback-in-colorado-governors-race-721020.

83. Eli Stokols, "How Colorado Gun-Control Advocates Beat the NRA," New Yorker, February 22, 2018, https://www.newyorker.com/news/news-desk/how-colorado-gun-control-advocates-beat-the-nra.

84. Jesse Paul, "Coloradans Would Be Able to Carry Concealed Weapons without a Permit under Measure That Passed GOP-Controlled State Senate," Denver Post, March 8, 2018, https://www.denverpost.com/2018/03/08/colorado-concealed-carry-without-permit-bill/.

85. Jesse Paul, "Colorado 'Red Flag' Gun Bill Passes Democratic-Controlled House—but with Almost No GOP Support," *Denver Post*, May 4, 2018, https://www.denverpost.com/2018/05/04/colorado-red-flag-bill-passes-house/.

86. Grace Hood, "Colorado's New Gun Laws Send Businesses Packing," National Public Radio, April 29, 2013, https://www.npr.org/2013/04/29/177806894/gunmaker-says-colorados-new-laws-will-send-it-packing.

87. "Colorado Gun Control: Over Half of State's Sheriffs Plan Lawsuit to Block Gun Control Laws," HuffPost, April 10, 2013, https://www.huffingtonpost.com/2013/04/09/colorado-sheriffs-lawsuit-block-gun-control-laws_n_3050162.html.

88. Robert Allen, "Few Violations of Colorado's 'Unenforceable' Gun Laws," *USA Today*, January 30, 2014, https://www.usatoday.com/story/news/nation/2014/01/30/colorado-gun-laws-enforcement/5055523/.

89. "Ronald Reagan: A Time for Choosing (aka 'The Speech')," air date October 27, 1964, American Rhetoric, updated August 16, 2018, https://www.americanrhetoric.com/speeches/ronaldreaganatimeforchoosing.htm.

Chapter Three: Political Impacts on Receiving States

1. Kevin McPherson and Bruce Wright, "Gone to Texas: Migration; Who's Coming and Where They're Going," *FiscalNotes*, Texas Comptroller website, October 2017, https://comptroller.texas.gov/economy/fiscal-notes/2017/october/migration.php.

2. Jeremy Wallace, "Post-Primary Surge Pushes Texas Voter Registration to 15.6 Million," *Houston Chronicle*, September 26, 2018, https://www.houstonchronicle.com/news/politics/texas/article/Texas-sets-voter-registration-record-with-1-6-13258057.php.

3. Tony Cantu, "Austin Is America's Fastest-Growing City: Report," Patch, October 8, 2018, https://patch.com/texas/downtownaustin/austin-americas-fastest-growing-city-report.

4. "#47 Connecticut," 2019 State Business Tax Climate Index, Tax Foundation, https://statetaxindex.org/state/connecticut/.

5. Patrick Gleason, "25 Years Ago Connecticut Became the Last State to Adopt an Income Tax, with Disastrous Results," *Forbes*, August 24, 2016, https://www.forbes.com/sites/patrickgleason/2016/08/24/ctincometax/.

6. Marc E. Fitch, "Connecticut Government Spending Grows Faster Than the State Economy," Yankee Institute for Public Policy, November 2, 2017, https://www.yankeeinstitute.org/2017/11/connecticut-government-spending-grows-faster-than-the-state-economy/.

7. Marc E. Fitch, "Ninety-Four Percent of Connecticut State Workforce Is Union-Controlled," Yankee Institute for Public Policy, March 16, 2018, https://www.yankeeinstitute.org/2018/03/ninety-four-percent-of-connecticut-state-workforce-is-union-controlled/.

8. Ken Dixon, "Are State Workers Overpaid?" *Connecticut Post*, August 30, 2010, https://www.ctpost.com/local/article/Are-state-workers-overpaid-637431.php.

9. Marc E. Fitch, "Bill Seeks to Lower Teacher Pension Contribution," Yankee Institute for Public Policy, April 11, 2018, https://www.yankeeinstitute.org/2018/04/bill-seeks-to-lower-teacher-pension-contribution/; Keith M. Phaneuf, "Shifting Pension Costs from State to Teachers Costs CT $20M," *Connecticut Mirror*, December 26, 2017, https://ctmirror.org/2017/12/26/shifting-pension-costs-from-state-to-teachers-costs-ct-20m/.

10. Bob Woods, "Another Fleeing Corporate Giant: Connecticut Is Facing a Business Migration Crisis," America's Top States for Business, CNBC, July 11, 2017, https://www.cnbc.com/2017/07/11/connecticut-is-facing-a-corporate-migration-crisis.html.

11. "What Will the Austin-San Antonio Corridor Look Like in 2030?" LawnStarter, https://www.lawnstarter.com/san-antonio-lawn-care/what-will-austin-san-antonio-corridor-look-like-2030.

12. Alex Samuels, "Hey, Texplainer: How Does Texas' Budget Use Taxes from Oil and Natural Gas Production?" *Texas Tribune*, January 5, 2018, https://www.texastribune.org/2018/01/05/hey-texplainer-how-does-texas-budget-use-taxes-oil-and-natural-gas-pro/.

13. "Release: Texas Oil and Natural Gas Industry Paid More Than $11 Billion in Taxes and Royalties in 2017, up from 2016," Texas Oil and Gas Association, https://www.txoga.org/release-texas-oil-natural-gas-industry-paid-11-billion-taxes-royalties-2017-2016/.

14. Tom Benning, "Fact Check: Is Ted Cruz Correct That Beto O'Rourke Supported a $10 per Barrel Tax on Oil?," *Dallas News*, October 9, 2018, https://www.dallasnews.com/news/2018-elections/2018/10/08/fact-check-ted-cruz-correct-beto-orourke-supported-10-per-barrel-tax-oil.

15. "A Brief Summary of What Happened This Morning at the San Patricio County Exxon/SABIC Public Hearing and Tax Abatement Vote," Portland Citizens United, March 20, 2017, https://portlandcitizensunited.com/a-brief-summary-of-what-happened-this-morning-at-the-san-patricio-county-exxonsabic-public-hearing-and-tax-abatement-vote/.

16. Patrick Michels, "Free Lunch," *Texas Observer*, accessed February 16, 2019, https://www.texasobserver.org/chapter-313-texas-tax-incentive/.

17. Bureau of Economic Analysis, "Gross Domestic Product by State: Second Quarter 2018," News Release no. BEA 18-62, November 14, 2018, https://www.bea.gov/system/files/2018-11/qgdpstate1118.pdf.

18. Lawrence J. Hogan Jr. and Boyd K. Rutherford, *Maryland Budget Highlights: Fiscal Year 2019*, January 17, 2018, https://dbm.maryland.gov/budget/Documents/operbudget/2019/Proposed/BudgetHighlights.pdf.

19. Leticia Miranda, Nicole Nguyen, and Ryan Mac, "Here Are the Most Outrageous Incentives Cities Offered Amazon in Their HQ2 Bids," BuzzFeed

News, November 14, 2018, https://www.buzzfeednews.com/article/leticiamiranda/amazon-hq2-finalist-cities-incentives-airport-lounge.

20. Nicole Gelinas, "NYC Shouldn't Be Begging for Amazon's New Jobs," *New York Post*, November 13, 2018, https://nypost.com/2018/11/13/nyc-shouldnt-be-begging-for-amazons-new-jobs/.

21. Kenneth Lovett, "Cuomo Plans to Freeze Out Lawmakers by Bypassing Capital Board on Amazon Project," *Daily News*, November 15, 2018, https://www.nydailynews.com/news/politics/ny-pol-cuomo-amazon-mujica-pacb-20181115-story.html.

22. J. David Goodman and William Neuman, "Can New York City's Mayor Be an Amazon Booster and Still Be Progressive?" *New York Times*, November 16, 2018, https://www.nytimes.com/2018/11/16/nyregion/mayor-de-blasio-amazon-progressive-nyc.html.

23. Anand Giridharadas, "The New York Hustle of Amazon's Second Headquarters," *New Yorker*, November 17, 2018, https://www.newyorker.com/tech/annals-of-technology/the-new-york-hustle-of-amazons-second-headquarters.

24. Lucas Nolan, "Report: Amazon Rethinks NYC Headquarteres in the Face of Growing Opposition," Breitbart, February 9, 2019, https://www.breitbart.com/tech/2019/02/09/report-amazon-rethinks-nyc-headquarters-in-the-face-of-growing-opposition/.

25. The Editorial Board, "Amazon Escapes from New York," *Wall Street Journal*, February 14, 2019, https://www.wsj.com/articles/amazon-escapes-from-new-york-11550189053.

26. Sophia Barnes and Christian Paz, "Amazon HQ2: $23 Million Incentives Package Approved in Virginia," Governing, March 18, 2019, https://www.governing.com/topics/finance/23-Million-Incentives-Package-Approved-in-Amazon-HQ2-Deal-With-Virginia.html.

27. Daphne A. Kenyon and Adam H. Langley, *Payments in Lieu of Taxes: Balancing Municipal and Nonprofit Interests* (Cambridge, MA: Lincoln Institute of Land Policy, 2010), https://www.lincolninst.edu/sites/default/files/PILOTs%2520PFR%2520final.pdf.

28. Amy Sherman, "Are the Miami Dolphins the Only Property Tax-Paying Team in the NFL?" *Miami Herald*, April 24, 2013, Politics, https://www.miamiherald.com/news/politics-government/article1950671.html.

29. Sean Williams, "The 5 Largest Corporate Subsidy Megadeals of the Past Decade," The Motley Fool, March 15, 2014, https://www.fool.com/investing/general/2014/03/15/the-5-largest-corporate-subsidy-megadeals-of-the-p.aspx.

30. Patrick Lohmann, "Massena to Lose 500 Jobs as Alcoa Closes Smelting Plant," Syracuse.com, November 2, 2015, https://www.syracuse.com/news/index.ssf/2015/11/massena_to_lose_500_jobs_as_alcoa_closes_smelting_plant.html.

31. Joseph Spector, "600 Upstate Alcoa Jobs Preserved with NY Bailout," *Press & Sun-Bulletin* (Binghamton, New York), November 25, 2015, https://www.pressconnects.com/story/news/local/new-york/2015/11/25/alcoa-jobs-saved/76356278/.

32. Angelo Young, "Taxpayer-Funded Capitalism: Here Are the Biggest Corporate Subsidy Deals of 2016," Salon, December 27, 2016, https://www.salon.com/2016/12/27/taxpayer-funded-capitalism-here-are-the-biggest-corporate-subsidy-deals-of-2016/.

Chapter Four: The Rise of the Purple State

1.   Deirdre Fernandes, "State Economy Slows as Labor Force Tightens," *Boston Globe*, January 27, 2017, https://www.bostonglobe.com/business/2017/01/27/state-economy-slows-labor-force-tightens/AUN7nDksvWyyIM8lYcV2tM/story.html.

2.   NH Division of Economic Development Business and Economic Affairs, "Study: New Hampshire Shows Strong Population Growth," Manchester Ink Link, September 4, 2018, https://manchesterinklink.com/study-new-hampshire-shows-strong-population-growth/.

3.   Holly Ramer, "Domestic Migration Fuels New Hampshire Population Growth," *Seattle Times,* December 27, 2017, https://www.seattletimes.com/nation-world/domestic-migration-fuels-new-hampshire-population-growth/.

4.   Tim Camerato, "Claremont Man Says Councilor Threatened Him over Holiday Display," *Valley News*, December 20, 2018, https://www.vnews.com/Councilor-s-Role-Question-in-Holiday-Debate-22302773.

5.   "Sam Killay, 37 – Claremont, NH," MyLife.com, https://www.mylife.com/sam-killay/e441945039336.

6.   Dick Berry, "Village of Elmore Threatened with Lawsuit over Nativity Scene," WTOL 11 News, December 14, 2017, http://www.wtol.com/story/37071224/village-of-elmore-threated-with-lawsuit-over-nativity-scene/.

7.   Christian Sheckler, "U.S. Judge Rules Concord High School's Live Nativity Was Unconstitutional," *South Bend Tribune*, March 7, 2017, https://www.southbendtribune.com/news/education/u-s-judge-rules-concord-high-school-s-live-nativity/article_6de62bb2-0355-11e7-8f31-d71c7e964e78.html.

8.   "Somerville: Sanctuary City since 1987," City of Somerville, https://www.somervillema.gov/sanctuary.

9.   Jeff McMenemy, "Portsmouth and Durham Debate Sanctuary City Status," Fosters, February 1, 2017, https://www.fosters.com/news/20170201/portsmouth-and-durham-debate-sanctuary-city-status.

10. Creede Newton, "New Hampshire Struggles with Sanctuary Cities," Al Jazeera, March 6, 2017, https://www.aljazeera.com/news/2017/03/hampshire-struggles-sanctuary-cities-170306145624879.html.

11. Kenneth M. Johnson, Dante J. Scala, and Andrew E. Smith, *First in the Nation: New Hampshire's Changing Electorate*, Carsey Research, National Issue Brief #96, Winter 2016, https://scholars.unh.edu/cgi/viewcontent.cgi?article=1263&context=carsey.

12. Johnson, Scala, and Smith, *First in the Nation.*

13. Jess Bravin, Brent Kendall, and Laura Stevens, "Supreme Court Rules States Can Collect Sales Tax on Web Purchases," *Wall Street Journal*, June 22, 2018,

https://www.wsj.com/articles/us-supreme-court-rules-states-can-require-online-merchants-to-collect-sales-taxes-1529591376.

14. "Delegates to the Constitutional Convention: New Hampshire," National Archives and Records Administration, http://law2.umkc.edu/faculty/projects/ftrials/conlaw/marrynewhamp.html.

15. Justine Paradis, "You Asked, We Answered: Why Is New Hampshire So against Having an Income Tax?" New Hampshire Public Radio, February 9, 2018, https://www.nhpr.org/post/you-asked-we-answered-why-new-hampshire-so-against-having-income-tax#stream/0.

16. F. Lauriston Bullard, "Two States Plan New Tax Systems; New Hampshire Board Would Levy on Incomes, Franchises and Cut Timber. Relief for Real Estate Graded Payments on Incomes Is Suggested in Massachusetts—Both Reports Criticized. Neither State Favors Move. Utilities Tax Proposed. Two States Plan New Tax Systems Advisory Board Suggested. Graded Tax for Bay State," *New York Times*, January 6, 1929, https://www.nytimes.com/1929/01/06/archives/two-states-plan-new-tax-systems-new-hampshire-board-would-levy-on.html.

17. Todd Bookman, "Lawmaker, Understanding What He's up Against, Backs Income Tax in NH," New Hampshire Public Radio, December 30, 2016, https://www.nhpr.org/post/lawmaker-understanding-what-hes-against-backs-income-tax-nh#stream/0.

18. Chris Kolmar, "These Are the 10 New Hampshire Cities with the Largest Latino Population for 2019," HomeSnacks, December 9, 2018, https://www.homesnacks.net/most-hispanic-cities-in-new-hampshire-1210775/.

19. Mark Hugo Lopez, Ana Gonzalez-Barrera, Jens Manuel Krogstad and Gustavo López, "4. Latinos and the Political Parties," *Hispanic Trends*, Pew Research Center, October 11, 2016, http://www.pewhispanic.org/2016/10/11/latinos-and-the-political-parties/.

20. Caitlin Hendee and 9News, "Colorado Closeup: Why This Northern Community Is Growing So Fast (Photos)," *Denver Business Journal*, February 9, 2018, https://www.bizjournals.com/denver/news/2018/02/09/why-this-northern-colorado-community-is-growing-so.html.

21. Associated Press, "Study Finds Change in Colo. ER Rates after Pot Legalization," CBS News, February 25, 2016, https://www.cbsnews.com/news/colorado-marijuana-complaints-tourists-emergency-rooms-new-england-journal-of-medicine/.

22. Mona Zhang, "Legal Marijuana Is a Boon to the Economy, Finds Study," *Forbes*, March 13, 2018, https://www.forbes.com/sites/monazhang/2018/03/13/legal-marijuana-is-a-boon-to-the-economy-finds-study/.

23. Marshall Cohen and Jeff Simon, "Colorado Is Not a Battleground This Year; Is It the Next Blue State?" CNN Politics, October 25, 2016, https://www.cnn.com/2016/10/25/politics/election-2016-colorado-battleground-swing-state-trend/index.html.

24. Jesse Paul, "Colorado's Partisan Voters Don't Appear to Be Strategically Voting En Masse in Their Rival Party's Primaries," *Denver Post*, June 25, 2018, https://www.denverpost.com/2018/06/25/colorado-unaffiliated-voters-party-switching/.

25. Jon Caldara, "Welcome to Colorful East California," *Denver Post*, December 8, 2017, https://www.denverpost.com/2017/12/08/welcome-to-colorful-east-california/.

26. "Poll: Californians Rank High Cost-of-Living/Housing as Top Issue; Large Majority Supports Immigrants," Press Room, November 10, 2017, https://pressroom.usc.edu/23127-2/.

27. Robert Frank, "800,000 People Are About to Flee New York and California Because of Taxes, Say Economists," CNBC, April 28, 2018, https://www.cnbc.com/2018/04/26/800000-people-are-about-to-flee-new-york-california-because-of-taxes.html.

28. Meredith Gunter, "U.Va. Assesses 2010 Census Data on Virginia's Hispanic Population," UVA Today, February 16, 2011, https://news.virginia.edu/content/uva-assesses-2010-census-data-virginias-hispanic-population.

Chapter Five: The New City-States

1. William H. Frey, "US Population Disperses to Suburbs, Exurbs, Rural Areas, and 'Middle of the Country' Metros," *The Avenue* (blog), Brookings Institution, March 26, 2018, https://www.brookings.edu/blog/the-avenue/2018/03/26/us-population-disperses-to-suburbs-exurbs-rural-areas-and-middle-of-the-country-metros/.

2. "New Census Bureau Population Estimates Show Dallas-Fort Worth-Arlington Has Largest Growth in the United States," United States Census Bureau, News Release no. CB18-50, March 22, 2018, https://www.census.gov/newsroom/press-releases/2018/popest-metro-county.html.

3. BND Editorial Board, "Illinois Lawmakers Need to Back Their Education Ideas with Cash," *Belleville News-Democrat*, May 5, 2018, https://www.bnd.com/opinion/editorials/article210379124.html.

4. John Klingner, "Illinois' Statewide, Unfunded Mandates Limit School-District Budget Flexibility," Illinois Policy, September 21, 2015, https://www.illinoispolicy.org/illinois-statewide-unfunded-mandates-limit-school-district-budget-flexibility/.

5. David L. Brown and Robin Blakely-Armitage, "Changing Composition of Upstate New York Communities" PowerPoint presentation, Community Development Institute: Informed Communities, Informed Decisions, Cornell University, July 16–17, 2011, https://cardi.cals.cornell.edu/sites/cardi.cals.cornell.edu/files/shared/documents/Changing-Composition-of-Upstate-NY-Communities.pdf.

6. Bryce Hill and Austin Berg, "More Than 80 Percent of Illinois Counties Saw Population Loss in 2017," Illinois Policy, March 22, 2018, https://www.

illinoispolicy.org/more-than-80-percent-of-illinois-counties-saw-population-loss-in-2017/.

7. "California's Population Increases by 215,000, Continuing State's Moderate Growth Rate," California Department of Finance news release, December 21, 2018, http://www.dof.ca.gov/Forecasting/Demographics/Estimates/E-2/documents/PressReleaseJul2018.pdf.

8. Beacon Economics, *California Migration: A Comparative Analysis*, Next 10, 2018, https://next10.org/sites/default/files/California-Migration-Final2.pdf.

9. Mike Maciag, "Population Declines Accelerate in Many Large Urban Areas," *Governing*, March 23, 2017, http://www.governing.com/topics/urban/gov-urban-counties-lose-population-2016.html.

10. Richard Craver, "N.C. Remains Top 10 for People Relocating within the United States, Led by Work Moves," *Winston-Salem Journal*, January 3, 2018, https://www.journalnow.com/news/local/n-c-remains-top-for-people-relocating-within-the-united/article_67e22098-2fe0-5efa-8bfb-e654a55f5a73.html.

11. J. Peder Zane, "For NC, Changing Demographics Point toward a Daunting Tomorrow," *News & Observer*, October 24, 2017, https://www.newsobserver.com/opinion/op-ed/article180691351.html.

12. Rebecca Tippett, "NC Demographic Trends through 2035," PowerPoint presentation, House Select Committee on Strategic Transportation Planning and Long Term Funding Solutions, February 22, 2016, https://www.ncleg.gov/documentsites/committees/house2015-172/2-22-16_Meeting/Demographic_Trends_through_2035.pdf.

13. Rob Christensen, "NC Natives Are Now Outnumbered among Voters. What Does That Mean for Tar Heel Politics?" *News & Observer*, April 13, 2018, https://www.newsobserver.com/news/politics-government/politics-columns-blogs/rob-christensen/article208570729.html.

14. Michael Bitzer, "Another Aspect of NC's Shifting Politics: Natives vs. Non-Natives," *Old North State Politics* (blog), March 30, 2018, http://www.oldnorthstatepolitics.com/2018/03/NC-native-non-native-registered-voters.html.

15. Will Doran, "Voter Turnout Soars in NC. Insiders Say It's Due to Women and Young People," *News & Observer*, November 7, 2018, https://www.newsobserver.com/news/politics-government/article221299945.html.

16. Jim Morrill and Paul A. Specht, "Blue Waves in Urban North Carolina Help Democrats Break GOP 'Supermajorities,'" *Charlotte Observer*, November 7, 2018, https://www.charlotteobserver.com/news/politics-government/election/article221279270.html; Steve Harrison, "After Recount, Rachel Hunt Wins Mecklenburg NC House Seat," WFAE 90.7, November 20, 2018, https://www.wfae.org/post/after-recount-rachel-hunt-wins-mecklenburg-nc-house-seat#stream/0.

17. Daniel Nichanian, "2018 Election Preview: Sheriff of Wake County, North Carolina," The Appeal: Political Report, October 10, 2018, https://www.appealpolitics.org/2018/wake-co-north-carolina-sheriff/.

18. Josh Delk, "ACLU to Spend $25 Million in 2018 Elections: Report," *The Hill*, January 6, 2018, https://thehill.com/blogs/ blog-briefing-room/367743-aclu-to-spend-25-million-in-2018-elections-report.

19. Burgess Everett, "ACLU Spending More Than $1M to Oppose Kavanaugh," *Politico*, October 1, 2018, https://www.politico.com/story/2018/10/01/ aclu-kavanaugh-ad-buy-854859.

20. Michael Perchick, "New Wake County Sheriff Vows to End Cooperation with Feds over Deportation," WTVD ABC11News, November 7, 2018, https:// abc11.com/politics/new-wake-county-sheriff-vows-to-end-cooperation-with-feds-over-deportation/4643615/.

21. Eric Mandel, "Georgia Sees Heavy 'In-Migration' from Florida, New York (Slideshow)," *Atlanta Business Chronicle*, May 15, 2018, https://www. bizjournals.com/atlanta/news/2018/05/15/georgia-sees-heavy-in-migration-from-florida-new.html.

22. James Salzer, "Democrats Gain 13 Seats in Legislature, Mostly in North Metro Atlanta," *Atlanta Journal-Constitution*, November 7, 2018, https://www.ajc. com/news/state—regional-govt—politics/democrats-gain-seats-legislature-mostly-north-metro-atlanta/Gi7vayO8PUq6OJkuZ27m1I/.

23. Thomas Wheatley, "Georgia Is Moving in Democrats' Direction. For Stacey Abrams, Will It Be Fast Enough?" *Atlanta*, October 2, 2018, https://www. atlantamagazine.com/news-culture-articles/ georgia-is-moving-in-democrats-direction-for-stacey-abrams-will-it-be-fast-enough/.

24. Alana Semuels, "Reverse Migration Might Turn Georgia Blue," *The Atlantic*, May 23, 2018, https://www.theatlantic.com/politics/archive/2018/05/reverse-migration-might-turn-georgia-blue/560996/; Michael E. Kanell, "Fed Says That Florida Leads the South, but Georgia Too Draws Millions," *Atlanta Journal-Constitution*, September 6, 2017, https://www.ajc.com/business/fed-says-that-florida-leads-the-south-but-georgia-too-draws-millions/ gr4xV2Oq6qk7m5BEodBHVI/.

25. Wendell Cox, "The Migration of Millions: 2017 State Population Estimates," New Geography, December 30, 2017, http://www.newgeography.com/ content/005837-the-migration-millions-2017-state-population-estimates.

26. Elizabeth Whalen, "Where Are All the New Residents of Nashville Moving From?" *SpareFoot Moving Guides* (blog), Spare Foot, September 6, 2017, https://www.sparefoot.com/moving/moving-to-nashville-tn/ nashville-moving-trends-2017/.

27. Rachel Rippetoe, "Where Did They Come From, Where Did They Go: Tennessee's Changing Population," *Nashville Business Journal*, June 6, 2018, https://www.bizjournals.com/nashville/news/2018/06/06/where-did-they-come-from-where-did-they-go.html.

28. "Reservoirs," New York City Department of Environmental Protection, https:// www1.nyc.gov/html/dep/html/watershed_protection/reservoirs.shtml.

29. Downeast Development Consulting Group, *The New York City Watershed Economic Impact Assessment Report: Determining Impacts and Developing*

Options Regarding NYC's Land Acquisition Program in Delaware County, May 2009, http://dev.co.delaware.ny.us/wsa/wp-content/uploads/sites/2/2017/06/NYCWatershedImpactStudy-FinalReport2.pdf.

30. "History of New York City's Water Supply System," New York City Department of Environmental Protection, https://www1.nyc.gov/html/dep/html/drinking_water/history.shtml.

31. John P. D. Wilkinson, *The Schoharie Valley* (New York: Arcadia Publishing, 2012).

32. A. J. Loftin, "The Ashokan Reservoir: The Creation of the Ashokan Reservoir Changed the Catskills Forever," *Hudson Valley*, July 17, 2008, http://www.hvmag.com/Hudson-Valley-Magazine/August-2008/History-The-Ashokan-Reservoir/.

33. Loftin, "The Ashokan Reservoir."

34. Julia Reischel, "DEP Drains Cannonsville Reservoir after Drilling Incident," Watershed Post, July 20, 2015, http://www.watershedpost.com/2015/dep-drains-cannonsville-reservoir-after-drilling-incident.

35. Kelly C. Owens, "The Gilboa Dam and Its Possible Failure: What It Means for NYC and Upstate New York," (thesis), Union College, 2008, https://digitalworks.union.edu/cgi/viewcontent.cgi?article=2711&context=theses

36. Molly Crane-Newman, Shayna Jacobs, and James Fanelli, "DEP Manager Took Gifts for Info That Led to $250M in Contracts: DA," *Daily News*, April 18, 2018, https://www.nydailynews.com/new-york/nyc-crime/dep-manager-gifts-info-leading-250m-contracts-da-article-1.3942200.

37. "Flood Resiliency," New York State Water Resources Institute, accessed February 17, 2019, https://wri.cals.cornell.edu/mohawk-river-basin/flood-resiliency/.

38. Anthony DePalma, "New York's Water Supply May Need Filtering," *New York Times*, July 20, 2006, https://www.nytimes.com/2006/07/20/nyregion/20water.html.

39. Edward Munger Jr., "Gilboa Dam Siren System Fixed," *Daily Gazette*, April 11, 2012, https://dailygazette.com/article/2012/04/11/0411_siren.

40. NYC DEP Bureau of Water Supply, *Long-Term Land Acquisition Plan: 2012 to 2022*, New York City Department of Environmental Protection, September 30, 2009, https://www1.nyc.gov/html/dep/pdf/resources/lt_plan_final.pdf.

41. NYC DEP Bureau of Water Supply, *Long-Term Land Acquisition Plan.*

42. "Upstate Population Drop Continues; 46 of 62 NY Counties Down Since 2010," Empire Center, March 23, 2017, https://www.empirecenter.org/publications/Upstate-population-drop-continues-46-of-62-ny-counties-down-since-2010/.

43. "New Perspectives on the West: Fred Eaton," Public Broadcasting Service, accessed February 17, 2019, https://www.pbs.org/weta/thewest/people/d_h/eaton.htm.

44. City of Los Angeles and the Owens Valley, "Owens Valley Water History (Chronology)," Inyo County Water Department, January 2008, https://www.inyowater.org/documents/reports/owens-valley-water-history-chronology/.

45. Ann Stansell, "Roster of St. Francis Dam Victims," SaintFrancisDam.com, updated January 17, 2018, https://scvhistory.com/scvhistory/annstansell_damvictims022214.htm.

46. E. J. McMahon, "New York's Uneven Economic Recovery," Empire Center, October 23, 2018, https://www.empirecenter.org/publications/new-york-uneven-economic-recovery/.

47. "Divide NYS into One State with Three Completely Autonomous Regions," Divide NYS Caucus Inc, https://www.newamsterdamny.org/.

48. Matthew Avitabile, "Push to Divide State through Constitutional Convention," *Mountain Eagle* (Schoharie, New York), October 13, 2017, https://drive.google.com/file/d/0B1j9dGzXZL_2VEdOTWl2aHFzaVk/view.

49. Adam Brinklow, "Plan to Split California into Three States Barred by State Supreme Court," *Curbed San Francisco* (blog), Curbed, July 19, 2018, https://sf.curbed.com/2018/7/19/17590594/california-supreme-court-three-californias-cal3-split-divide.

50. John Myers, "Radical Plan to Split California into Three States Earns Spot on November Ballot," *Los Angeles Times*, June 12, 2018, https://www.latimes.com/politics/la-pol-ca-california-split-three-states-20180612-story.html.

51. Bob Egelko, "Splitting Up California: State Supreme Court Takes Initiative Off Ballot," *San Francisco Chronicle*, July 18, 2018, https://www.sfchronicle.com/politics/article/Splitting-up-Calif-State-Supreme-Court-takes-13085880.php?psid=8wer0.

52. Valley Central School District, "Unfunded New York State and Federal Mandates and Mandatory Reporting Requirements," https://www.vcsd.k12.ny.us/cms/lib/NY24000141/Centricity/Domain/1/Unfunded%20Mandates%20in%20NYS%20Education.pdf.

53. Joseph Spector, "Poof! How New York Could Eliminate 50% or More of Your County Tax Bill," *Democrat & Chronicle*, July 11, 2018, https://www.democratandchronicle.com/story/news/politics/albany/2018/07/11/poof-how-new-york-could-eliminate-50-more-your-county-tax-bill/774960002/.

54. Bill Hammond, "Shifting Shares: The Costly Challenge of a State Medicaid Takeover," Empire Center, July 10, 2018, https://www.empirecenter.org/publications/shifting-shares/.

55. Greg Bishop, "Dozens of Cities Need Bankruptcy Because of Unfunded Mandates, Group Says," *Journal-Courier*, May 10, 2018, https://www.myjournalcourier.com/news/article/Dozens-of-cities-need-bankruptcy-because-of-12903198.php.

56. Dan McCaleb, "The Financial Collapse in Harvey, Illinois," *Effingham Daily News*, April 20, 2018, https://www.effinghamdailynews.com/opinion/columns/the-financial-collapse-in-harvey-illinois/article_9b24e0e4-b01d-5749-9fad-a6d4b601cb23.html.

57. Benjamin VanMetre, "Illinois Lawmakers Propose 59 New Unfunded Mandates for Local Governments," Illinois Policy, March 30, 2015, https://

www.illinoispolicy.org/illinois-lawmakers-propose-59-new-unfunded-mandates-for-local-governments/.

Chapter Six: Washington, D.C.

1. Mike Patton, "The Growth of Government: 1980 to 2012," *Forbes*, January 24, 2013, https://www.forbes.com/sites/mikepatton/2013/01/24/the-growth-of-the-federal-government-1980-to-2012/.

2. Jeff Clabaugh, "A 10-Year History of DC's Housing Market in One Chart," WTOP, August 16, 2016, https://wtop.com/business-finance/2016/08/a-10-year-history-of-dcs-housing-market-in-one-chart/.

3. Terence Jeffrey, "Gallup: Washington, D.C., Is Most Liberal Place in USA," CNS News, January 31, 2014, https://www.cnsnews.com/news/article/terence-p-jeffrey/gallup-washington-dc-most-liberal-place-usa.

4. John Reid Blackwell, "Report: Virginia's Economy Looking Good, but Dependence on Federal Spending Still Problematic," *Richmond Times-Dispatch*, December 16, 2018, https://www.richmond.com/business/local/report-virginia-s-economy-looking-good-but-dependence-on-federal/article_c3c2f954-c562-5159-9a5f-262df9a6e56e.html.

5. Jeff Clabaugh, "Exactly How Many Washingtonians Work for the Federal Government?" WTOP, February 19, 2018, https://wtop.com/business-finance/2018/02/exactly-many-washingtonians-work-federal-government/.

6. Joe Perticone, "The Most Ridiculous Projects the Government Funded in 2017," Business Insider, November 28, 2017, https://www.businessinsider.com/james-lankford-federal-fumbles-report-of-government-waste-2017-11.

7. "U.S. Department of Transportation Announces $1 Billion to Expand Trolley Service in San Diego," (news release) Federal Transit Administration, September 14, 2016, https://www.transit.dot.gov/about/news/us-department-transportation-announces-1-billion-expand-trolley-service-san-diego.

8. Perticone, "The Most Ridiculous Projects."

9. Casey Harper, "Congressman Publishes 10 Worst Examples of Government Waste," The Daily Caller, April 8, 2015, https://dailycaller.com/2015/04/08/congressman-publishes-10-worst-examples-of-government-waste/.

10. Marissa Laliberte, "11 Bizarre Things the U.S. Government Actually Spent Money On," *Reader's Digest*, accessed February 17, 2019, https://www.rd.com/culture/wasteful-government-spending-examples/.

11. Tom Kertscher, "Uncle Sam Spends Six Figures to Study Coked Birds Copulating, Wisconsin GOP Senate Candidate Mark Neumann Says," PolitiFact Wisconsin, February 20, 2012, https://www.politifact.com/wisconsin/statements/2012/feb/20/mark-neumann/uncle-sam-spends-six-figures-study-coked-birds-cop/.

12. "Washington, DC," Data USA, https://datausa.io/profile/geo/washington-dc/.

13. Ester Bloom, "Here's How Much Members of Congress Pay for Their Health Insurance," CNBC Make It, July 25, 2017, https://www.cnbc.com/2017/07/25/heres-how-much-members-of-congress-pay-for-their-health-insurance.html.

14. John Malcolm and Michael F. Cannon, "Congress' Illegal and Egregious Obamacare Exemption, Explained," *Washington Examiner*, September 5, 2017, https://www.washingtonexaminer.com/congress-illegal-and-egregious-obamacare-exemption-explained.

15. Katelin P. Isaacs, *Retirement Benefits for Members of Congress*, Congressional Research Service, December 5, 2017, https://www.senate.gov/CRSpubs/ac0d1dd5-7316-4390-87e6-353589586a89.pdf.

16. Samuel Taube, "Why Congressional Insider Trading Is Legal—and Profitable," Investment U, July 22, 2017, https://www.investmentu.com/article/detail/55695/why-congressional-insider-trading-legal-profitable.

17. Sean Williams, "10 Perks Congress Has That You Don't," Motley Fool, October 20, 2013, https://www.fool.com/investing/general/2013/10/20/10-perks-congress-has-that-you-dont.aspx.

18. "Congressional Salaries and Allowances: In Brief," EveryCRSReport.com, April 11, 2018, https://www.everycrsreport.com/reports/RL30064.html.

19. Paul Singer, "Taxpayers Fund a First-Class Congressional Foreign Travel Boom," *USA Today*, February 27, 2017, https://www.usatoday.com/story/news/politics/2017/02/27/taxpayers-fund-first-class-congressional-foreign-travel-boom-overseas/98351442/.

20. James D. Agresti, "A Look at Pay for Federal Employees Compared to Their Private-Sector Counterparts," Foundation for Economic Education, September 5, 2018, https://fee.org/articles/a-look-at-pay-for-federal-employees-compared-to-their-private-sector-counterparts/.

21. Editorial, "Government Shutdown: Pampered Federal Workers Don't Deserve Anyone's Pity," *Investor's Business Daily*, January 16, 2019, https://www.investors.com/politics/editorials/federal-workers-government-shutdown/.

22. Philipp Bewerunge and Harvey S. Rosen, "Wages, Pensions, and Public-Private Sector Compensation Differentials," Griswold Center for Economic Policy Studies, Working Paper No. 227, June 2012, https://www.princeton.edu/ceps/workingpapers/227rosen.pdf.

23. Andrew G. Biggs, "How Generous Are Federal Employee Pensions?" *AEIdeas* (blog), American Enterprise Institute, September 30, 2011, http://www.aei.org/publication/how-generous-are-federal-employee-pensions/.

24. Kathryn Watson, "Here's Why It's All but Impossible to Fire a Fed," The Daily Caller, March 3, 2016, https://dailycaller.com/2016/03/03/heres-why-its-all-but-impossible-to-fire-a-fed/.

25. John W. York, "Firing a Bad Federal Employee May Get a Little Easier," Heritage Foundation, July 19, 2018, https://www.heritage.org/government-regulation/commentary/firing-bad-federal-employee-may-get-little-easier.

26. Paul C. Light, "What Federal Employees Want from Reform," *Brookings Reform Watch* No. 5, March 2002, https://www.brookings.edu/wp-content/uploads/2016/06/rw05.pdf.

27. Jill R. Aitoro, "Here's Why Federal Employees Rarely Get Fired," *Washington Business Journal*, March 10, 2015, https://www.bizjournals.com/washington/blog/fedbiz_daily/2015/03/heres-why-federal-employees-rarely-get-fired.html.

28. Robert Goldenkoff, "Federal Workforce: Distribution of Performance Ratings Across the Federal Government, 2013," (letter to the Honorable Ron Jonson), May 9, 2016, https://www.gao.gov/assets/680/676998.pdf.

29. Nancy Cordes, "Bribes, Kickbacks in GSA Scandal?" CBS News, April 17, 2012, https://www.cbsnews.com/news/bribes-kickbacks-in-gsa-scandal/.

30. Eric Katz, "OPM Seeks to Curb Use of 'Often' Abused Paid Administrative Leave," Government Executive, June 1, 2015, https://www.govexec.com/pay-benefits/2015/06/opm-seeks-curb-use-often-abused-paid-administrative-leave/114175/.

31. "FERS Information," U.S. Office of Personnel Management, https://www.opm.gov/retirement-services/fers-information/types-of-retirement/#url=Early-Retirement.

32. Dennis Cauchon, "Select Group of Federal Retirees Collect Six-Figure Pensions," CNBC, August 15, 2012, https://www.cnbc.com/id/48678353.

33. Daniel Bier, "In Government, Nobody Quits—And You Can't Get Fired," Foundation for Economic Education, October 15, 2015, https://fee.org/articles/in-government-nobody-quits-and-you-cant-get-fired/.

34. "Why Trump Shouldn't Cave on Border Wall, by the Numbers," *Investor's Business Daily*, January 2, 2019, https://www.investors.com/politics/editorials/government-shutdown-trump-border-wall-2/.

Chapter Seven: The New Exurbs

1. Sabrina Tavernise and Robert Gebeloff, "They Voted for Obama, Then Went for Trump. Can Democrats Win Them Back?" *New York Times*, May 4, 2018, https://www.nytimes.com/2018/05/04/us/obama-trump-swing-voters.html.

2. Angelly Carrión, "New York to Philly Among Largest Metro-to-Metro Migration Flows, Says Census Bureau," *Philadelphia*, August 26, 2015, https://www.phillymag.com/property/2015/08/26/new-york-philadelphia-mobility/.

3. Kyle Plantz, "New Hampshire Sanctuary Churches, Cities, Colleges Seek to Resist Trump's Immigration Policies," NH Journal, April 16, 2017, https://www.insidesources.com/sanctuary-church-nh-trump-immigration/.

4. Luis Gomez, "Leaving California: Here's Who's Moving Out, Who's Moving In," *San Diego Union-Tribune*, February 22, 2018, https://www.sandiegouniontribune.com/opinion/the-conversation/sd-california-losing-low-income-people-gaining-wealthy-people-per-report-20180221-htmlstory.html.

5. Kenneth Lovett, "New York Is No. 1 in Losing Residents Who Move to Other States, Study Shows," *Daily News*, December 20, 2017, https://www.

nydailynews.com/news/
politics/n-y-no-1-losing-residents-move-states-article-1.3712413.

6. Bryce Hill and Austin Berg, "More Than 80 Percent of Illinois Counties Saw Population Loss in 2017," Illinois Policy, March 22, 2018, https://www.illinoispolicy.org/more-than-80-percent-of-illinois-counties-saw-population-loss-in-2017/.

7. Wendell Cox, "The Migration of Millions: 2017 State Population Estimates," New Geography, December 30, 2017, http://www.newgeography.com/content/005837-the-migration-millions-2017-state-population-estimates.

8. Nia Harden, "Local District Defends Removal of Christmas Scene from Classroom Door," KWTX-TV News 10, December 9, 2016, https://www.kwtx.com/content/news/Local-district-defends-removal-of-Christmas-scene-from-classroom-door-405680675.html.

9. Liam Stack, "How the 'War on Christmas' Controversy Was Created," *New York Times*, December 19, 2016, https://www.nytimes.com/2016/12/19/us/war-on-christmas-controversy.html.

10. Associated Press, "How AP Tallied the Cost of North Carolina's 'Bathroom Bill,'" AP News, March 27, 2017, https://apnews.com/ec6e9845827f47e89f40f33bb7024f61.

11. "New Census Data Show Differences Between Urban and Rural Populations," United States Census Bureau (News Release no. CB16-210), December 8, 2016, https://www.census.gov/newsroom/press-releases/2016/cb16-210.html.

12. Andrew Follett, "Obama Kept His Promise, 83,000 Coal Jobs Lost and 400 Mines Shuttered," The Daily Caller, September 5, 2016, https://dailycaller.com/2016/09/05/obama-kept-his-promise-83000-coal-jobs-lost-and-400-mines-shuttered/.

13. Bucksright, "Barack Obama Admits: Energy Prices Will Skyrocket under Cap and Trade," YouTube, June 23, 2009, https://www.youtube.com/watch?v=BqHL404zhcU.

14. America Rising ICYMI, "Hillary Clinton: 'We Are Going to Put a Lot of Coal Miners & Coal Companies out of Business,'" YouTube, March 13, 2016, video, https://www.youtube.com/watch?v=ksIXqxpQNt0.

15. C. Eugene Emery and Lauren Carroll, "Does Hillary Clinton Want to Shut Down Fracking?" Daily Beast, September 25, 2016, https://www.thedailybeast.com/does-hillary-clinton-want-to-shut-down-fracking.

16. "Displaced Workers Summary," Bureau of Labor Statistics, (News Release no. USDL-18-1370), August 28, 2018, https://www.bls.gov/news.release/disp.nr0.htm.

17. Mary Jo Dudley, "These U.S. Industries Can't Work without Illegal Immigrants," CBS News, January 10, 2019, https://www.cbsnews.com/news/illegal-immigrants-us-jobs-economy-farm-workers-taxes/.

18. Tamar Haspel, "Illegal Immigrants Help Fuel U.S. Farms. Does Affordable Produce Depend on Them?" *Washington Post*, March 17, 2017, https://www.washingtonpost.com/lifestyle/food/in-an-immigration-crackdown-who-will-pick-our-produce/2017/03/17/cc1c6df4-0a5d-11e7-93dc-00f9bdd74ed1_story.html.

19. Vernon M. Briggs Jr., "Illegal Immigration: The Impact on Wages and Employment of Black Workers," Center for Immigration Studies, April 4, 2008, https://cis.org/Testimony/Illegal-Immigration-Impact-Wages-and-Employment-Black-Workers.

Chapter Eight: More Divided Than Ever

1. Eyewitness News, "Man Wearing Donald Trump Hat Choked, Pinned on NYC Subway 5 Train," WABC-TV, November 15, 2016, https://abc7ny.com/politics/man-wearing-trump-hat-choked-pinned-on-nyc-subway/1608588/.
2. "Woman's Trump MAGA Hat Causes Stir at New York City Bar, Earns Her $150," Fox News, March 20, 2017, https://www.foxnews.com/food-drink/womans-trump-maga-hat-causes-stir-at-new-york-city-bar-earns-her-150.
3. Irene Plagianos (@IrenePlagianos), "And then Trump supporter shows up, gets pushed out to chants of 'racist,' #ShutdownCityHallNYC @DNAinfoNY," Twitter, August 1, 2016, 5:13 p.m., https://archive.is/GOcoS; newyorkist (@Newyorkist), "#SHUTDOWNCITYHALLNYC," Twitter, August 1, 2016, 4:34 p.m., https://archive.is/DGdmN.
4. John Annese and Chris Sommerfeldt, "Police Arrest 11 People at NYU Protest over Controversial Right-Wing Speaker's Event," *Daily News*, February 3, 2017, https://www.nydailynews.com/new-york/11-arrested-nyu-protest-right-wing-vice-media-co-founder-article-1.2963179.
5. Dean Balsamini, "I Was Attacked with a Glass Bottle Because of My MAGA Hat," *New York Post*, July 22, 2017, https://nypost.com/2017/07/22/i-was-attacked-with-a-glass-bottle-because-of-my-maga-hat/.
6. Sarah Taylor, "Int'l Tourist Mugged at Knifepoint While Wearing MAGA Hat—and Attackers Wouldn't Give Hat Back," The Blaze, April 13, 2018, https://www.theblaze.com/news/2018/04/13/intl-tourist-mugged-at-knifepoint-while-wearing-maga-hat-and-attackers-wouldnt-give-hat-back.
7. Ciara McCarthy, "Milo Yiannopoulos Shouted out of Murray Hill Bar," Patch, April 23, 2018, https://patch.com/new-york/gramercy-murray-hill/milo-yiannopoulos-shouted-out-murray-hill-bar.
8. Mike Brest, "'Fox & Friends' Host Brian Kilmeade Stalked and Harassed All Day," The Daily Caller, October 5, 2018, https://dailycaller.com/2018/10/05/kilmeade-harrassed-nyc/.
9. Grant Burningham, "Cruz Is Wrong and Trump Is Right: New York Has a Long History of Conservatives," *Newsweek*, January 14, 2016, https://www.newsweek.com/cruz-wrong-and-trump-right-new-york-has-long-history-conservatives-416041.
10. Justin Davidson, "Cities vs. Trump," *New York Magazine*, April 17, 2017, http://nymag.com/intelligencer/2017/04/the-urban-rural-divide-matters-more-than-red-vs-blue-state.html.
11. Davidson, "Cities vs. Trump."

12. H.B. 628-FN, 2017 Legislation, New Hampshire.

13. Kathleen Elkins, "New York City Is Home to Nearly 1 Million Millionaires, More than Any Other City in the World," CNBC Make It, January 18, 2019, https://www.cnbc.com/2019/01/18/new-york-city-has-more-millionaires-than-any-other-city-in-the-world.html.

14. Gary Buiso, "Welfare Rolls Increasing, Even as Economy Improves," *New York Post*, March 8, 2015, https://nypost.com/2015/03/08/welfare-rolls-increasing-in-city-even-as-economy-improves/.

15. Anna M. Tinsley, "Here's How Ted Cruz Won Texas Despite Beto O'Rourke Taking Tarrant County," *Fort Worth Star-Telegram*, November 7, 2018, https://www.star-telegram.com/article221281350.html.

16. Alexa Ura, Chris Essig, and Darla Cameron, "Are Texas Suburbs Slipping away from Republicans?" Texas Tribune, November 7, 2018, https://www.texastribune.org/2018/11/07/are-texas-suburbs-slipping-away-republicans/.

17. Nolan McCarty, "What We Know and Don't Know about Our Polarized Politics," *Monkey Cage* (blog), *Washington Post*, January 8, 2014, https://www.washingtonpost.com/news/monkey-cage/wp/2014/01/08/what-we-know-and-dont-know-about-our-polarized-politics/.

18. Bill Bishop, *The Big Sort: Why the Clustering of Like-Minded America Is Tearing Us Apart* (New York: Mariner Books, 2009).

19. James A. Thomson and Jesse Sussell, "Is Geographic Clustering Driving Political Polarization?" *Monkey Cage* (blog), *Washington Post*, March 2, 2015, https://www.washingtonpost.com/news/monkey-cage/wp/2015/03/02/is-geographic-clustering-driving-political-polarization/.

20. David Wasserman, "Purple America Has All but Disappeared," FiveThirtyEight, March 8, 2017, https://fivethirtyeight.com/features/purple-america-has-all-but-disappeared/.

21. Tom Dart, "Your Place or Mine? Texas Liberals and California Conservatives Swap States," *The Guardian*, July 3, 2017, https://www.theguardian.com/us-news/2017/jul/03/texas-california-conservatives-liberals-switch-places.

22. Ross Douthat, "We Should Treat Big Cities Like Big Corporations, and Bust Them Up," *Dallas News*, March 28, 2017, https://www.dallasnews.com/opinion/commentary/2017/03/28/treat-big-cities-like-big-corporations-bust.

23. Karlyn Bowman, "The Decline of the Major Networks," *Forbes*, July 27, 2009, https://www.forbes.com/2009/07/25/media-network-news-audience-opinions-columnists-walter-cronkite.html.

24. Rich Lowry, "From Carson to Kimmel: The Collapse of the Late-Night Empire," *New York Post*, October 16, 2017, https://nypost.com/2017/10/16/from-carson-to-kimmel-the-collapse-of-the-late-night-empire/.

25. Bill Higgins, "Throwback Thursday: When Johnny Carson Said Goodbye to TV," *Hollywood Reporter*, May 21, 2015, https://www.hollywoodreporter.com/news/throwback-thursday-johnny-carson-said-797310.

26. "Most Americans Get News from Social Media, Despite Doubts: Survey," Phys. org, September 10, 2018, https://phys.org/news/2018-09-americans-news-social-media-survey.html.

27. Sarah Griffiths, "Unfriended on Facebook? You Were Probably a School Friend Who Had Different Political Beliefs," *Daily Mail*, April 23, 2014, https://www.dailymail.co.uk/sciencetech/article-2611226/Unfriended-Facebook-You-probably-school-friend-different-political-beliefs.html.

28. Justin Ellis, "Where You Get Your News Depends on Where You Stand on the Issues," NiemanLab, October 21, 2014, http://www.niemanlab.org/2014/10/where-you-get-your-news-depends-on-where-you-stand-on-the-issues/.

29. Hadas Gold, "Study: Facebook Main Source of Political News for Millennials, Gen X-ers," *On Media* (blog), *Politico*, June 1, 2015, https://www.politico.com/blogs/media/2015/06/study-facebook-main-source-of-political-news-for-millennials-gen-x-ers-208005.

30. Sara Gonzales, "Liberal Actress Calls for Military Coup Against Trump," The Blaze, February 2, 2017, https://www.theblaze.com/news/2017/02/02/liberal-actress-calls-for-military-coup-against-trump.

31. Katie Reilly, "How Violent Protests at Middlebury and Berkeley Became a Warning for Other Schools," *Time*, March 13, 2017, http://time.com/4697066/campus-protests-controversial-speakers/.

32. "Civil War Casualties," American Battlefield Trust, https://www.battlefields.org/learn/articles/civil-war-casualties.

33. Wikipedia, s.v. "1967 Detroit Riot," last modified February 17, 2019, https://en.wikipedia.org/wiki/1967_Detroit_riot.

34. Bryan Burrough, "The Bombings of America That We Forgot," *Time*, September 20, 2016, http://time.com/4501670/bombings-of-america-burrough/.

35. Eric Alterman, "Remembering the Left-Wing Terrorism of the 1970s," *The Nation*, April 14, 2015, https://www.thenation.com/article/remembering-left-wing-terrorism-1970s/.

Chapter Nine: Reading the Tea Leaves

1. History.com editors, "Roosevelt Announces 'Court-Packing' Plan," History.com, February 9, 2010, https://www.history.com/this-day-in-history/roosevelt-announces-court-packing-plan.

Chapter Ten: The Case for Optimism

1. Jonathan Williams, "Americans Continue Their March to Low-Tax States," *The Hill*, February 12, 2019, https://thehill.com/opinion/finance/429623-americans-continue-their-march-to-low-tax-states.

2. Alana Semuels, "Indiana's Medicaid Experiment May Reveal Obamacare's Future," *The Atlantic*, December 21, 2016, https://www.theatlantic.com/business/archive/2016/12/medicaid-and-mike-pence/511262/.

3. "Medicaid Waiver Tracker: Approved and Pending Section 1115 Waivers by State," Kaiser Family Foundation, October 9, 2019, https://www.kff.org/medicaid/issue-brief/medicaid-waiver-tracker-approved-and-pending-section-1115-waivers-by-state/.

4. "Our Team," Conservative Move, https://conservativemove.com/our-team.

5. Vanessa Romo, "Texas Becoming a Magnet for Conservatives Fleeing Liberal States Like California," NPR, August 27, 2017, https://www.npr.org/2017/08/27/546391430/texas-becoming-a-magnet-for-conservatives-fleeing-liberal-states-like-california, .

6. Ana Campoy and Youyou Zhou, "Conservative Californians Are Fleeing to Texas. Data Show They're in for a Surprise," Quartz, February 17, 2018, https://qz.com/1189388/conservative-californians-are-moving-to-texas-for-the-home-prices-and-politics/.

7. Kyle Munzenrieder, "Florida Has the Second Fewest Native Residents of Any State," *Miami New Times*, August 18, 2014, https://www.miaminewtimes.com/news/florida-has-the-second-fewest-native-residents-of-any-state-6548292.

8. Marc Caputo, "'Florida Is Trump's State to Lose,'" *Politico*, January 25, 2019, https://www.politico.com/story/2019/01/25/trump-2020-elections-florida-1125442.

9. Florida Department of Transportation Office of Policy Planning, *Florida Transportation Trends and Conditions*, June 2014, https://fdotwww.blob.core.windows.net/sitefinity/docs/default-source/content/planning/trends/tc-report/population.pdf?sfvrsn=9c976c9f_0.

10. Rhodes Cook, "Registering by Party: Where the Democrats and Republicans Are Ahead," Rasmussen Reports, July 12, 2018, http://www.rasmussenreports.com/public_content/political_commentary/commentary_by_rhodes_cook/registering_by_party_where_the_democrats_and_republicans_are_ahead.

11. United States Census Bureau, *State-to-State Migration Flows*, 2017 American Community Survey, https://www2.census.gov/programs-surveys/demo/tables/geographic-mobility/2017/state-to-state-migration/State_to_State_Migrations_Table_2017.xls.

12. G. Jeffrey MacDonald, "Secession Theology Runs Deep in American Religious, Political History," *St. Louis Post-Dispatch*, November 30, 2012, https://www.stltoday.com/lifestyles/faith-and-values/secession-theology-runs-deep-in-american-religious-political-history/article_dda5a49c-0d6f-537b-a727-8163f6d0b28c.html.

13. "Has Ron Paul Interested You in Liberty in Your Lifetime?" Free State Project, https://web.archive.org/web/20130519122424/http:/freestateproject.org/intro/ron_paul.

14. "Difference Makers—The Keene Squad," *The Colbert Report*, November 19, 2014, http://www.cc.com/video-clips/dvppp6/the-colbert-report-difference-makers—-the-free-keene-squad.

15. Matt Welch, "New Hampshire Democrat: 'Free Staters Are the Single Biggest Threat the State Is Facing Today,'" *Reason*, December 27, 2012, http://reason.com/blog/2012/12/27/new-hampshire-democrat-free-staters-are.

16. Welch, "New Hampshire Democrat."

17. Robert Taylor, "The Police in This Small Town Are Cracking Down on Citizens—With a Tank," Mic, August 16, 2013, https://mic.com/articles/59831/the-police-in-this-small-town-are-cracking-down-on-citizens-with-a-tank.

18. Madison Pauly, "Why Libertarians Are (Still) Plotting to Take Over New Hampshire," *Mother Jones*, February 1, 2016, https://www.motherjones.com/politics/2016/02/libertarians-new-hampshire-free-state/.

19. Holly Ramer, "Domestic Migration Fuels New Hampshire Population Growth," *Concord Monitor*, December 27, 2017, https://www.concordmonitor.com/Domestic-migration-fuels-New-Hampshire-population-growth-14559300.

20. Amanda Loder, "New Hampshire, a Low-Cost Massachusetts?" NPR, August 27, 2012, https://www.npr.org/2012/08/27/160092192/new-hampshire-a-low-cost-massachusetts.

21. Richard Fry, "Millennials Projected to Overtake Baby Boomers as America's Largest Generation," *FactTank* (blog), Pew Research Center, March 1, 2018, http://www.pewresearch.org/fact-tank/2018/03/01/millennials-overtake-baby-boomers/.

22. John Fleming, "Gallup Analysis: Millennials, Marriage and Family," Gallup News, May 19, 2016, https://news.gallup.com/poll/191462/gallup-analysis-millennials-marriage-family.aspx.

23. Richa Chaturvedi, "A Closer Look at the Gender Gap in Presidential Voting," *FactTank* (blog), Pew Research Center, July 28, 2016, http://www.pewresearch.org/fact-tank/2016/07/28/a-closer-look-at-the-gender-gap-in-presidential-voting/.

24. Celinda Lake and Joshua E. Ulibarri, *Comparing the Voting Electorate in 2012-2016 and Predicting 2018 Drop-Off: How the Electorate Has Changed over the Years and How That Informs the 2018 Cycle* (Washington, D.C.: The Voter Participation Center, June 2017), https://data.voterparticipation.org/wp-content/uploads/2017/07/Report.VPC_.Drop-Off.fi_.2017.06.29.pdf.

25. Editorial, "Why Are Millennials Turning Against Democrats? The Answer Is Simple," *Investor's Business Daily*, May 1, 2018, https://www.investors.com/politics/editorials/millennials-democrats-poll-economy/.

26. "Continued Bipartisan Support for Expanded Background Checks on Gun Sales," Pew Research Center, August 12, 2015, http://www.people-press.org/2015/08/13/continued-bipartisan-support-for-expanded-background-checks-on-gun-sales/8-12-2015-3-58-40-pm/.

27. Frank Newport, "Majority Say More Concealed Weapons Would Make U.S. Safer," Gallup News, October 20, 2015, https://news.gallup.com/poll/186263/majority-say-concealed-weapons-safer.aspx.

28. Jacqueline Howard, "Millennials More Conservative Than You May Think," CNN, September 7, 2016, https://www.cnn.com/2016/09/07/health/millennials-conservative-generations/index.html.

29. Becky Nicolaides and Andrew Wiese, "Suburbanization in the United States after 1945," Oxford Research Encyclopedia of American History, April 2017,

http://oxfordre.com/americanhistory/view/10.1093/
acrefore/9780199329175.001.0001/acrefore-9780199329175-e-64.

30. "Exit Polls," CNN Politics, https://www.cnn.com/election/2018/exit-polls/
texas/senate.

31. Graham Vyse, "Democratic Socialists Rack Up Wins in States," *Governing*,
November 9, 2018, http://www.governing.com/topics/politics/gov-ocasio-
cortez-tlaib-Democratic-Socialists-state-level.html.

32. Frank Newport, "Democrats More Positive about Socialism Than Capitalism,"
Gallup News, August 13, 2018, https://news.gallup.com/poll/240725/
democrats-positive-socialism-capitalism.aspx.

Index

A

Abbott, Greg, 58, 142
Abrams, Stacey, 96
Amazon Prime Video, 63
Amazon, 32, 38, 40, 62–66, 68
America Alone (Steyn), 22
American Civil Liberties Union
   (ACLU),
American Federation of Government
   Employees, 118
American Redoubt, 176
American Revolutionary War, 111
Arlington, 33–34, 66, 110, 159

B

baby boomers, 179–80, 184–85
Baca, Lee, 13
Baker, Gerald, 95–96
Baldwin, Chuck, 176
Bezos, Jeff, 62–65
Bitcoin, 178
Blue Wall, 54
Boeing, 32, 36, 38, 157
boutique economies, 29, 31, 42
Brown, Jerry, 16, 184
Brown, Pat, 184
Brown, Scott, 173, 187
Buckley, William F., 139
building policies, 20, 39
bureaucrats, 12, 14, 20, 34–35, 38,
   40–41, 56, 79, 104, 109, 114–17,
   119, 132
Bush, George H. W., 58, 186, 188
Bush, George W., 33, 175
BuzzFeed, 63

C

California Supreme Court, 18, 106
California, 3, 5–6, 8–9, 11–13, 15–23,
   36–37, 44–46, 49, 51, 55, 67, 81,
   85–86, 91–93, 95–98, 104–107,
   111, 114, 126, 128, 130–31, 133,
   136, 144, 152, 157–59, 169, 173,
   176, 183–84, 190
Cannonsville Reservoir, 101
capital gains, 46, 158
carbon tax, 37
Carolina Panthers, 10
Carolina Population Center, 95
Carson, Johnny, 145–46
Castro, Fidel, 49, 182
Catholic Church, 169–70, 172, 181
Cato Institute, 68, 160
Chabot, Paul, 173
Chase, Cynthia, 177
Chesterfield County, VA, 87
Chicago, 8, 19, 28, 43, 63–64, 89,
   92–94, 97, 107, 125, 127, 139–40,
   149, 157, 183
China, 11, 18, 44, 150
Choice Scholarship Pilot Program, 83
cigarette taxes, 37
Civil War, 148–49, 167
Claremont, NH, 72–73
Clinton, Bill, 16, 110, 129, 186, 188
Clinton, Hillary, 33, 51, 54, 89, 114,
   121, 123, 144, 174, 179–80
CNN, 146, 152
Colorado Supreme Court, 83–84
Concord Community Schools, 73

Congress, 22, 24, 53, 104, 112, 114–15, 119, 143, 152, 156–58, 164, 168, 184, 187–88
Connecticut Hedge Fund Association, 8
Connecticut, 4, 9–10, 13, 19–20, 22, 55–58, 61, 67–68, 87, 96–97, 128, 130–31
Conservative Move, 173
Conway, Kellyanne, 148
corporate growth, 2, 4, 58, 65, 69, 144
Cronkite, Walter, 145
Cruz, Ted, 51, 53, 60, 141–42, 148, 152, 186
Cuomo, Andrew, 7–8, 65, 158

D

Dartmouth College, 76, 124
Dartmouth Medical School, 80
Dartmouth-Hitchcock Medical Center, 80
Davis, Jefferson, 88
Davis, Wendy, 142
de Blasio, Bill, 4, 30, 65–66, 98, 141
Declaration of Independence, 111
Decline of the West, The (Spengler), 22
Democracy Vouchers, 40
democracy, 22, 162, 188
Democratic Party, 14, 34, 41, 54, 80, 88–89, 108, 168, 180–81, 184, 186–87, 188
Democratic votes, 5–6, 34, 52, 59, 85, 96, 111, 125, 152, 180–81
Denver, CO, 29, 45, 48–49, 81, 84, 135, 162–64, 185
Department of Agriculture, 145
Department of Commerce, 161
Department of Environmental Protection (DEP), 99–101
Department of Health and Human Services, 109, 117
Dickinson, John, 112
Douglas County School District, 83
Douthat, Ross, 144

Draper, Tim, 106
Dukakis, Michael, 187

E

economic boom, 26–27, 29, 31, 35, 45, 158, 162, 184
Economic Opportunity Institute, 38
Edelman Intelligence, 12
Edwards, John, 66
Edwards, Lucy, 177
Electoral College, 112, 168
Environmental Protection Agency (EPA), 117, 161
Erie County, PA, 122–23

F

Facebook, 118, 146–47
Fairfax County, VA, 33–34, 49
federal government, 10, 22, 33, 35, 79, 110–12, 114–19, 157–58, 160–62, 186
Federal Override, 156–58, 160–61, 164
federal workers, 12, 33, 110, 114–19
Federalist no. 43, 112
First Amendment, 84
First Continental Congress, 111
Florida, 3–4, 7–8, 10, 12, 14, 21, 55, 77, 100, 128, 151–52, 154, 168, 174–76, 190
free market, 64, 68
Free State Project, 177–78
Freedom From Religion Foundation (FFRF), 72–73
Friedman, Milton, 35

G

General Electric, 58, 67
General Motors, 132
Generation X, 180
Generation Z, 179
Georgia, 55, 63, 92, 94, 96, 106, 152, 168, 176, 182, 186, 189

Gibbon, Edward, 22
Gillespie, Ed, 34, 89
Giuliani, Rudy, 30, 189
Goueli, Hisam, 40
Government Services Administration
    (GSA), 118
Graham, Lindsey, 155
Grapes of Wrath, The (Steinbeck), 126
Great American Beer Festival, 31
Great Depression, 126
Great Recession, 35–37, 62, 106
Greatest Generation, 183, 185
Green New Deal, 24, 103, 155
gun control, 47–48, 85–86, 131, 180
gun rights, 35, 129, 180

H

Hamilton, Alexander, 112
Harris County, TX, 27–28, 141
Harris, Kamala, 151–54, 156–158,
    161–62
Harrison, Donnie, 95
Harvard Law School, 53
Hauswirth, Heather, 137–38
Hays County, TX, 141–42
Henle, Paul, 79
Hickenlooper, John, 45, 47
*History of the Decline and Fall of the
    Roman Empire, The* (Gibbon), 22
homeless population, 1, 21, 30, 41–42
Houston, TX, 6, 27–29, 58–60, 141,
    144, 158–59
Hurricane Irene, 100
Hurricane Maria, 174

I

illegal immigrants, 12, 15, 29, 46, 92,
    96, 124, 134–35, 136
Illinois, 3–6, 9, 14, 18–23, 36, 46, 49,
    55, 89, 91–94, 96–97, 107, 111,
    127–28, 131, 136, 155, 157–58,
    168–69, 174, 176
income inequality, 17, 41, 153, 154

income taxes, 5, 7–14, 21, 32, 37–38,
    44, 55–57, 60–61, 64–67, 69,
    78–79, 86–87, 140, 190
Industrial Revolution, 98
Internal Revenue Service (IRS), 7, 13
invisible hand, 5
Iseman, Luke, 20

J

Jefferson, Thomas, 112
Johnson, Martha, 118

K

Kaine, Tim, 54, 89, 154
Kavanaugh, Brett, 96, 156
Kemp, Brian, 96
Kilmeade, Brian, 139
Knoxville, TN, 26–27, 29, 31
Ku Klux Klan, 148

L

Las Vegas, NV, 20, 118
Latin America, 51, 182
Lee, Robert E., 87
left-wing politics, 14, 20, 28, 30,
    36–37, 41, 92, 116–17, 119, 126,
    146, 171, 174, 188
legalization of marijuana, 31, 82, 85,
    178
LGBT community, 92, 123, 130
Lockheed Martin, 67
Long Island, NY, 106
Los Angeles, CA, 3, 8, 28, 92–93,
    97–98, 104–105, 140, 160
Lowey, Nita, 8

M

Madison, James, 112
Magpul Industries, 48
Malloy, Dannel, 57
marijuana entrepreneurs, 46, 82
Martinez, Susana, 45

Marx, Karl, 65
McAuliffe, Terry, 35, 54
McCrory, Pat, 130
McDonnell, Bob, 35
McGovern, George, 188
McGuire, Bruce, 8
McInnes, Gavin, 138
Medi-Cal, 15
Medicaid, 12, 14–16, 43–44, 107,
    171–72
Melville, Sam, 149
Merit Systems Protection Board
    (MSPB), 188
Metropolitan Transportation
    Authority (MTA), 2, 65
Microsoft, 36, 38, 80, 157
middle class, 3, 8–9, 14, 18, 23, 29, 35,
    45, 49, 57, 127, 135, 140, 142, 144,
    160, 182
millennials, 26, 113, 147, 162, 179–81,
    189
minimum wage, 3, 40–41, 124, 157,
    161, 163
moral hazard, 14
Mother Jones, 146, 178

N

National Endowment for the Arts, 113
Nativity scene, 72–73, 130
NATO, 150
Neely, Jeff, 118
New England, 24, 63, 70, 74
New Frontier Data, 82
New Hampshire, 9, 21, 23–24, 28, 30,
    36, 69–71, 74–80, 89, 113, 124–25,
    127–28, 135, 140, 142, 173,
    177–78
New Jersey, 3, 10, 13, 18–19, 21, 64,
    67, 87, 95–97, 100, 128
New Mexico, 16, 32, 44–45
New York City, 1–4, 7, 27–28, 30, 55,
    65–66, 71, 92–94, 98–104,

106–107, 110, 121, 125, 138–41,
    149, 162, 189
New York Times, 7, 63, 79, 121–22,
    144
Northam, Ralph, 34, 89
Northern Virginia, 29, 33–34, 88, 113,
    142
NPR, 48, 173, 178
Nunn, Michelle, 96

O

O'Neill, William, 57
O'Rourke, Beto, 23, 51, 60, 141–42,
    152, 186–87
Obama administration, 114, 133, 187
Obama, Barack, 28, 33, 36, 47, 84, 89,
    122, 133, 137, 155–56, 160, 169,
    186
Obamacare, 15, 114, 171–72
Ocasio-Cortez, Alexandria, 23–24,
    66, 152, 187
oil fracking, 32, 45, 60, 133, 162
Orange County, CA, 55, 173, 184
Owens Valley, 104

P

Patrick, Dan, 174
Paul, Rand, 152
Paul, Ron, 153, 177
payment in lieu of taxes (PILOT), 65,
    67
Pelosi, Nancy, 161
Pence, Mike, 54, 152, 156, 172
Pennsylvania Mutiny, 112
pension system, 12, 16–18, 23, 56–57,
    92, 107, 114, 116, 119, 129, 158–
    59, 162, 170, 185, 190
Pew Research Center, 147, 180
Polis, Jared, 45, 47
political correctness, 130–31
Politico, 175

population boom, 28–29, 31, 33, 45, 52, 81, 183
Portland, OR, 29, 31–32, 36, 42–44, 49
Potomac River, 112
property taxes, 7, 9, 39, 55, 61, 67, 102–104, 107, 171
Proposition 9, 106
Puerto Rico, 174–75

R

Race and Social Justice Initiative, 39–40
Rauner, Bruce, 92
Rawles, Wesley, 176
Reagan, Ronald, 34, 49, 55, 67, 122, 150, 168, 182–86, 188–90
regressive taxes, 38, 42
Republican Party, 53, 59, 80, 85, 88, 171, 175
Road to Serfdom, The (Hayek), 160
Roman Empire, 22
Roosevelt, Franklin, 126, 156
Rowland, John, 57
Rust Belt, 98, 122

S

Sacramento, CA, 8, 19, 45
San Francisco, CA, 12, 19–20, 23, 27–28, 78, 84, 93–94, 122, 125, 140, 142, 149, 185
San Patricio County, TX, 61
Sanders, Sarah, 148
Santillan, Tanya, 144
Scalise, Steve, 148
Scott, Rick, 154, 174, 182
Seattle Times, 41
Seattle, WA, 26, 29, 32, 36, 38–41, 49, 157
Secrest, Sheley, 40
Silicon Valley, 81, 106
Sixteenth Amendment, 79
Smith, Adam, 5

Smith, Justin, 49
social justice programs, 39, 92
Social Security benefits, 46, 116, 157, 188
social welfare programs, 9, 15–16, 160
socialism, 24, 153, 182, 188
Soviet Union, 150
St. Louis, MO, 37
state and local tax (SALT) deductions, 7–9
Steinbeck, John, 126
Steyer, Tom, 154–55
Steyn, Mark, 22

T

Tax Cuts and Jobs Act, 7
Tepper, David, 10–11
Texas Enterprise Fund, 61
The Colbert Report, 177
The Hill, 92
Tlaib, Rashida, 187
Trump administration, 7, 172
Trump, Donald, 7–8, 18, 21, 35, 45, 51, 54, 87, 96, 114, 121–23, 129–34, 137–40, 144, 148, 151–52, 154, 156, 172, 174–75, 179–80, 185
Twenty-Third Amendment, 111–12

U

U-Haul, 3, 29, 108, 155
U.S. Census Bureau, 4, 176
U.S. Supreme Court, 78, 83–84, 96, 130, 153, 155–57, 160–61, 171
unemployment rates, 36, 44
United Van Lines, 94
University of California system, 16–17
Upstate New York, 91, 93, 98–101, 103–104, 106, 122

V

von Bismarck, Otto, 169–70, 172, 181

W

Walden, Michael, 94
Walker, Scott, 171–72, 187
Wall Street Journal, 10
Wall Street, 18
Warner, Mark, 54, 89
Washington Post, 63
Washington, D.C., 32–33, 60, 64–65,
    88–89, 109–17, 119, 142, 149, 159
Weicker, Lowell, 57
World War II, 140, 183, 185

Y

Yiannopoulos, Milo, 139